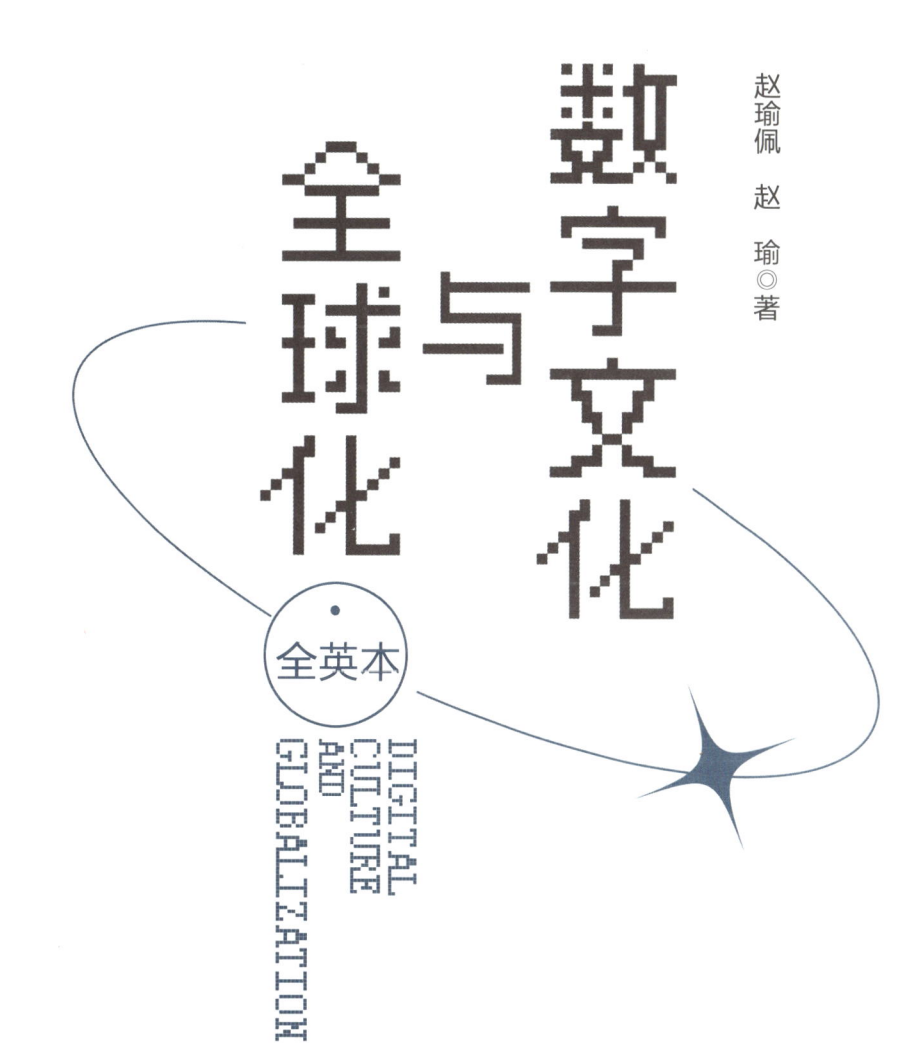

赵瑜佩 赵 瑜 ◎ 著

数字文化与全球化

·全英本·

DIGITAL CULTURE AND GLOBALIZATION

浙江大学出版社
·杭州·

图书在版编目（CIP）数据

 数字文化与全球化 ：英文 / 赵瑜佩，赵瑜著. —杭州 ：浙江大学出版社，2023.10
 ISBN 978-7-308-23273-9

 Ⅰ. ①数… Ⅱ. ①赵… Ⅲ. ①数字技术－应用－文化产业－研究－英文 Ⅳ. ①G114-39

 中国版本图书馆CIP数据核字(2022)第216932号

数字文化与全球化
SHUZI WENHUA YU QUANQIUHUA

赵瑜佩　赵　瑜　著

责任编辑	郑成业
责任校对	李　晨
封面设计	闰江文化
出版发行	浙江大学出版社
	（杭州市天目山路148号　邮政编码310007）
	（网址：http://www.zjupress.com）
排　版	杭州林智广告有限公司
印　刷	杭州捷派印务有限公司
开　本	787mm×1092mm　1/16
印　张	13
字　数	353千
版 印 次	2023年10月第1版　2023年10月第1次印刷
书　号	ISBN 978-7-308-23273-9
定　价	55.00元

版权所有　侵权必究　　印装差错　负责调换

浙江大学出版社市场运营中心联系方式：0571－88925591；http://zjdxcbs.tmall.com

前　言

在人类社会数字化转型的过程中，数字文化和全球化成为一个重要议题。数字技术的革新正在并将持续赋能媒体文化和全球化中的数字领域。从人工智能到物联网，从区块链到虚拟现实，数字技术不断突破界限，日益融入人类生产、生活和生态的各领域和全过程，成为加速经济和社会结构升级进程、改变国际竞争格局的关键变量之一。

而随着数字技术深度嵌入传播实践、全球化水平不断提高，数字文化急需更加适应行业发展趋向的教材和教学体系，对于数字传播实践的研究不能再局限于国内，而应将视点放大至全球。自2018年起，浙江大学传媒与国际文化学院以"全球传播"为优势特色学科推进"双一流"建设。通过深入学习贯彻习近平总书记加强和改进国际传播工作重要讲话精神，围绕"五个力"要求，2021年，学院制定优势特色学科2.0计划，将"全球传播"升级为"数字全球沟通"，努力打造世界一流、中国特色、浙大风格的新闻传播学派，探索中国特色新闻传播学学科体系、学术体系和话语体系。

本教材将探讨技术、文化和全球化的关系，以及与之相关的理论和实证问题，尤其关注全球数字技术的进步对文化的发展带来的影响，涉及数字平台、数字鸿沟、青年文化、数字身份等全球数字文化的研究重点，覆盖电影、电视剧、音乐、短视频、电子竞技、数字游戏、虚拟现实等数字领域内容，辅之以典型案例，对数字技术的演进与数字文化产业新现象等多个方面进行深入剖析。

教材秉持立德树人的教学理念，精心编写内容积极、时代感强、具有国际视野的内容，且严谨挑选具有新时代青年数字文化代表性的实证研究作为教材案例，每章都围绕以下三条主线叙述：

（1）数字叙事时代国际传播生态研究；

（2）国际本土化理论与实践探索研究；

（3）数字叙事时代中外多元主体形象塑造的比较研究。

教材对标跨学院跨专业的研究生课程，尤其是广播电视专业、传播学专业的课程及全球传播等硕士研究生课程。教材将多角度解读数字文化与国际化本体，并介绍相关研究范式，引导学生进行批判性思考，提高文化自信。为讲好中国故事、传播好中国声音，展示真实、立体、全面的中国贡献力量。

CONTENTS

LECTURE & SEMINAR 1

Communication, Technology and Society

1.1	Introduction	2
1.2	Theory	3
	1.2.1 What Is Globalization?	3
	1.2.2 What Is Technology?	9
	1.2.3 What Is Culture?	12
	1.2.4 Culture and Globalization	16
1.3	Conclusion	17
1.4	Extended Readings	17
1.5	Post Questions and Discussion	17
1.6	Bibliography	18

LECTURE & SEMINAR 2

Digital Divide

2.1	Knowledge Gap and Digital Divide	22
	2.1.1 Knowledge Gap Hypothesis	22
	2.1.2 New Media vs. Old Media	23
2.2	ICT and Digital Divide	26
	2.2.1 Types of ICT	27
	2.2.2 ICT and Digital Access	29
	2.2.3 Digital Divide: From Access to Use	30
2.3	Digital Access and Digital Divide	35
	2.3.1 Access as a Method of Technology Appropriation	36
	2.3.2 The Theoretical Framework for Analyzing Access	37
	2.3.3 Determinants in a Successive Phase of Access	37
2.4	Conclusion	39
2.5	Extended Readings	40
2.6	Post Questions and Discussion	40
2.7	Bibliography	40

Digital Culture and Globalization

LECTURE & SEMINAR 3

Youth Culture, Audio-Visual Communication, and Platformalization

3.1 Digital Platform	46
3.1.1 The Creativity of Youth Culture	46
3.1.2 The Creativity of Audio-Visual Communication	49
3.2 Subculture	54
3.2.1 What Is Subculture?	54
3.2.2 Categories of Subculture	55
3.2.3 Subculture and Digital Platforms	60
3.3 Case Study	61
3.3.1 Case 1: An Example of Popular Revenge	61
3.3.2 Case 2: Urban Entertainment Subculture and Black Music: Blues, Ragtime and Jazz	62
3.3.3 Case 3: China's Cultural Evolution: Egao, Digital Parody, and Politics	63
3.3.4 Case 4: Harajuku Culture in Japan	64
3.4 Conclusion	65
3.5 Extended Readings	65
3.6 Post Questions and Discussion	65
3.7 Bibliography	66

LECTURE & SEMINAR 4

ESport, Platform Economy Career Development and Wellbeing

4.1 Background	70
4.2 Theory	72
4.2.1 Platformization and Infrastructuralization	72
4.2.2 Stigma Power	74
4.3 Case Study	76
4.3.1 Case 1: Tencent—The Platformizing ESports Conglomerate	76
4.3.2 Case 2: Challenges Faced by Chinese ESports Professional Players	85
4.4 Conclusion	91
4.5 Extended Readings	92
4.6 Post Questions and Discussion	92
4.7 Bibliography	93

LECTURE & SEMINAR 5

Hip-Pop, Music and Technological Power

5.1 Theory: Critical Transculturalism	97
5.1.1 Cultural Syncretism	97

	5.1.2	Cultural Hybridization	98
	5.1.3	Cultural Imperialism vs. Cultural Pluralism	99
5.2	Case Study: Hip-Hop in China		100
	5.2.1	Background: Keywords that Help to Understand Hip-Hop	101
	5.2.2	Globalization of Hip-Hop	103
	5.2.3	Chinese Hip-Hop Music	104
5.3	Conclusion		111
5.4	Extended Readings		112
5.5	Post Questions and Discussion		112
5.6	Bibliography		112

LECTURE & SEMINAR 6

Chinese Cinema History and Globalization

6.1	Background		115
6.2	Chinese Cinema History		115
	6.2.1	Beginning of Chinese Cinema	115
	6.2.2	Early Communist Era: 1949–1960s	118
	6.2.3	Cultural Revolution: 1967–1977	119
	6.2.4	The Fifth Generation: Mid-Late 1980s and 1990s	120
	6.2.5	The Sixth Generation: 1990s–	124
	6.2.6	Current Cinema Culture in China	125
6.3	Transnational Chinese Film Studies		128
	6.3.1	Transnationalism of Transnational Chinese Films	129
	6.3.2	Challenges of Transnational Chinese Film Studies	132
6.4	Conclusion		132
6.5	Extended Readings		133
6.6	Post Questions and Discussion		133
6.7	Bibliography		133

LECTURE & SEMINAR 7

Film Making, Communication, and Technical Skills

7.1	Visual Narration		136
	7.1.1	Cinematography vs. Mise-en-Scène	136
	7.1.2	Composition of the Frame	138
	7.1.3	Aspect Ratio	143
	7.1.4	Mobile Framing	146
	7.1.5	Cinematography and Perspective	148

7.2　Technical Narration 150
　　7.2.1　New Style: Virtual Reality 151
7.3　Interactive Narration 153
　　7.3.1　Case Study: Netflix and Interactive Films 154
7.4　Conclusion 156
7.5　Extended Readings 156
7.6　Post Questions and Discussion 156
7.7　Bibliography 156

LECTURE & SEMINAR 8

Consumption of Image Representation Discourses

8.1　How to Analyze Images 159
　　8.1.1　Theories of Signs: Linguistics and Semiotics Approaches . 159
　　8.1.2　Culture Study Approach: Hall's Representation Theory ... 166
　　8.1.3　Foucault's Discourse Theory: Power and Discursive Practices . 168
8.2　Case Study 169
　　8.2.1　Case 1: The Semiotics in Advertising 169
　　8.2.2　Case 2: Representation of Girlfriendship in the TV Drama . 170
8.3　Conclusion 171
8.4　Extended Readings 172
8.5　Bibliography 172

LECTURE & SEMINAR 9

AI in Media

9.1　Background 175
9.2　Theory 176
　　9.2.1　Machine Generated Content 177
　　9.2.2　Intelligent Recommendation 180
　　9.2.3　Extended Reality 182
9.3　Case Study 185
　　9.3.1　Case 1: Quakebot: Automated Earthquake Reports 185
　　9.3.2　Case 2: Douyin: Intelligent Recommendation for Short Video . 187
　　9.3.3　Case 3: Motion-Driven VUPs and Data-Based Virtual Anchors . 189
9.4　Conclusion 193
9.5　Extended Readings 193
9.6　Post Questions and Discussion 194
9.7　Bibliography 194

LECTURE & SEMINAR 1
Communication, Technology and Society

In the context of globalization, digital culture is integrating into all aspects of life around the world, bringing new opportunities and challenges to human society. Globalization, technology and culture are three interrelated concepts that are inseparable, mutually reinforcing, and can be interpreted from multiple perspectives. Through the study of this lecture, you will further deepen your understanding of the relationship between digital culture and globalization in the digital era, and understand the opportunities and development, risks and challenges brought by their interaction.

Framework

1.1 Introduction	1.2 Theory
	1.2.1 What Is Globalization?
	1.2.2 What Is Technology?
	1.2.3 What Is Culture?
	1.2.4 Culture and Globalization
1.3 Conclusion	1.4 Extended Readings
1.5 Post Questions and Discussion	1.6 Bibliography

Terms

communication, technology, ICT, culture, globalization, society

Pre-lecture Discussion

(1) This lecture is mainly talking about culture, technology and globalization. Before reading, how do you understand their relationships?

(2) What do you want to know about these two topics? For example, what are the advantages and disadvantages of globalization?

1.1　Introduction

The Internet has prompted fresh thinking about the social implications of technological changes. This lecture will explore various theoretical and empirical issues and debates in communication, technology and society, particularly focusing on the digital domain in media culture and globalization.

The ever-advancing technologies are changing the world and the way we understand it. What kind of communication revolution does the evolving technology herald, and what conceptual tools do we need to understand it? These are the central questions addressed by the lecture. To be specific, the lecture is going to interrogate power in the interaction of technological and communicational processes in the global society; it will explore dynamic **information and communication technology (ICT)** connecting governments, markets and the public; it will examine why technology is crucial to the historical understanding of globalization; it assesses the complexity of cultural exchanges in contemporary media, technical services and technical characteristics.

> **ICT**
> Technologies that support data and information processing, storage and analysis, as well as data and information transmission and communication, via the Internet and other means (Webber & Kauffman, 2011).

The questions mentioned above will be linked with media and communication practices in this lecture. New forms of sociability, participation and commerce resulting from the production and consumption of media will be investigated via relevant case studies. We will also analyze diverse youth cultures and explore how media voice previously unheard groups of individuals and engaged in cultural rituals. From the lecture, students will gain insights into the global patterns of media and communication.

The main contents we are going to talk about will help to analyze critical theoretical and empirical debates about the impact of new media on society, including the network society (Castells, 2001), networked individualism (Wellman, 2001), online public sphere (Habermas, 1991), digital media, local cultures and global communities (Miller, 2008), new media and democratization (Coleman, 2005; Morozov, 2012), and virtual identity and virtual communities (Turkle, 1996; Rheingold, 1993), from the perspectives of media production, media culture and media consumption.

After the study, you are expected to have learning outcomes as follows.

(1) Further develop an understanding of media culture and communication as technical information and social practices.

(2) Critically reflect on how technology articulates social interactions and global communication.

(3) Employ advanced research methodologies and critical perspectives in the analysis of contemporary media culture and global practices.

(4) Gain a sophisticated and critically informed understanding of how culture and society are produced and circulated through various media and technological forms.

(5) Have an understanding of technological factors intrinsic to contemporary communicational processes, the role of the Internet in the changing communication environment, the technical patterns shaping the country and market power in the global society, and vital technological dimensions of globalization (i.e., relations with cultural production and consumption)

(6) Develop critical thinking on how technology helps us understand different cultures and how it helps to transform global capitalism.

1.2 Theory

1.2.1 What Is Globalization?

1.2.1.1 Analytical Concepts and Definition of Globalization

Globalization is not a new concept. In ancient times, traders travelled vast distances to buy rare and expensive commodities for sale in their homelands. And the Industrial Revolution brought advances in transportation and communication in the 19th century, easing the trade across borders and connecting the world accordingly. Till then, globalization began to take shape.

Nowadays, the concept of globalization ripples out into various aspects of the world. Economically, it indicates a world where international trade, capital flows, technology transfer, service provision, etc., have formed a closely connected whole. Socially, it leads to more significant interactions among multiple populations. Culturally, it represents the exchange of ideas, values and artistic expressions among cultures, whose possible outcomes would be homogenization, heterogenization and hybridisation. Politically, globalization has shifted public attention to intergovernmental organizations such as the United Nations (UN) and the World Trade Organization (WTO). Legally, globalization has changed the way international law is created and enforced.

Compared to similar processes in the past (e.g. colonization), contemporary globalization takes on wider dimensions—it is more extensive, more intense, quicker and generates greater impact than previous, historical developments. In this regard, Held et al. (2003) argue that the effect of globalization is particularly important and they distinguish four distinct types of its impact: (a) decisional—costs/benefits at local level influenced by the global; (b) institutional—influence on organizational agendas; (c) distributive—distribution of power and wealth; (d) structural—conditioning of domestic social, economic and political behavior/organization. Keohane and Nye (2003) indicate that the fundamental distinction of globalization is problematic, "since absolute discontinuities do not exist in human history. Every era builds on others, and history can always find precursors for phenomena in the present" (Keohane & Nye, 2000: 108).

Before introducing the definition of "globalization", here are four keywords for its emerging features to help you better understand it.

> **Four Keywords to Better Understand "Globalization"**
> *Velocity*: speeding up of these processes thanks to the development of global transport and communication infrastructures. Ideas, goods, information, capital and people can be globally diffused in a very speedy manner.
> *Impact*: also tends to be global in the sense that local events may have global, wide-scale impact, i.e. not confined or contained, blurring boundaries between domestic and global affairs.
> *Extensity*: stretching of social, political and economic activities across frontiers. In other words, it refers to spatial dimension.
> *Intensity*: intensification (getting stronger) of interconnectedness in the sense of taking on the shape of durable patterns.

With that in mind, let's look at two standard definitions of "globalization".

Stevenson (2002: 21) defines globalization as "a process whereby the world's financial markets, political systems and cultural dimensions form increasingly intense relationships".

In Giddens's eyes, globalization is "the intensification of worldwide social relations which link distant localities in such a way that local happenings are shaped by events occurring many miles away, and vice versa" (Giddens, 1990: 64).

Many other scholars also give their definitions, like "a process (or set of processes) which embodies a transformation in the spatial organization of social relations and transactions—assessed in terms of their extensity, intensity, velocity, and impact—generating transcontinental or interregional flows and networks of activity, interaction, and the exercise of power" (Held et al., 2003: 68).

> **Question:**
>
> After reading the above materials, how will you define globalization?

1. 2. 1. 2 Approaches to Globalization Studies

There are three major paradigms that constitute globalization discourses: modernization, critical political economy, and cultural globalization, known as hybridization.

The first paradigm, i.e. the **modernization theory** is one of the oldest approaches. As Alberto Martinelli (2005:101) especially argues, "globalization is one of the most visible consequences of modernity and has reshaped the project of modernity". For him, "modernization is a global process". With several ICTs and the media, those developing countries are called for transformation from pre-modern to modern in social life technologically, culturally, politically, and economically by imitating the West (Curran, 2002). The major critique here is that the modernization process mode flows from a few developed and modernized countries to those less-developed. More importantly, what these modernized countries ask developing countries to alter into is their economic system or what we call capitalism.

The second paradigm is the **critical political economy approach**. This paradigm emphasizes it is the centrality of the economy that is in control of social and cultural change (Ampuja, 2004). Specifically, the new media and information technologies enable the transnational media corporations to "create a demand for commodities and deliver audiences to powerful advertisers" (Ampuja, 2004: 68), holding substantial economic and cultural power by dominating global media markets. The dominance of Walt Disney, Netflix, Google, and Apple in content production and distribution channels exemplifies the imbalance of cultural flows around the globe.

The third paradigm, i.e. the **cultural globalization approach** emphasizes the cultural elements of globalization. Instead of criticizing the cultural imperialism thesis, cultural globalization theorists see the positive, stating that globalization has been responsible for "increasing international dialogue, empowering minorities, and building progressive solidarity" (Curran & Park, 2000: 10). Cultural globalization emphasizes different cultures, redefining themselves as hybrids. This process is considered to be free from Western domination because, for example, in popular music, new stylistic innovations can come from the third world (Jin, 2020).

It is clear that globalization studies are an inherently interdisciplinary approach. It cannot just be studied from one perspective or academic tradition. In addition to the three methods mentioned above, researchers in the globalization studies also include geographers (e.g., Murray, 2006), sociologists (e.g., Giddens, 1990), media and communication scholars (e.g., Thussu, 2008).

1. 2. 1. 3 Globalization and "Glocalization": Origins and History of Globalization

There are generally five different perspectives on the history and origins of globalization (Ritzer, 2019), which are:

> **Question:**
> What other disciplines do you think would have something important to say about globalization/the globalized world?

(1) the idea that globalization is hardwired into human beings (desire for a better life);

(2) the idea that globalization proceeds in long-term "cycles";

(3) the idea that globalization is characterized by "epochs" or "waves" (e.g., European colonial conquests);

(4) the idea that globalization is a result of specific seminal historical events (e.g., 9/11);

(5) the idea that globalization results from more recent 20th-century events (e.g., the emergence of multinational corporations).

To be more specific, there is a strong relationship between "**glocalization**" and globalization, and the terminology of glocalization is perceived as the latter. It is noticeable that there are two words—"local" and "globalization"—in the combination word "glocalization". The term originally derives from business and marketing (buzzword in the 1990s). It was coined as a micro marketing term in dealing with the problem of how can global products and services be tailored to locally differentiated markets. It was not as simple as adapting to local market conditions and cultural traditions but required inventing or constructing consumers for the local setting.

If we switch to the media perspective on the term "glocal" or "glocalization", the closely-related **cultural imperialism** would be shed light on. In other words, glocalization is often perceived as synonymous with cultural imperialism, a homogenizing of culture (e.g., Americanization, Westernization, McDonaldization), which tends to be closely related to the **globalization of capitalism**. Capitalism is a class system that builds on the system of commodity production built around the relationship between private ownership of capital and property-less wage labor. Globalization of capitalism is owing to the capitalist countries, which always aspire to stretch beyond boundaries (which it has been able to do precisely because it is insulated). It has become the dominant production system worldwide and has led to the international division of labor.

But arguably, the global is not inimical to the local, an idea that it destroys local culture and traditions, but is part of it, just as the local is part of the global. As Robertson (1995: 26) said about the mutual integration of globalization and glocalization,

> "Much of the talk about globalization has tended to assume that it is a process which overrides locality... This interpretation neglects two things. First, it neglects the extent to which what is called local in large degree constructed on a trans- or supra-local basis."

In other words, there is very little that is "purely" local but the local is often shaped by the dynamics of the supra-local (e.g., nationalism and ethnic conflict). And he pointed out that local spaces are always, to some extent, constructed by the global, and they should not be seen in opposition (Robertson, 1995).

Other critiques of cultural imperialism argue against the strong media effects model it is based on. It is how people "read" global media (e. g., Hollywood movies) or the "interpretation" that matters (Tomlinson, 1991). People tend to explain what they receive from the perspective of their own culture, however "global" it is. The complexity of media flows needs to be understood as a counterpoint to "dependency theory", and there are "**counter flows**" to consider.

A more complex picture emerges when looking at the local and global interaction in the media sphere. One particularly striking example of glocalization is global media formats tailored to local markets. Media research has considered the importance of the local, national, regional, and global, with mass communication research focusing on adapting global media formats to local tastes. The mass communication theory has also moved to consider how audiences read and interact with exported forms of media. There is also a cross-cultural analysis of media forms (e.g., imported US soaps in Trinidad).

Counter Flows

There are also flows of communication from regions outside the US-UK axis to the West (Thussu, 2006):

- Bollywood, Nollywood, etc.

- Aljazeera Arabic: http://www.aljazeera.com/

- Australia exported to a number of countries-UK.

- "Scandi noir" detectives from Sweden and Denmark

- Mexico and Brazil for telenovelas

- *Big Brother* in a Dutch format

> **Questions:**
>
> (1) How relevant does the concept of glocalization to the contemporary media landscape?
>
> (2) Would you say that the cultural imperialism paradigm is outdated, or does it still have something useful to say about the digital age?

1. 2. 1. 4 Globalization and Western Hegemony

From the analysis we have conducted so far, it is clear that capitalism goes hand in hand with the **nation-state** when the acknowledgment of private ownership and requirement of a particular political order—democracy is brought with it. There also comes the strict separation between public and private and the recognition of fundamental liberties.

Nation-State

Where the state coincides with the nation (cultural/ethnic dimension) in an important geographical way, "coordinated control over delimited territorial areas" (Giddens, 1986). It basically means "sovereignty" and monopoly over means of violence (military dimension).

Globalization, in turn, has been understood for these reasons as a matter of Western (and more particularly the US) hegemony, within which the Western societies typically unite capitalism and liberalism. The Westernization of a country, place, or individual is the process by which they adopt the ideas and behaviors typical of Europe and North America, rather than retaining those traditional in their culture (*Collins Advanced Dictionary of the English Language*, 2023). In other words, Westernization is the reconstruction of the rest of the world on Western norms, values and institutions.

However, to what degree is globalization simply "Westernization"? Do we confuse globalization with "Westernization" or "Americanization"?

While the movement of globalization can be understood in one direction as Westernization or Americanization, globalization also includes processes that import the encounter with the postcolonial reality into Western societies (Schuerkens, 2003). Nowadays, with the emergence of many third world countries, especially China, the Western hegemony seems to some extent to be weakened. Therefore, Westernization is likely to be considered only as a part of globalization. What matters is that globalization should not have been equal to Westernization. In a globalizing age, the intracultural, intercultural, and transcultural exchange has become a global experience. As in the sense of intermingling, cultural diversity has spread around the entire globe. "It is not Westernization in the sense that the world is becoming more homogeneous and the non-Western world looks increasingly like the West." (Turner & Khondkher, 2010: 19) Instead, Globalization could principally take non-Western directions or possible future postmodern globalization (Scholte, 2002).

1. 2. 2 What Is Technology?

1. 2. 2. 1 Technology and Globalization

Everyone knows what technology means, but how about the relationship between technology and globalization? Maybe you'll say technology helps the world get together, but is it all true?

According to the *Digital 2022 Global Overview Report*, there had been about 4.95 billion people worldwide on the Internet at the start of 2022, accounting for some 62.5% of the world's total population. However, the percentage of unconnected population remains high, particularly in Southern Asia and Africa. The latest data reveals that more than 1 billion people remain offline across Southern Asia, while nearly 840 million people in Africa are yet to come online. Furthermore, 1 in 4 people across lower- and middle-income countries is still unaware of the existence of mobile Internet (GSMA, 2021). Mobile broadband connections were multiplying, though regional disparities in global Internet development are still in a grim situation. Under the general trend of globalization interconnection, further improvement of global Internet penetration needs to be continued in the future.

Here comes the concept of "**digital divide**". Granqvist (2005) describes the myth of the digital divide, which she claims as if the uneven global distribution of material wealth were not a new thing. The digital divide is often discussed as being isolated from the economic system and perpetuating such inequalities. Merely highlighting this so-called divide indicates a modernist worldview and approach to development, implying that the imperative thing is to fortify the deployment of ICTs in marginalized countries and therefore, adapting them to the socioeconomic patterns of the economically powerful regions.

Digital Divide

It refers to the disparity in access to information and communication technologies (ICTs) and the use of the Internet for various activities between individuals, households, businesses and geographic areas at different socioeconomic levels (OECD, 2001).

Technology can sometimes be a means of modernization. It is conceptualized as a significant causal factor for development within a theoretical perspective. Technology and the entire socio-political context of modernity should be transferred to developing countries. There's an argument that ICTs or "mass media" can contribute to literacy, urbanization, and industrialization (Zhao

Modernization Theory

Modernization refers to a pattern of gradual transition from a "pre-modern" or "traditional" society to a "modern" society. Originated from German sociologist Max Weber (1864–1920), modernization theory provided the basis for the modernization paradigm developed by Harvard sociologist Talcott Parsons (1902–1979). It emphasized internal factors while making an exception of science (Shrum, 2001).

Dependency Theory

Dependency theory is a school of contemporary social science that seeks to advance the understanding of underdevelopment, the analysis of its causes, and, to a lesser extent, the paths to overcome it. It derived from Latin America in the 1960s and spread rapidly to North America, Europe, and Africa, continuing to be relevant to contemporary debates (Sonntag, 2001).

Participatory Approach

Participatory methodologies originated from qualitative research approaches, which aim to reflect, explore, and communicate the views, concerns, feelings and experiences of research participants from their

& Hao, 2005). However, there is also much criticism. For example, **modernization theory** focuses on short-term quantifiable criteria and results and emphasizes a uniform general trajectory of development, which excludes deeper cultural and contextual factors that might limit longer-term growth. Communication is also viewed as one-directional in this approach since the technological solutions are often driven by the core and the problems in the periphery that the core perceives.

Concerned with social structures and exploitation, **dependency theory** reflects on another aspect of the impact of technology. When technology affects developments, the core (Western countries) benefits from its global links and experiences dynamic development, but the periphery (global south) is constrained by its dependence on the core. In terms of ICTs, intellectual property and technology development remain in the core, with the periphery encouraged to adopt and use limited "ownership" or empowerment, which feeds into the cycle of dependence.

The **participatory approach** challenges the view that communication is a one-way process from the rich to the poor. It favors grassroots movements for social change within developing countries that call for more attention. It holds the view that the context is vital for technology use, because the ICTs are often used for purposes that were not intended and are often modified to suit the local needs better. The local context tends to be idealized since the projects are usually initiated or driven by developed countries but implemented locally. Consequently, the existing relations of dominance fail to be challenged, and the participation of developing countries becomes a "box to tick".

1. 2. 2. 2 Approaches to Understand Technology and New Media[1]

Three main factors have contributed to the emergence of the technology and new media referred to as cyber-optimism and cyber-pessimism.

First of all, the last two decades have witnessed the opening up, through new media, of a new arena for grassroots political debate among individuals from across the political spectrum, which has broken down the boundaries to be the audiences between mass media and new media. The channels for communication—one to one, one to many then many to many—have both increased the complexity and intensified the proliferation of information. According to Lieroun and Livingstone (2006), **new media** is "those digital media that are interactive, incorporate two-way communication, and involve some form of computing as opposed to lad media such as telephone, radio and TV", then Socha (2012) further defined "new media" as a term englobing "all that is related to the Internet and the interplay between technology, images and sound". Interactivity is the core feature of new media, which could be defined as a new model for communication, relying on digital technology; the "new" component of the title highlights contrast with traditional forms of media such as television and printing newspapers.

perspectives (French & Swain, 2004). One of the most important principles of participatory research is research with rather than on people (Reason & Heron, 1986).

New Media

Media that depends on digital technology featured by interactivity and two-way communication.

Secondly, according to media experts Voltmer, Negrine and Stanyer, as far as political communication is concerned, the interactions between social actors (media, citizens and political organizations) "are frequently characterized by conflicts and disruptions, but equally by the compromises and cooperation that are required to maintain the relationship" (Voltmer, 2006; Negrine & Stanyer, 2007). New media has an effect, for instance, on the shifting of relationships between parties and voters, typically including the voices of citizens in party decision-making, although there is an on-going discussion about whether this is happening in practice (David, 2000; Van Dijk & Hacker, 2000).

Thirdly, scholars have interpreted the dialectical interactions between technology and society in widely differing ways, from Barlow's cyber-libertarian vision of a digital utopia of the

---

[1] Extracted from Zhao, Y. (2014). New Media and Democracy: 3 Competing Visions from Cyber-Optimism and Cyber Pessimism. *Journal of Political Sciences & Public Affairs*, 2(1), 114-118.

future to the dystopian nightmare envisioned by Davies, who believes that technology will lead to ubiquitous surveillance. In other words, different people are evaluating the benefits and drawbacks of new media upon politics from radically different perspectives. The interrelationships between actors involved in political communication through new media warrant close scrutiny. That is to say, the emergence of conflicting views between cyber-optimism and cyber-pessimism is inevitable.

1.2.3 What Is Culture?

1.2.3.1 Concepts and Characteristics

Many definitions have changed historically. For a long time, culture was understood as a fixed, bounded concept (Servaes, 2007). "A culture" was viewed as a "Thing", a homogeneous entity that involved a list of "traits", while "certain cultures" were seen as more advanced, developed or civilized than others. Now, culture is seen as being dynamic, open-ended and heterogeneous. The definition changes from within, through deviance, disagreements, etc., and from outside, through influences from other cultures. If these traits of culture were seen to be incompatible with aspects of development, it was then seen as an obstacle to development—something that needs to be overcome.

To conceptualize culture, scholars propose lots of characteristics. The following are some of them.

> **Key Characteristics of Culture**
> (1) Culture manifests at different levels. It is expectable to distinguish three basic levels of cultural expression when analyzing the culture at an organizational level: (a) observable artifacts, (b) values, and (c) basic underlying assumptions (Schein, 1990).
> (2) Culture is learned, not inherited. It derives from one's social environment, not from one's genes. It is a social construct.
> (3) Culture is shared. It never occurs in isolation; instead, it emerges with the shared experience of durable groups. Culture results from social interaction. It is common for individuals to belong to multiple cultures such that they may share culture with a large number of people (i.e., global culture).

Culture and globalization also interact. As Edward Said (2008: 8) noted, "The thing to be noticed about this kind of contemporary discourse, which assumes the primacy and even the complete centrality of the West, is how totalizing is its form, how all-enveloping its attitudes and gestures, how much it shuts out as it includes, compresses and consolidates." So, it is assumed that globalization will result in the creation of a global village. Some people think that different cultures will become less distinct because of their constant interaction, and cultural differences will vanish.

Among all perspectives, the multi-perspectival approach is a pragmatic contextualist approach. It uses critical theories for certain specific tasks and others for different ones. It combines Marxism, feminism, post-structuralism, and other contemporary theoretical optics.

1. 2. 3. 2 How to Study Culture?

There are three primary schools to culture research: Frankfort School, British Cultural Studies, and Postmodern Cultural Studies.

(1) Frankfurt School

Frankfurt School pioneered critical communication studies in the 1930s, combining the political economy of the media, cultural analysis of texts, and audience reception studies with the social and ideological effects of mass culture and communications.

Max Horkheimer, Theodor Adorno, Walter Benjamin and Jürgen Habermas.

They proposed the concept of "**culture industries**", which means all mass-mediated cultural artifacts within the context of industrial production. These artifacts exhibited the same features as other mass production products: commodification, standardization, and massification.

Frankfurt School is the first to systematically analyze and criticize the mass-mediated culture and communications within critical social theory. They are also the first to unpack the significance of what they called "cultural industry" in the reproduction of contemporary societies. It is an essential agent of socialization, a mediator of political reality, and should therefore be seen

Culture Industries

A term used for the first time in the book *Dialectic of Enlightenment*, published by Horkheimer and Adorno in 1947. Firstly, it is used to replace the expression "mass culture" to outset its disadvantages. In cultural industries, products customized for mass consumption largely determine the nature of such consumption, and are manufactured more or less according to plan (Adorno & Rabinbach, 1975).

🌐 Digital Culture and Globalization

Scan the QR code to learn more about Frankfurt School.

as a significant institution of modern societies with various economic, political, cultural, and social effects. Positively, their research dissected the interconnection of culture and communication in artifacts that reproduced the existing society, thoroughly presented the social norms and practices, and legitimized the social organization of state capitalism.

Their limitation is the preliminary analysis of the political economy of the media and the processes (audience reception) of culture production. Also, their dichotomy between high culture and low culture has problems contrasted with an ideal of "authentic art" that limits critical moments to high culture. The third limitation is the lack of experience and historical research on the construction of the media industry and its interaction with other social institutions. Many suggestions are given to them to distinguish between the encoding and decoding of media artifacts. From the 1930s to the 1950s, schoolers excluded new cultural theories and methods into a reconstructed critical theory.

(2) British Cultural Studies

British Cultural Studies emerged in the 1960s, led by the Birmingham Center for Contemporary Cultural Studies. It places culture in a theory of social production and reproduction, illustrating how culture fosters social domination or enables people to resist and struggle against authority. Society is conceived as a hierarchical and antagonistic set of social relations characterized by the oppression of subordinate class, gender, race, ethnicity, and national hierarchies. In such a situation, individuals striving for more freedom and power must fight.

In British Cultural Studies, **Antonio Gramsci** proposed the **hegemony theory**. Based on his model of hegemony and counterhegemony, cultural studies analyze "hegemonic", social and cultural forms of domination and seek "counter-

Antonio Gramsci (1891–1937)

Hegemony Theory

Hegemony, the dominance of one group over another, is of-

14

hegemonic" forces of resistance and struggle.

Richard Johnson, who worked at the University of Texas and conferenced on cultural studies, proposed a postmodern concept of "difference" (Johnson, 2002) to compete with the Birmingham notion of "antagonism", including the workers and bosses, men and women, whites and blacks and so on. It is a struggle against domination.

The limitations of British Cultural Studies are as follows. (a) It is a fetishism of the audience's reception and construction of meanings. (b) It is a fetishism of resistance without distinguishing between types and forms of resistance. (c) It is a fetishism of struggle, while the political battle is displaced into the struggle for meanings and pleasure and resistance equated with the evasion of social responsibility. Such opposition does not challenge the existing structure. (d) It is a fetishism of audience pleasure. It valorizes certain forms of culture which bind individuals to conservative, sexist or racist positions. And finally, (e) it has generally failed to engage modernism or other forms of high culture, therefore overlooking the potential for opposition, subversion, and ideology.

Comparing the Frankfurt School with the British Cultural Studies, they develop theoretical models of the relationship between the economy, country, society, culture, and everyday life, thus depending on contemporary social theory's problematics. One of the prominent features of British Cultural Studies is that it subverts the high and low culture distinction.

(3) Postmodern Cultural Studies

Postmodern Cultural Studies are a kind of underdefined theory. It is simply used as a buzzword without a real definition pointing out what is at stake, or justifying why their approach or subject is indeed "postmodern". For example, Denzin (1991) proposes that everything that occurred

ten supported by legitimating norms and ideas (Rosamond, 2020).

Cultural hegemony is a philosophical and sociological theory proposed by Gramsci, which refers to the domination of a social class over the whole society through social cultures, such as beliefs, interpretations, perceptions, values, etc.

Scan the QR code to learn about Stuart Hall, one of the representative scholars of British Cultural Studies.

in American society after World War II is "postmodern". He lists many defining characteristics of the term, many of which could be assimilated to modern phenomenalists. Technological determinism and postmodernism of resistance all belong to Postmodern Cultural Studies.

Compared with the other two approaches, Postmodern Cultural Studies is on the break or rupture: "a result of revolution and history" vs. "a result of new technologies". Postmodernism replicates the old discourses of technological determinism. It is an aesthetic reaction against high modernism that mixed high and low culture features.

Scan the QR codes to learn more about Postmodern Cultural Studies, with representative theories from Jean Baudrillard and Michel Foucault respectively.

1. 2. 4 Culture and Globalization

Cultural difference, the fact of objective existence, is one of the major obstacles to globalization. However, as we discussed before, there are assumptions that the constant interaction of different cultures in the process of globalization will result in the global village, where different cultures become less distinct and cultural differences vanish. This is what we call "homogenization". But leaning to the other extreme, heterogenization (e.g., "glocalization") or "cultural infusion" is also what should be avoided. Another common consequence of globalization is "hybridization", a state where users could manipulate cultural products to fit their own needs, like transnationalism, creolization, traveling cultures, etc. Therefore, the balance of cultural diversity and globalization seems to be a thorny issue and those consequences going to any of the extremes are not what we should have originally longed for.

The relationship between cultural diversity and globalization should not be conflictive. Actions like trying to unify the world with one ideology and value should be intrinsic to so-called "radical globalization", which doesn't contribute to globalization but fuels ethnic conflicts and cultural divisions. For example, Europe's handling of refugees has led to chaotic and disorderly social consequences for lack of careful consideration of developmental differences. What needs to be changed is not the long-term trend of global contact, circulation, exchange and integration, but the globalization that eliminates differences; the world should be not only a multi-source fusion but also a colorful one.

With the concept of "**human community with a shared future**" put forward by the president of PRC Xi Jinping, we are supposed to look at the overall and long-term interests of development, respect the differences and pluralistic forms of the international community, and strive to build a new globalization value with the consensus of tolerance, mutual appreciation and win-win cooperation.

Scan the QR code to read a paper concerning the notion "human community with a shared future" by Zhang Xiaochun (2018).

1.3 Conclusion

In this lecture, we briefly introduced several concepts and theories related to globalization, technology and culture, and three approaches in studying culture. On top of that, relations between technology & globalization and culture & globalization were briefly investigated.

From now on, you need to start thinking about the possible connections between "theory" "globalization" "culture" "technology" and "new media" from the perspective of what and how "new globalization" actually is, and the extent of the communicative process taking places within.

1.4 Extended Readings

Scan the QR code to get extended reading materials.

1.5 Post Questions and Discussion

(1) Scan the QR code and watch a video. American President Donald Trump announced a ban on TikTok in the US in 2020. What do you think of the current anti-globalization phenomenon?

(2) What events do you think exemplify the four characteristics mentioned above of globalization (velocity, impact, extensity, and intensity)?

(3) Has the digital divide been narrowed down during technological improvement?

(4) Some people assume that globalization will create a global village, where different cultures will become less distinct and cultural differences will vanish because of their constant interaction. What's your opinion?

(5) Regarding the technological determinism debate, which do you agree with more? Technology shapes humanity or humanity shapes technology? And why?

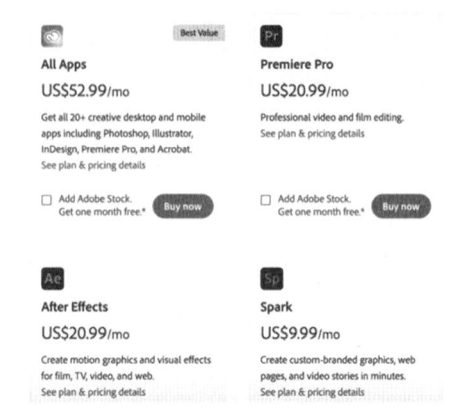

1.6 Bibliography

Adorno, T. W., Rabinbach, A. G. (1975). Culture Industry Reconsidered. *New German Critique*, (6): 12-19.

Ampuja, M. (2004). Critical Media Research, Globalisation Theory and Commercialisation. *Javnost—The Public*, 11(3): 59-76.

Coleman, S. (2005). New Mediation and Direct Representation: Reconceptualizing Representation in the Digital Age. *New Media & Society*, 7(2): 177-198.

Curran, J. (2002). *Media and Power*. London: Routledge.

Curran, J., Park, M. J. (eds.). (2000). *De-Westernizing Media Studies*. New York: Routledge.

Dai Y. J. (2020). *Globalization and Media in the Digital Platform Age.* London: Routledge.

David, R. (2000). *The Political Impact of the Internet: The American Experience in Reinvigorating Democracy: British Politics and the Internet.* London: Ashgate Publishing Limited.

Giddens, A. (1986). The Nation-State and Violence. *Capital & Class*, 10(2): 216-220.

Giddens, A. (1990). The Consequences of Modernity. Cambridge: Polity Press.

Global System for Mobile Communications Association (GSMA). (2021). The State of Mobile Internet Connectivity 2021. https://www.gsma.com/r/wp-content/uploads/2021/09/The-State-of-Mobile-Internet-Connectivity-Report-2021.pdf.

Habermas, J. (1991). *The Structural Transformation of the Public Sphere: An Inquiry into a Category of Bourgeois Society*. Cambridge: MIT Press.

Held, D., McGrew, A., Goldblatt, D., & Perraton, J. (2003). *Global Transformations: Politics, Economics and Culture*. Cambridge: Polity Press.

International Telecommunications Union (ITU). (2019). Measuring the Information Society Report. https://www.itu.int/en/ITU-D/Regional-Presence/AsiaPacific/Documents/Events-/2016/Mar-ICTStats/Presentations/Session%201a.%20MIS-Report-2015%20Es-pie.pdf.

Jinqiu, Z., Xiaoming, H. (2005). Modernization in the Information Age. *Media Asia*, 32(4): 191-196.

Johnson, R. (2002). *Exemplary Differences: Mourning (and Not Mourning) a Princess*. London: Routledge.

Lievrouw, L. A., Livingstone, S. (2006). *The Handbook of New Media* (updated student edition). London, Thousand Oaks and New Delhi: Sage Publications.

Martinelli, A. (2005). *Globalization and Modernity. Global Modernization: Rethinking the Project of Modernity*. Thousand Oaks: Sage.

Miller, V. (2008). New Media, Networking and Phatic Culture. *Convergence*, 14(4): 387-400.

Negrine, R. M., Stanyer, J. (2007). "Introduction: Political Communication Transformed?" in *The Political Communication Reader* (pp. 1-10). London: Routledge.

OECD. (2001). Understanding the Digital Divide. OECD Digital Economy Papers, No. 49. Paris: OECD Publishing. http://dx.doi.org/10.1787/236405667766.

Reason, P., Heron, J. (1986) Research with People: The Paradigm of Co-operation Experiential Enquiry. *Person-Centred Review*, 1(4): 456-476.

Rheingold, H. (1993) *The Virtual Community: Homesteading on the Electronic Frontier*. New York: Harper Collins.

Robertson, R. (1995). Glocalization: Time-Space and Homogeneity-Heterogeneity. *Global Modernities*, 2(1): 25-44.

Rosamond, B. (2020). Hegemony. Encyclopedia Britannica. https://www.britannica.com/topic/hegemony.

Schein, E. H. (1990). Organizational Culture. American Psychological Association, 45(2): 109.

Schuerkens, U. (2003). The Sociological and Anthropological Study of Globalization and Localization. *Current Sociology*, 51(3-4): 209-222.

Servaes, J. (ed.). (2007). *Communication for Development and Social Change*. Delhi: Sage Publications.

Sonntag. H. R. (2001). Dependency Theory. *International Encyclopaedia of the Social & Behavioral Sciences*: 3501-3505.

Thussu, D. K. (2006). *Media on the Move: Global Flow and Contra-Flow*. London: Routledge.

Thussu, D. K. (ed.). (2009). *Internationalizing Media Studies*. London: Routledge.

Tomlinson, J. (1991). *Cultural Imperialism: A Critical Introduction*. London: Pinter.

Van Dijk, J. A., Hacker, K. L. (2000). What Is Digital Democracy?. In *Digital Democracy, Issues of Theory and Practice* (pp. 1-9). New York: Sage Publications.

W. Shrum. (2001). Science and Development. *International Encyclopaedia of the Social & Behavioral Sciences*: 13607-13610.

Weber, D. M., Kauffman, R. J. (2011). What Drives Global ICT Adoption? Analysis and Research Directions. *Electronic commerce research and applications*, 10(6): 683-701.

Wellman, B. (2001). Little Boxes, Glocalization, and Networked Individualism. In *Kyoto Workshop on Digital Cities* (pp. 10-25). Berlin, Heidelberg: Springer.

Xiaochun, Z. (2018). In Pursuit of a Community of Shared Future: China's Global Activism in Perspective. *China Quarterly of International Strategic Studies*, 4(01): 23-37.

Zhao, Y. (2014). New Media and Democracy: 3 Competing Visions from Cyber-Optimism and Cyber Pessimism. *Journal of Political Sciences & Public Affairs*, 2(1): 114-118.

LECTURE & SEMINAR 2
Digital Divide

The "digital gap" is the disparity between people with and without access to the Internet. Who can easily access information and communication technology tools and the knowledge that these technologies supply and who cannot? This wide gap in most modern countries might result from socio-economic, geographical, educational, behavioral, generational, and other factors. Within the global community, there is still a disparity in technology adoption between the industrialized and developing worlds, which may be even more significant.

Framework

2.1 Knowledge Gap and Digital Divide
2.1.1 Knowledge Gap Hypothesis
2.1.2 New Media vs. Old Media

2.2 ICT and Digital Divide
2.2.1 Types of ICT
2.2.2 ICT and Digital Access
2.2.3 Digital Divide: From Access to Use

2.3 Digital Access and Digital Divide
2.3.1 Access as a Method of Technology Appropriation
2.3.2 The Theoretical Framework for Analyzing Access
2.3.3 Determinants in a Successive Phase of Access

2.4 Conclusion
2.5 Extended Readings
2.6 Post Questions and Discussion
2.7 Bibliography

Terms

knowledge gap hypothesis, digital divide, SES, usage gap, digital access

Pre-lecture Discussion

(1) Do new types of inequality exist or rise in the information society?

(2) What is new about the inequality of access to and use of ICTs as compared to other scarce material and immaterial resources?

(3) Can you share some examples about technology narrowing or widening digital divide?

2.1 Knowledge Gap and Digital Divide

2.1.1 Knowledge Gap Hypothesis

The **knowledge gap hypothesis** was initially proposed in 1970 by Philip J. Tichenor, George A. Donohue, and Clarice N. Olien. As more information becomes available through mediated communication, there is a widening knowledge gap between specific societal sectors. This point of view is frequently expressed concerning an individual's comprehension of political and public events and how they may influence their ability for civic participation (Eveland, 2002; Tichenor et al., 1970).

According to the knowledge gap hypothesis, social class gaps in information flow are created by underlying disparities and inequalities in the social structure, notably in the educational system (Bonfadelli, 2002). Tichenor and his colleagues identify five key factors that contribute to **knowledge gaps**: communication skills (i.e., higher education improves one's ability to understand information), existing subject knowledge, relevant social contacts (i.e., the increased social reference provides more opportunities to discuss and absorb information), selective information exposure and retention, and the media system's structure (i.e., certain information is more widely distributed) (Bonfadelli, 2002; Tichenor et al., 1970).

Although Tichenor and his colleagues were the first to express such ideas publicly, their argument was based on years of mass media research. Hyman and Sheatsley noted in 1947 that providing more information does not always result in greater understanding. They also highlighted that learning motivation on an individual level is crucial to the success of information efforts.

Another line of scholarship, **digital divide** research,

As the infusion of mass media information into a social system rises, parts of the population with greater socio-economic class tend to learn this information at a faster rate than lower status segments, causing the knowledge gap between these segments to widen rather than close.

Knowledge Gap Hypothesis

This concept explains how information is frequently disseminated differently within a social system.

Knowledge Gap

When a new thought enters the society, the people in the higher strata understand it better, and so the divide widens.

Digital Divide

Digital divide is commonly characterized as the difference between those who have and do not have access to various types of information and communication technologies.

supports the knowledge gap argument. It implies that measuring information availability and exposure does not accurately reflect potential socio-economic disparities among particular people or areas. Even though all groups have equal access to information, knowledge gaps might exist when respective mediums are used differently (Bonfadelli, 2002). The increased fragmentation of the media environment may also impact knowledge gaps.

According to Bonfadelli (2002), the Internet encourages more customized information searching, which can result in a decline in the amount of common knowledge. Prior (2005: 587) observed that although some people use expanded access and diversity of media sources to improve their political knowledge, others "take advantage of additional choice and shut out politics completely". Wei and Hindman (2011) observed a similar pattern, discovering that increased Internet use amplifies an education-based knowledge gap, causing disparities in political knowledge to widen as Internet use increases. The emphasis of the knowledge gap hypothesis in the digital era is more concerned with one's ability to identify, critically analyze, and retain information rather than just gaining access to it, analogous to the shift from a first to second-level digital divide perspective (Bonfadelli, 2002). The same data might be processed and retained differently due to the underlying expected media satisfaction, according to Bonafadelli (2002: 72). The Internet has contributed significantly to the current understanding of the knowledge gap; nevertheless, emphasizing the Internet as a method of information distribution must not eclipse the value of more conventional media outlets. Some scholars employ conceptualizations of uses and gratifications to explore potential differences in expectations that facilitate such a transition (LaRose & Eastin, 2004).

2. 1. 2 New Media vs. Old Media

The study discovered that traditional media viewers differ depending on their thematic interests and the type of material they access. For example, children from higher **socio-economic status (SES)** homes were more likely to watch instructional television programs such as *Sesame Street* (Cook et al., 1975). Similarly, lower-income persons are more likely to read the newspaper's sports section. Higher status focuses more on the disturbing news or opinion and analysis pages (Newspaper Association of America, 1998). Disparities in selective exposure, acceptability, and retention across education levels (Tichenor et al., 1970) indicate a disparity in media content consumption between high SES (Eveland & Scheufele, 2000).

SES

It refers to socio-economic status, a central feature or measure of a social structure including economic and social status, which tends to be positively associated with better health.

However, this difference may be more pronounced for Internet users than conventional media consumers. While traditional media consumers engage in selective exposure, its format, organization, and content have some limitations. Newspapers, for example, provide readers with obvious cues about the day's essential issues by stressing the size and prominence of the headlines, as well as the position and length of the articles (Graber, 1988). Television also impacts viewers' agendas through story sequencing, length, and frequency cues. Furthermore, research has indicated that conventional media place a relative priority on either news (such as newspapers) or entertainment (such as television) (Chaffee & Frank, 1996; Lee & Wei, 2008; Postman, 1986), resulting in a broadly consistent supply of material from traditional mass media. As a result, the nature of ancient media weakens the relationship between selective exposure and education. Simply put, there are few options available to consumers in certain outdated media.

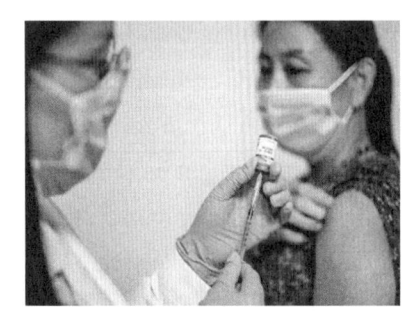

The Chinese populace has a Covid-19 digital knowledge gap. The usage of digital media may significantly predict the difference in Covid-19 knowledge level. On the other hand, interpersonal and public communication, as well as the usage of conventional media like newspaper, radio, and television, did not raise knowledge levels. In the establishment of a Covid-19 knowledge gap, there is an interaction link between education level and online media consumption.

New media, like the Internet, offer significantly more variety of content and unheard-of user control than traditional mass media. Because journalists do not structure the material supply on the Internet, it is diverse and possibly limitless (Bonfadelli, 2002). The Internet provides a broader choice of possibilities and fewer obvious indications than conventional media. According to Tewksbury and Althaus (1999), online readers are less exposed to pieces regarding worldwide, national, or political concerns. They are less likely to pay attention to topics generally clustered on the front page of print newspapers. They discovered this by comparing the print and online versions of the *New York Times*. Furthermore, Internet use, as opposed to conventional media, necessitates a significantly more involved and experienced user (Hargittai & Hinnant, 2008; Wei & Zhang, 2008). Integrating these variables leads to a more fantastic range of distinct content-specific consuming habits differentiated by the user's background and position (Bonfadelli, 2002; Scheufele & Nisbet, 2002).

The Internet's immense openness is expected to break the limits imposed by conventional media, transforming how people use it into a critical indicator of their socio-economic status and favor content. Therefore, it is conceivable that status indicators would affect Internet usage patterns more so than traditional media usage trends.

The social inclusion agenda has welcomed the conceptual shift from access to utilization, focusing scholarly emphasis on the social consequences of "engagement" (or lack thereof) with **information and communication technology (ICT)** (Livingstone & Helsper, 2007; Selwyn, 2004). According to Warschauer (2003: 14), a technological paradigm for social inclusion allows us to change the emphasis from bridging equipment gaps to boosting social development through effective ICT integration into institutions and communities.

ICT

ICT (Information and communication technology) is a larger acronym for IT (information technology), which includes the Internet, wireless networks, mobile phones, computers, and other digital media applications and services.

Knowledge is an essential component of social inclusion linked to various media usage. Again, this applies to both new and old media. The knowledge gap hypothesis, which has a long history in communication studies, provides a framework for understanding unequal knowledge distribution. According to Tichenor et al. (1970: 159-160), when mass media knowledge spreads across a social system, those with higher SES tend to absorb this information more rapidly than those with lower SES. The knowledge gap between these groups tends to widen.

Selective exposure to traditional media is one of the five explanations Tichenor et al. (1970) offered as to why there are knowledge gaps across sectors of society with high and low SES. Newton (1999) discovered a very weak correlation between tabloid reading mobilization and depression using data from the British Social Attitudes survey conducted in 1996, but a strong correlation between broadsheet newspaper reading and higher levels of political knowledge and self-assessed interest and understanding. Holz-Bacha and Norris (2001) revealed that a preference for public television was associated with increased political experience. On the other hand, commercial television was associated with lower knowledge levels. Furthermore, research indicated that viewing television news was favorably associated with political knowledge, but preferring entertainment was adversely associated with learning (Eveland et al., 2003; Prior, 2005; Putnam, 2000). This study concludes that informed uses of mass media, such as reading newspapers or watching news broadcasts, have repercussions (Shah et al., 2005).

Internet usage and political awareness are related (Drew & Weaver, 2006; Kim, 2008). How individuals use a medium and how they utilize new and old media differently are more important questions, though. The responses would be connected to the user's SES (Wei, 2009). The previously mentioned stronger association between SES and Internet information intake might be one way in which new and old media affect knowledge acquisition differently. People with high socio-economic status, in particular, learn more quickly when exposed to information media because they are more likely to pay attention to information-oriented content. Traditional media's broadly consistent content supply, such as newspapers or television, limits users' freedom of choice. As a result, the knowledge disparity between SES groups will close. The Internet's diverse and unlimited content alternatives reduce the external effect of media form on the user's active choice. As a result, Internet users rather than consumers of conventional media will likely see the SES-based knowledge gap widen. According to Bonfadelli (2002: 73), "In contrast to traditional media, the Internet supports audience dispersion and individualized information seeking, and this could result in an increasing breakdown of personal agendas and the quantity of shared knowledge."

2. 2 ICT and Digital Divide

Since the late 1990s, the "digital gap" between those who have access to computers and the Internet and those who do not have dominated the intellectual and political agenda for developing new media. The difference between individuals who have access to computers and the Internet and those who do not is commonly used to describe this disparity. The digital gap and other inequality indicators, such as income, gender, race or ethnicity, and geography, are related. Different social, economic, and political isolation will be made worse by a lack of access to computers, the Internet, and related information flows. This disparity in ICT access affects the economic growth and productivity of industrialized and developing nations.

ICTs as a tool may change the way societies work, entertain, govern, and live if they are accessible and inexpensive (at all levels).

ICT as a sector of the economy: ICTs encompass a sizable and expanding economic sector that includes hardware, software, telecom/datacom, and consultancy services.

Instead of its earlier, more limited emphasis on unequal access to computers and the Internet, the phrase "digital divide" today refers to a broader understanding of access in terms of infrastructure and consumption. While policymakers have continued to focus on ICTs in terms of insufficient infrastructure access, information flows via discovering methods to provide people and communities access to computers, Internet service, and training in computer literacy. The essential knowledge of ICT access, adoption, and use, as well as associated ideas and conversations on the digital divide, are therefore introduced in this section.

ICTS AS INSTRUMENT VS. INDUSTRY

India
- Thriving IT industry based on exported ICT services
- But... internal "digital divide"

China
- ICT powerhouse
- Concerns about impact of Internet information flows on political system

2. 2. 1 Types of ICT

The new ICT may be broadly categorized as (1) computing, (2) communication, and (3) Internet-enabled communication and computing, depending on the type of usage.

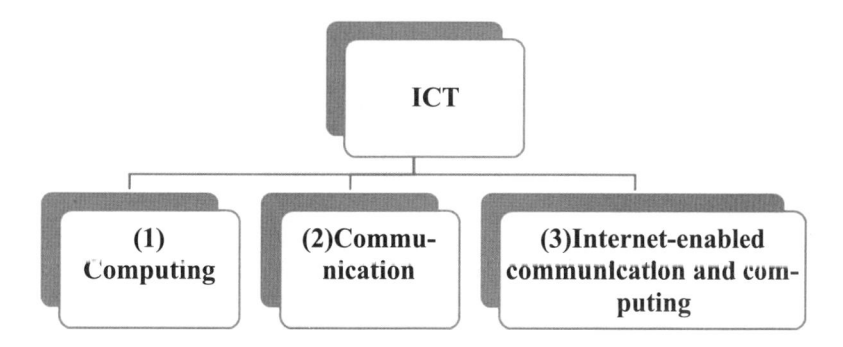

```
                    ICT
         ┌───────────┼───────────┐
    (1)           (2)Commu-    (3)Internet-enabled
   Computing      nication    communication and com-
                                     puting
```

New methods of information generation, organizing, and display (including multimedia) are made possible by the Internet (through collaborative and distance work). In contrast to many other media that depict consumers as passive, the Internet is an active medium that requires more reasoning and critical thinking.

All fields, including scientific computing and business automation, have seen a substantial shift in communications, commerce, and computing due to the Internet's rapid spread from PCs to palmtops, mobile phones, and appliances.

The degree to which an economy has adopted ICT reveals whether it will be able to capitalize on the commercial potential given by new technology or, more broadly, if it will be able to transition to the "new economy". ICT adoption varies significantly among countries, as is to be anticipated. In recent years, Asia has experienced an explosion in the usage of personal computers, although the growth rate has changed from government to country.

Following globalization, the emergence of new ICT types has led to fresh possibilities for social and economic reforms, from which both developed and developing countries might greatly benefit. Two essential characteristics of emergent ICT have been identified in this context. In contrast to earlier technical advancements, emerging countries may nearly instantly access new technology and the benefits it may provide. Even if the statistics now available prevent a complete cost-benefit analysis, new ICT may be utilized wisely and creatively to enhance the welfare of the underprivileged directly. Besides, it is projected that the development of new ICT forms would result in a more seamless integration of the world's labor markets than was previously possible. Even as forces of globalization quickly remove trade and investment restrictions, new forms of ICT enable the migration of manufacturing and service sectors to locations with comparative advantages. The new ICT kinds enable more effective service delivery, particularly when services can be digitalized and market data transfer might be sped up. This tendency has the potential to eradicate absolute poverty by facilitating a more seamless integration of the global labor markets, particularly for unskilled people.

Many academics believe that the digital gap will not disappear abruptly or automatically, despite the enormous promise of new ICT forms. Additionally, it is thought that an aggressive strategy of investing in ICT at the expense of other crucial developmental objectives to close the digital gap would backfire. Such an approach will detract from the core development issues that many nations must quickly address. They include improving the core infrastructure, opening new markets, dismantling telecom monopolies, establishing a solid legal and regulatory framework, and educating everyone. Given the potential for more effective use of limited investable resources in other areas of the economy, nations attempting to sidestep these difficulties may find that their computerization and Internet access investments are ineffective or even a prescription for financial catastrophe.

Assume that governments in developing countries use their few financial and political resources to create social and human capital, build essential infrastructure, and provide fair business conditions. This will significantly aid in developing the ICT sector in this setting. Underdeveloped nations can progressively proceed to more difficult software development and hardware innovation demands by starting simply with industries like data processing and teleworking. Therefore, emerging countries should carefully weigh their competing requirements to accept new technology and create the groundwork for economic success, despite worries about falling behind in the digital world.

How do ICTs help to eradicate poverty?

Governments in the Asia-Pacific area have long recognized the benefits of ICTs, and many have promoted investments in ICT infrastructure, which has resulted in increased Internet connection. Despite substantial advances in ICT development, 930 million people in Asia-Pacific still lack Internet access or the e-literacy necessary to fully capitalize on ICT-enabled possibilities.

In Bangladesh, for example, UNDP's early assistance through the "Access to Information (a2i)" project has decreased the cost of access to services such as health and education, agricultural information, and physical mobility. Every month, 5,000+ digital centers give over 100 services to 5 million underprivileged persons as part of the program. On average, the time it takes to get benefits has been reduced by 85 percent, while the cost has been reduced by 63 percent. A six-year study of 23 services found that streamlining and digitalization saved rural Bangladeshis half a billion dollars.

2. 2. 2 ICT and Digital Access

Many analysts believe that ICT will support nations' social and economic development in the early 21st century. Over the last two decades, many pundits have discussed how new computer and telecommunications technology would turn countries into "knowledge economies" and "network societies". The governments of (over) developed nations worldwide have embraced this usually religious passion with equal zeal. Politicians have hailed ICT proficiency as "the necessary grammar of modern life" and a critical component of citizenship in the digital age (Wills, 1999: 10). Indeed, in reaction to the seeming inevitability of the information society, several governments in developed countries have launched ICT-based initiatives to ensure that their citizens are not "left behind" and can "win" in the new global era.

ICT's revolutionary potential has also been lauded as a once-in-a-lifetime opportunity to transcend existing social barriers and injustices in academia's generally less spectacular confines. Many academic observers believe that ICT may "empower" individuals (D'Allesandro & Dosa, 2001), improve social connection and civic participation (Katz et al., 2001), and improve education and other public and government services accessible and widely available. "Access to information technology and the ability to utilize it has increasingly become part of the toolset required to participate and thrive in an information-based society," Servon and Nelson (2001: 279) write.

Meanwhile, concerns about the potentially polarizing aspects of the information age have dampened such "techno-enthusiasm." Relations about the "emergent" between social groups have been prompted, especially by uneven access to technology and information difficulties. It is suggested that denying some persons or groups access to ICT will reject many of the benefits that ICT may provide.

As a result, generic worries about "knowledge inequalities" have gained importance in public and political debate during the last ten years (e.g., Hansard, 1997; Thomas, 1996). Questions about who is "connected" to information and technology have become more prominent. They are now a crucial component of the information age policy agenda in industrialized, technologically sophisticated nations such as the United States and the United Kingdom. As a result, a strange alliance of academics, IT executives, politicians, and social welfare organizations have been zealously supporting the concept of the digital divide, albeit for very opposite reasons (Strover, 2003). Even though significant initiatives are being enacted to fight the digital divide, much of the surrounding discourse is conceptually simplistic and logically undeveloped. As Ba (2001: 4) found, "little has been done... to build comprehensive theoretical frameworks and research assessment agendas to understand the nature of quality access (to ICT)."

2. 2. 3 Digital Divide: From Access to Use

The digital gap may be regarded as practically embodying the broader notion of social inclusion, which has lately been prominent in policymaking among center-left governments in Western nations. During the Clinton/Gore administration in the 1990s, nations such as the United Kingdom, France, and the United States witnessed a gradual shift toward a more socially inclusive legislative agenda. Indeed, in many countries, combating social isolation and building an "inclusive society" is now the focal point of intellectual and political debate. The addresses' convergence of the information and inclusive society into ongoing public and political discussions about the potential for ICTs to either exacerbate or alleviate social exclusion has been one of the fascinating aspects of recent social policy formation in nations such as the UK (Selwyn, 2002).

2. 2. 3. 1 The Concept

Access can have both particular and broad consequences. As previously stated, physical access is the most common limiting reason. A more general definition is preferable for effectively describing and explaining all digital divide manifestations. This refers to the complete process of employing a particular technology. In this case, the desire for and attitude toward acquiring physical access takes precedence over allowing physical access.

Furthermore, physical access, rather than a single decision to accept and purchase a specific technology, is a continual process of gaining access to new hardware and software versions, associated equipment, and subscriptions. When people are unable to control the technology, physical access is unneeded. As a result, access necessitates unique talents or capacities. When humans have mastered the use and knowledge of technology, the reason for access and the ultimate goal of appropriating it will be sought: practical utilization.

2. 2. 3. 2 Questions of World Divide

Recently, worries about social isolation have been compounded by strong concerns from all political parties about **digital exclusion** and the digital divide. Although the concept of digital exclusion initially emerged in Western advanced capitalist societies with the technical divide between developed and underdeveloped nations, the transnational focus of these talks swiftly changed to the problem of technological inequality inside individual countries. Consequently, the 1990s witnessed the birth of mainstream political debates over "information haves" and "information have-nots" (Wresch, 1996), "information and communication poverty" (Balnaves et al., 1991), and, most recently, the "digital divide" (BECTa, 2001; Jurich, 2000; Parker, 2000). In doing so, the dominant political viewpoint is essentially resolved by opposing a dichotomous gap between those who are "connected" to technological knowledge and those who are "disconnected" from it. It corresponds to the current or postmodern society.

Digital Exclusion

It is where a segment of the population continues to have uneven access to and capacity to use information and ICT, which are required to fully participate in society (Warren, 2007).

Several official data and scholarly investigations over the last ten years have backed up this dichotomous image of "haves" and "have-nots". Individual citizens' access to ICT, for example, is unequally distributed both socially and geographically, according to research (Warf, 2001), with discrepancies in access to ICT substantially connected with socio-economic position, income, gender, level of education, age, location, and ethnicity (e.g., BRMB, 1999; MORI, 1999; DTI, 2000; RSGB, 2001; National Statistics, 2001, 2002). Despite variances in these numbers' magnitude, certain social classes are substantially less likely to have easy access to ICT even in "technologically developed" locations like the US, Western Europe, and Southeast Asia (e.g., NTIA, 1995, 1999, 2000; Dickinson & Sciadas, 1999; Jung et al., 2001; Loges & Jung, 2001; Reddick, 2000; UCLA, 2000; Bonfadelli, 2002). In terms of socio-economic position, for example, these opportunity gaps are stark and persistent, with more "poor" people having much lower access rates to various forms of technology. Men are more likely to report crimes than women. Access to ICTs such as the Internet is inversely proportional to age, as is access to all three technologies. Access to technologies such as personal computers, the Internet, and digital television appears to be structured by gender, family composition, and age, in addition to inequalities in socio-economic level and money (Households most likely to have access include those with two adults and one or two children). Access to ICT also seems to vary geographically within nations, favoring areas with greater economic prosperity. It would seem that any information society would be famous for having a digital divide.

Nonetheless, this representation of the digital divide appears to have a simple base. Political and public perceptions of the digital divide are typically binary: You either have access to ICT, or you don't; you're connected or not. Given the political will to assist those who are "without", the digital gap is simply defined from this standpoint and, as a result, is rapidly closed, bridged, and defeated (Edwards-Johnson, 2000; Devine, 2001). As a result, by providing public and subsidized access to ICT for those social groups that would otherwise be excluded, the benefits of the information age may be amplified for those segments of the population who have access to it and the requisite capacities to use it. This argument supports the UK government's initiative to improve access to ICT, based on a commitment to achieve both "universal service" and "universal access" to the Internet by 2005. The ambitious target set by the government's Policy Action Team on Information Technology is that "75 percent of people living in underprivileged neighborhoods will have the capabilities to access electronically delivered public services and the skills to do so if they wish" (DTI, 2000: 59). This will be achieved by establishing networks of community ICT centers and points of access in a range of previously existing venues, such as schools and community centers, to provide individuals who lack home access to technology or work with flexible access to new technology. These initiatives are supplemented with grants to cover the cost of home technology purchases and IT basics teaching for low-income persons. Thus, nations such as the United Kingdom may progress toward becoming information societies with confidence that the majority, if not all, of their citizens, will be on board.

This skewed representation of the digital divide appeals to both short-term practical and political interests. To base our understanding of inequality in the information age just on a contentious set of technologically "rich" and "poor" persons is, in the long term, too limited and naive, as we will now demonstrate. Even with this little explanation, it is evident that concepts such as "universal access" and "digital divide", which are mainly founded on economic assumptions, are "simplistic, formalistic, and so utopian" (Burgelman, 2000: 56).

Despite its shortcomings, the concept of a dichotomous digital gap is important because it brings up the issue of information inequality in today's social debate. However, we must continue the discussion now that the realities of an ICT-based society are more visible than they were ten years ago. Politicians must recognize that the fundamental issues with the digital divide are social, economic, cultural, and political.

Researchers have begun to rethink the idea of the digital divide as more people have gone online and begun to use the Internet for a broader range of activities. Some researchers provided a more sophisticated digital divide perspective by viewing it as a multifaceted, complicated, and dynamic phenomenon (Van Dijk, 2002; Van Dijk & Hacker, 2003). Kling (1999) divided access into two categories: technical access (physical availability of technology) and social access (the mix of professional knowledge, economic resources, and technical skills required for productive use of technology). Attewell established two division levels in 2001: the "first digital gap", which relates to uneven access to computers and the Internet, and the "second digital divide", which considers unequal computer and Internet use. Hargittai (2002) proposed a similar distinction between access and capacity to utilize as the "first-level digital gap" and "second-level digital divide".

2. 2. 3. 3 Usage Gap

The study objective has shifted dramatically from material access to the diversity and quality of use, surpassing simple binary distinctions of access/no-access or usage/non-use (Gunkel, 2003; Selwyn, 2004; Livingstone & Helsper, 2007). A general understanding that was merely having connections does not guarantee that possible sources of inequality will be eliminated. While considering possible splits, the types of activities people take up when using the Internet will matter the most (Hargittai & Hinnant, 2008). For instance, if the Internet is utilized as a game instead of a tool, it might not improve the user's chances in life (Jung et al., 2001). When evaluating potential divides, the sorts of activities individuals engage in on the Internet will be the most critical factor (Hargittai & Hinnant, 2008). For example, if the Internet is used as a game rather than a utility, it may not boost the user's prospects in life (Jung et al., 2001). Many researchers believe that there is a "**usage gap**" between those who use digital technologies for entertainment and those who use them for knowledge (Bonfadelli, 2002; Hargittai & Hinnant, 2008; Livingstone & Helsper, 2007; Van Dijk, 2002). Most individuals agree that

Usage Gap

The difference between the overall market potential and the actual present utilization by all market consumers.

information uses are preferable since they are more likely to increase a user's political understanding, engagement, life opportunities, and social inclusion (despite some claims to the contrary) (Livingstone & Helsper, 2007; Sandvig, 2001; Clark, 2003; Hargittai & Hinnant, 2008; Warschauer, 2003).

How to comprehend the "second-level digital gap" in comparison to the first is the logical next step. According to research, social standing is still essential. According to Howard, Rainie, and Jones (2001), online behaviors like sending emails, looking up financial, political, or governmental information, and banking positively correlate with education. Individuals with higher education and money are less likely to download music or utilize instant messaging. According to Madden's (2003) research, they are more likely to use the Internet for news, work, travel planning, and shopping. Hargittai and Hinnant (2008) observed that persons with higher levels of education use the Web for more "capital-enhancing" activities, such as investigating occupations, studying financial and health services, and checking up on political or governmental material.

Inequality and Empowerment:
Social Impact of ICT—Comparison between EU and Other Parts of the World

The majority of foreign research is based on data acquired in North America, particularly the prominent Pew Internet Project investigations. There is a risk that study findings from the United States may be regarded entirely transferable to other Western countries, ignoring the extent to which major cultural distinctions exist between US Americans and Europeans. Dread of random crime and fear of one's neighbors motivates many to retreat into the private realm, and therefore the line between public and private is not a pleasant zone for many. Because Europeans differ, conclusions from US studies on telework... and other changes that directly alter the boundary between the public and private spheres may not apply to European situations.

However, when it comes to the Internet and mobile phone usage trends, existing evidence reveals that disparities within EU member states are more substantial than those between North America and the EU average. Users from Southern Europe, for example, mostly utilize the Internet for entertainment and communication. At the same time, other Europeans are more inclined to utilize it for practical purposes such as eBanking and online shopping.

The Horizontal Domain Report compares trends in social applications of ICT and their societal implications in Europe and chosen other countries of the world, particularly the United States, Australia, Canada, Japan, and the ROK.

In recent years, the ROK and Japan have seen significant growth in ICT infrastructure and applications, particularly in mobile (personal) communication technology and broadband (fiber to the curb). Significant governmental investment in ICT is mostly viewed as essential for economic development. Applications for building modern societies, on the other hand, are lacking. Plans for employing ICT (e.g., ubiquitous computing) to address contemporary difficulties in the social domain are ambitious. Nonetheless, it appears that they may be directed by technical determinism without taking the implementation circumstances into consideration. One example is ICT-based remote work, which has long been pushed by the Japanese government and several enterprises. However, take-up is extremely low in practice, owing to working cultures that continue to rely on face-to-face connection. On the other hand, ICTs have been avidly adopted to foster social bonds, particularly among close-knit groups of people such as families and friends. Individuals who used to suffer from strong societal control, such as adolescents and, to a lesser extent, women, regard the liberty provided by mobile phones as extremely liberating.

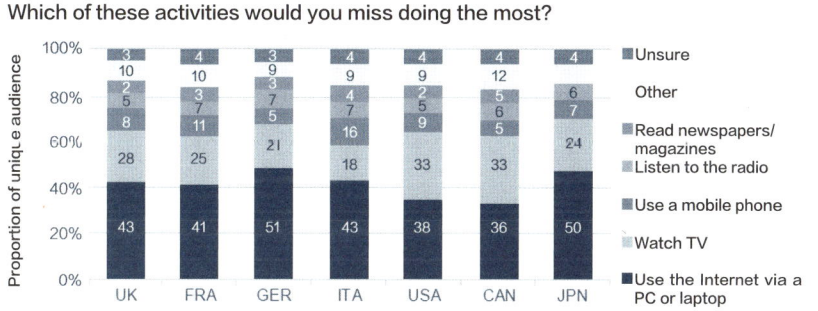

Which of these activities would you miss doing the most?

Country	Use the Internet via a PC or laptop	Watch TV	Use a mobile phone	Listen to the radio	Read newspapers/magazines	Other	Unsure
UK	43	28	8	5	2	10	3
FRA	41	25	11	7	3	10	4
GER	51	21	5	7	3	9	3
ITA	43	18	16	7	4	9	4
USA	38	33	9	5	2	9	4
CAN	36	33	5	6	5	12	4
JPN	50	24	7	6	—	—	4

Base: All adults aged 18+ who use the Internet (UK 1001, France 1000, Germany 1002, Italy 1003, USA 1010, Canada 1000, Japan 1003)
Notes: As the questionnaire was answered online, it may not reflect the attitudes of a representative sample of the whole population

The ROK and Japan have lower penetration of high-speed Internet, implying that broadband has a substantial impact on the degree to which the Internet is ingrained in daily life. In The ROK, the Internet, in conjunction with mobile ICTs, has become a critical component in how people deal with daily difficulties as well as their recreational activities. The growth of the information society throughout Europe is likely to follow basically similar pathways. National disparities, however, will continue to be large.

2. 3 Digital Access and Digital Divide

The digital divide is commonly characterized as the difference between people with access to information and communication technology and those without access. These are primarily computers and the Internet. In this context, inclusion and exclusion in specific social units are common ideas.

Digital Access

The capacity to fully participate in the digital society, including access to tools and technologies that enable full involvement, such as the Internet and computers.

The term "digital divide" initially arose in the United States in the mid-1990s. It was coined by the US Department of Commerce's National Telecommunications and Information Administration, removing much uncertainty. It is a misperception caused by at least four misunderstandings. First, the misconception is a clear separation between two disparate groups separated by a vast chasm. Second, it suggests that it will be difficult to close this deficit. Third, it may mean absolute disparities between those included and those excluded, although differences are more typical of a relative nature. Last, the digital divide is also a dynamic phenomenon that changes over time. The following sections will provide clarification on these misconceptions.

2.3.1 Access as a Method of Technology Appropriation

The term "access" is defined more precisely and broadly. The most common limiting definition is physical access. A broad time is preferable to describe and illustrate all digital divides, including the second-level gap. The complete process of utilizing a particular technology is referred to here. In this instance, getting a physical permit takes precedence over getting access.

Furthermore, physical access is a constant process of accessing new hardware and software versions, additional equipment, and subscriptions rather than a single decision to accept and purchase a particular technology. Physical access is not necessary if people are unable to use the technology. Access so necessitates both knowledge and skills. When individuals have mastered the use and comprehension of the technology, "actual usage"—the reason for access, and the ultimate goal of adoption will be considered.

Technology acceptance theories deal with these access stages in social and communication science. More psychological theories, such as the technology acceptance model and the concept of planned behavior, deal with access and are more concerned with motivation and attitudes. Perceived usefulness, usability, and subjective norms impact behavioral intention to access digital media. Adoption theories such as innovation diffusion are used as acceptance progresses to the decision-making stage. These ideas are based on sociology and communication, emphasizing social and contextual issues in the postadoption phase (first and continued use). Domestication theory, usefulness and enjoyment theory, and social cognitive theory, which led to the media attendance model, are a few examples (LaRose & Eastin, 2004).

Each of these theories of acceptance or access corresponds to a particular methodological approach by evaluating social and information (in)equality. The descriptive nature of digital divide research is driven mainly by methodological individualism, which leads to individualistic concepts of (in)equality. In this case, unequal access is determined by an individual's demographics. An alternative definition of (in)equality takes a relational or network approach

(Wellman & Berkowitz, 1988). Persons are not the fundamental units of study here, but rather locations and interactions between individuals. Inequality is often caused by categorical distinctions between groups of people, such as managers and executive staff, men and women, and blacks and whites, rather than by individual characteristics; these groups attempt to appropriate the technology first, hoard its opportunities, and reinforce their positions regarding the other category. This notion was developed in 1998 by sociologist Charles Tilly and is backed by a network approach (Kadushin, 2012). The development of social networking and the Internet is driving this technique. In this example, all-access phases are related to social support and connections rather than individual qualities.

2. 3. 2 The Theoretical Framework for Analyzing Access

Van Dijk has developed a framework for investigating access based on a specific hypothesis. It is also helpful as a stepping stone for a fair presentation of the significant research results on the digital divide due to its breadth. Van Dijk refers to his idea as resources and appropriation theory. It combines structuration and acceptance theories (appropriation).

The statements that follow give a concise description of the theory's core argument:

(1) Inequal distribution of resources results from categorical inequities in society.

(2) Unequal access to digital technologies results from an uneven allocation of resources.

(3) The qualities of digital technologies also affect how equally accessible they are.

(4) Unequal engagement in society results from unequal access to digital technologies.

(5) The allocation of resources and absolute inequality are strengthened by uneven participation in society.

2. 3. 3 Determinants in a Successive Phase of Access

Any new technology comes with a low level of acceptance in terms of motivation, attitude, and intention. Many people replied to surveys in the 1980s and 1990s since they did not require a computer or an Internet connection. Many individuals were concerned about the future computer era; negative and critical perspectives predominated. However, as technology became more generally available in society, the desire to get digital material grew rapidly. Even those who were considerably older and less educated were motivated to gain access because they were often afraid of being excluded from society or losing contact with their grandkids, relatives, or friends. For instance, surveys conducted in Germany and the US (ARD/ZDF-Arbeitsgruppe Multimedia, 1999; National Telecommunications and Information Administration, 2000) found that lack of demand or significant usage opportunities, distaste for or rejection of the medium (the drawbacks of the Internet and computer gaming), a lack of skills, and a lack of resources were the leading causes of refusal. The majority of respondents without Internet connections rejected access to these surveys. Ten years later, the picture changed dramatically; for example, in 2012, 96 percent of Dutch people were encouraged to use the Internet (Van Deursen & Van Dijk, 2013).

Social or cultural aspects, as well as mental or psychological qualities, explain sufficient access to motivation. "Low-income and low-education folks have little interest in the Internet", according to one early cultural interpretation (Katz & Rice, 2002: 93). To dive deeper into the roots of this lack of interest, it became necessary to augment the large-scale surveys with qualitative studies in local communities and cultural groupings. Laura Stanley, for example, accomplished this in a San Diego study of low-income Latino and African-American working-class communities (Stanley, 2003), as did the University of Texas in low-income districts of Austin (Rojas et al., 2004). They recognized the importance of traditional macho cultures (such as dismissing computer work as "not cool" and "something girls do"), as well as minority and working-class lifestyles (leaving computer work as "not cool" and "something girls do"). Working-class and low-educated people have caught up with the other classes and spent more time on the Internet than highly educated people in the mid-2010s (Van Deursen & Van Dijk, 2013).

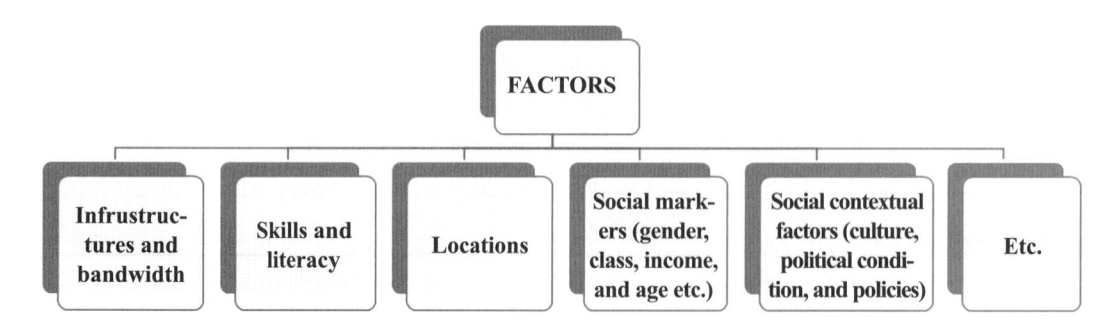

```
                        FACTORS
    ┌──────────┬──────────┬──────────┬──────────┬──────────┐
 Infrustruc-  Skills and            Social mark-  Social contextual
 tures and    literacy    Locations  ers (gender,  factors (culture,   Etc.
 bandwidth                           class, income, political condi-
                                     and age etc.) tion, and policies)
```

The motivation and purpose behind adoption are influenced by social norms and social support from one's neighborhood or social network (Stewart, 2007). These elements influence physical, material, skill, and user access. Being a member of a particular household, business, school, nation, or neighborhood is a positional category that can facilitate or impede access to all types of resources. Families with school-aged children are encouraged to purchase, use, and learn about computers and Internet access. They are required by both businesses and schools. Students and employees assist each other in understanding the necessary skills and operating specific programs. Lastly, opportunities and support vary across affluent and impoverished regions and developed and developing nations.

The use gap idea is comparable to the knowledge gap thesis of the 1970s (Tichenor, Donohue & Olien, 1970), which argued that better-educated individuals obtained more knowledge from mass media such as television and newspapers than less educated individuals. However, the use gap is broader and potentially more effective in alleviating social inequality than the knowledge gap, as it incorporates varied uses and activities in multiple sectors of daily life and not only the perception and comprehension of mass media.

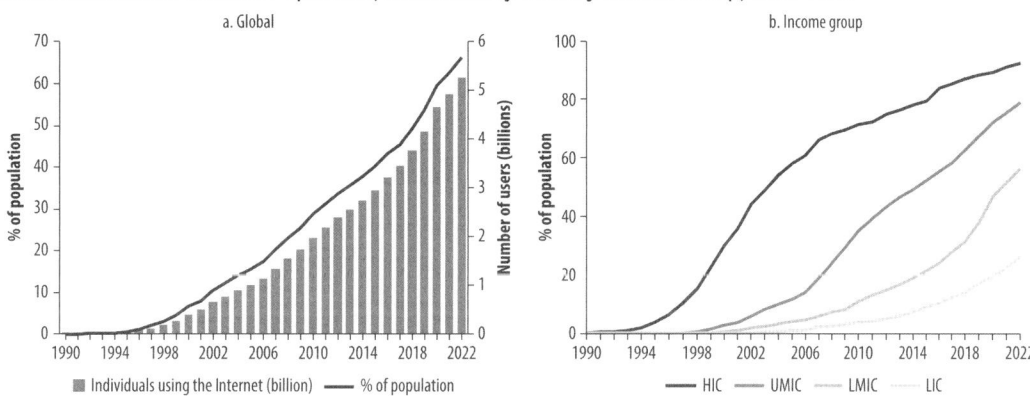

Internet Users as a Share of Population, Global and by Country Income Group, 1990–2022

Sources: World Development Indicators and International Telecommunication Union data (https://www.itu.int/en/ITU-D/Statistics/Pages/stat/default.aspx).
Note: HIC = high-income countries; LIC = low-income countries; LMIC = lower-middle-income countries; UMIC = upper-middle-income countries.

Global Internet Usage Surge: Covid-19's Impact on Digital Growth in Low- and Middle-Income Countries

The latest Digital Progress and Trends Report indicates that the world added 1.5 billion new internet users between 2018 and 2022, with the Covid-19 pandemic boosting and accelerating growth in low- and middle-income countries. By 2022, internet users numbered 5.3 billion, covering two-thirds of the global population. In 2020, the initial year of the Covid-19 pandemic, internet usage among the global population surged by 6 percent (500 million people), marking the largest increase in history, propelled by mobility restrictions that shifted numerous activities online. Although growth decelerated in 2021 and 2022, it continued at a pace faster than most years in the past two decades, as significant numbers in both low-income and lower-middle-income countries started accessing the internet (World Bank Group, 2023).

2. 4 Conclusion

This lecture introduced the term "digital divide". To provide a clear illustration, the author describes the relationship between a knowledge gap, ICT, and digital access.

The digital divide is the gap between persons with and without access to information and communication technology. People lacking access to the Internet and other ICTs are disadvantaged socioeconomically, a recurring issue throughout the lecture. The author presented the knowledge gap hypothesis to explain how a knowledge gap originates and grows due to information and the Internet. From access to utilization, the gap is mainly determined by skills, literacy, geography, etc.

Multiple factors have both accelerated and slowed the global expansion of the Internet. The Internet is one example of technological dissemination. Similar to the diffusion of earlier technologies, the Internet has spread unevenly across nations, creating concerns about a "digital divide". The new information economy also reflects this disparity between the wealthy and the poor. Between the North and South, a digital divide is rising—the gap in information resources. As Internet access approaches universality, the digital divide can be characterized more correctly as differences in the actual application of information and communication technology. This disparity is more remarkable among Internet users of socioeconomic status than users of conventional media.

2.5 Extended Readings

Scan the QR code to get extended reading materials.

2.6 Post Questions and Discussion

(1) What form of inequality does the digital divide concept refer to?

(2) Is the digital divide a valuable framework for thinking about global development?

(3) What relationship exists between "access to ICT" and "usage of ICT"?

(4) To what extent does SE (socioeconomic status) affect the diversity of Internet use and its outcomes?

2.7 Bibliography

American Psychological Association, Presidential Task Force on Educational Disparities [APA]. (2012). Ethnic and Racial Disparities in Education: Psychology's Contributions to Understanding and Reducing Disparities. http://www.apa.org/ed/resources/racial-disparities.aspx.

Arunachalam, S. (2004). Information and Communication Technologies and Poverty Alleviation. *Current Science*, 87(7): 960-966. http://www.jstor.org/stable/24109401.

Attewell, P. (2001). The First and Second Digital Divides. *Sociology of Education*, 74: 252-259.

Bandura, A. (1995). Exercise Personal and Collective Efficacy in Changing Societies. In A. Bandura (ed.), *Self-Efficacy in Changing Societies* (pp. 1-45). New York: Cambridge University Press.

Bargh, J. A., McKenna, K. Y. (2004). The Internet and Social Life. *Annual Review of Psychology*, 55: 573-590.

Beaudoin, C. E. (2009). Exploring the Association between News Use and Social Capital: Evidence of Variance by Ethnicity and Medium. *Communication Research*, 36: 611-636.

Blumler, J. (1979). The Role of Theory in Uses and Gratifications Studies. *Communication Research*, 6: 9-36.

Bonfadelli, H. (2002). The Internet and Knowledge Gaps: A Theoretical and Empirical Investigation. *European Journal of Communication*, 17: 65-84.

Caplan, S. E. (2003). Preference for Online Social Interaction: A Theory of Problematic Internet Use and Psychosocial Well-being. *Communication Research*, 30: 625-648.

Caplan, S. E., Turner, J. S. (2007). Bringing Theory to Research on Computer-Mediated Comforting Communication. *Computers in Human Behavior*, 23: 985-998.

Chaffee, S. H., Frank, S. (1996). How Americans Get Political Information: Print versus Broadcast News. *Annals of the American Academy of Political and Social Science*, 546: 48-58.

Charney, T., Greenberg, B. (2001). Uses and Gratifications of the Internet. In C. Lin & D. Atkin (Eds.), *Communication, Technology and Society: Audience Adoption and Uses*. Creskill: Hampton Press.

Chou, C., Hsiao, M. C. (2000). Internet Addiction, Usage, Gratification, and Pleasure Experience: The Taiwan College Students' Case. *Computers & Education*, 35: 65–80.

Conway, J., Rubin A. (1991). Psychological Predictors of Television Viewing Motivation. *Communication Research*, 4: 443-463.

Cook, T. D., Appleton, H., Conner, R. F., Shaffer, A., Tamkin, G., & Weber, S. J. (1975). *"Sesame Street" Revisited*. New York. Russell Sage.

D'Allesandro, D., Dosa, N. (2001) Empowering Children and Families with Information Technology. *Archives of Paediatric & Adolescent Medicine*, 155(10): 1131-1136.

Diddi, A., LaRose, R. (2006). Getting Hooked on the News: Uses and Gratifications and Forming News Habits among College Students in an Internet Environment. *Journal of Broad-

casting & Electronic Media, 50: 193-210.

DiMaggio, P., Hargittai, E., Celeste, C., & Shafer, S. (2004). Digital Inequality: From Unequal Access to Differentiated Use. In K. M. Neckerman (ed.), *Social Inequality* (pp. 355-400). New York: Russell Sage Foundation.

DiMaggio, P., Hargittai, E., Neuman, W. R., & Robinson, J. P. (2001). Social Implications of the Internet. *Annual Review of Sociology*, 27: 307-336.

Drew, D., Weaver, D. (2006). Voter Learning in the 2004 Presidential Election: Did the Media Matter? *Journalism & Mass Communication Quarterly*, 83: 25-42.

Eastin, M. S., LaRose, R. (2000). Internet Self-Efficacy and the Psychology of the Digital Divide. *Journal of Computer-Mediated Communication*. doi:10.1111/j.1083-6101. 2000. tb00110.x.

Eastin, M. S., Cicchirillo, V. J., Cunningham, N. R., & Liang, M. C. (2014). Managing Media: Segmenting Media through Consumer Expectancies. *International Journal of Business and Social Research*, 4: 8-19.

Eveland, W., Scheufele, D. (2000). Connecting News Media Use with Gaps in Knowledge and Participation. *Political Communication*, 17: 215-237.

Ferguson D., Perse, E. (2000). The World Wide Web as a Functional Alternative to Television. *Journal of Broadcasting & Electronic Media*, 44: 155-174.

Flanagin, A., Metzger, M. (2001). Internet Uses in the Contemporary Media Environment. *Human Communication Research*, 27: 153-181.

Gaziano, C. (1997). Forecast 2000: Widening Knowledge Gaps. *Journalism & Mass Communication Quarterly*, 74: 237-264.

Graber, D. A. (1988). *Processing the News: Taming the Information Tide* (2nd ed.). New York: Longman.

Gunkel, D. J. (2003). Second Thoughts: Toward a Critique of the Digital Divide. *New Media & Society*, 5: 499-522.

Hargittai, E., Hinnant, A. (2008). Digital Inequality: Differences in Young Adults' Use of the Internet. *Communication Research*, 35: 602-621.

Holz-Bacha, C., Norris, P. (2001). "To Entertain, Inform, and Educate": Still the Role of Public Television. *Political Communication*, 18: 123-140.

Howard, P. N., Rainie, L., & Jones, S. (2001). Days and Nights on the Internet: The Impact of a Diffusing Technology. *American Behavioral Scientist*, 45: 383-404.

Hyman, H. H., Sheatsley, P. B. (1947). Some Reasons Why Information Campaigns Fail. *Public Opinion Quarterly*, 11: 412-423. https://doi.org/10.1086/265867.

Jung, J.-Y., Qiu, J. L., & Kim, Y.-C. (2001). Internet Connectedness and Inequality: Beyond the "divide". *Communication Research*, 28: 507-535.

Katz, J., Rice, R. (2002). Project Syntopicial Consequences of Internet Use. *IT & Society*, 1(1): 166-179.

Kim, S.-H. (2008). Testing the Knowledge Gap Hypothesis in South Korea: Traditional News Media, the Internet, and Political Learning. *International Journal of Public Opinion Research*, 20: 193-210.

Kling, R. (1999). What Is Social Informatics and Why Does It Matter? *D-Lib Magazine*, 5(1). http://www.dlib.org/dlib/january99/kling/01kling.html.

Lee, T.-T., Wei, L. (2008). How Newspaper Readership Affects Political Participation. *Newspaper Research Journal*, 29: 8-23.

Livingstone, S., Helsper, E. (2007). Gradations in Digital Inclusion: Children, Young People and the Digital Divide. *New Media & Society*, 9: 671-696.

Loges, W. E., Jung, J. Y. (2001). Exploring the Digital Divide: Internet Connectedness and Age. *Communication Research*, 28: 536-562.

Madden, M. (2003). America's Online Pursuits. Washington, DC: Pew Internet and American Life Project.

Newton, K. (1999). Mass Media Effects: Mobilization or Media Malaise? *British Journal of Political Science*, 29: 577-599.

Parker, B. J., Plank, R. E. (2000). A Uses and Gratifications Perspective on the Internet as a New Information Source. *American Business Review*, 18: 43-49.

Postman, N. (1986). *Amusing Ourselves to Death: Public Discourse in the Age of Show Business*. London: Methuen.

Prior, M. (2005), News vs. Entertainment: How Increasing Media Choice Widens Gaps in Political Knowledge and Turnout. *American Journal of Political Science*, 49: 577-592. https://doi.org/10.1111/j.1540-5907.2005.00143.x.

Putnam, R. D. (2000). *Bowling Alone: The Collapse and Revival of American Community*. New York: Simon and Schuster.

Scheufele, D. A., Nisbet, M. C. (2002). Being a Citizen Online: New Opportunities and Dead Ends. *Harvard International Journal of Press and Politics*, 7: 55-75.

Selwyn, N. (2004). Reconsidering Political and Popular Understandings of the Digital Divide. *New Media & Society*, 6: 341-362.

Servon, L. J., Nelson, M. K. (2001). Community Technology Centers and the Urban Technology Gap. *International Journal of Urban and Regional Research*, 25(2): 419-426.

Shah, D. V., Cho, J., Eveland, W. P., Jr., & Kwak, N. (2005). Information and Expression in a Digital Age: Modeling Internet Effects on Civic Participation. *Communication Research*,

32: 531-565.

Tewskbury, D., Althaus, S. (1999). Differences in Knowledge Acquisition among Readers of the Paper and Online Versions of a National Newspaper. Paper presented at the Annual Meeting of the International Communication Association, San Francisco.

Tichenor, P. J., Donohue, G. A., & Olien, C. N. (1970). Mass Media Flow and Differential Growth in Knowledge. *Public Opinion Quarterly*, 34: 159-170.

Wang, H., Li, L., Wu, J., & Gao, H. (2021). Factors Influencing COVID-19 Knowledge Gap: A Cross-Sectional Study in China. *BMC Public Health*, 21. 1826. 10.1186/s12889-021-11856-9.

Warschauer, M. (2003). Technology and Social Inclusion: Rethinking the Digital Divide. Cambridge: MIT Press.

Wei, L. (2009). Filter Blogs vs. Personal Journals: Understanding the Knowledge Production Gap on the Internet. *Journal of Computer-Mediated Communication*, 14: 532-558.

Wei, L., Zhang, M. (2008). The Impact of Internet Knowledge on College Student's Intention to Continue to Use the Internet. *Information Research*, 13(3). http://InformationR.net/ir/13-3/paper348.html.

Wei, L., Hindman, D. (2011). Does the Digital Divide Matter More? Comparing the Effects of New Media and Old Media Use on the Education-Based Knowledge Gap. *Mass Communication and Society*. 14: 216-235. 10.1080/15205431003642707.

Wills, M.A. (1999). Congruence between Phylogeny and Stratigraphy: Randomization Tests and the Gap Excess Ratio. *Syst. Biol*. 48: 559-580.

Wresch, W. (1996) *Disconnected: Haves and Have-Nots in the Information Age*. Piscataway: Rutgers University Press.

LECTURE & SEMINAR 3
Youth Culture, Audio-Visual Communication, and Platformalization

This lecture is mainly about the relationship between Youth Culture, subculture and platforms. Nowadays, digital platforms are developing faster than ever before. Teenagers have been especially prominent on social media sites, frequently dictating trends and creating online subcultures with other site members. This lecture will discuss this trend in youth culture and subculture, including the types of subcultures worldwide, why these subcultures would emerge and exist, and how they affect digital platforms. Read the lecture with cases, and you will learn about all kinds of fantastic subcultures.

Framework

3.1 Digital Platform

3.1.1 The Creativity of Youth Culture

3.1.2 The Creativity of Audio-Visual Communication

3.2 Subculture

3.2.1 What Is Subculture?

3.2.2 Categories of Subculture

3.2.3 Subculture and Digital Platforms

3.3 Case Study

3.3.1 Case 1: An Example of Popular Revenge

3.3.2 Case 2: Urban Entertainment Subculture and Black Music: Blues, Ragtime and Jazz

3.3.3 Case 3: China's Cultural Evolution: Egao, Digital Parody, and Politics

3.3.4 Case 4: Harajuku Culture in Japan

3.4 Conclusion

3.5 Extended Readings

3.6 Post Questions and Discussion

3.7 Bibliography

Terms

subculture, Youth Culture, Generation Z, TikTok, Douyin, Type-O Negative

Pre-lecture Discussion

What causes the narcissi and sociopathy of the youth in media culture? What symptoms do they have?

3.1 Digital Platform

3.1.1 The Creativity of Youth Culture

Digital media and platforms are becoming an integral part of our everyday life. They are a part of extensive changes in how we generate information, communicate, and express ourselves creatively. In contrast to the early phases of computer and computer-based media development, digital media are now pervasive and employed by individuals and institutions from all walks of life. Digital platforms have escaped the limitations of professional and formal practice and the academic, governmental, and economic organizations that first supported their development. They have been embraced by various demographics and non-institutionalized means, including teenage peer activities. A generation is developing in an era where digital media are woven into the social and cultural fabric of learning, play, and social communication, notwithstanding the vast diversity of specific technology use.

Digital skills are essential for the youth to navigate the world and obtain mobility successfully. Mobility refers to the ability to communicate and engage in cross-cultural forums or conversations (into new types of cultural "spaces" through online platforms or digital technologies) and move across socioeconomic and cultural groupings in daily life.

If we want to talk about the digital platform, we first introduce Youth and **Youth Culture**. Young generations are playing an essential role in digital platforms, not only because they grew up as "digital natives" of the tools of technology but also they bring creativity and diversity into new spaces.

Youth Culture

It refers to the corpus of norms, beliefs, and practices acknowledged and accepted by members of adolescent society as suitable guides for activities (Gracious & Sibanda).

3.1.1.1 Youth Culture

Culture has several levels, including the historical position of ideas and ideals, the level of meaning, and the subsequent influences on art, popular culture, sport, symbolism, and signs (Brake, 1985: 8).

We may build a concept of youth or youthful subcultures based on age, which has been commonly encapsulated by the phrase "Youth Culture". It has been informally used as a structural monolith of all individuals under 30, regardless of class, race, or even gender (Brake, 1985: 7).

Talcott Parsons developed the term "young culture", whereby this tradition got entangled with structural functionalism in the United States (Merton, 1968; Buckingham & Kehily, 2014: 1). During the 1950s, the growth of adolescent misbehavior sparked grave worries (Goodman, 1960). Consequently, early theories associated subculture creation with juvenile habits related to unlawful acts, deviance, and irresponsibility. However, the "natural" relationship between "lost" youth and subculture is entirely false. Nonetheless, it is still a common assumption in several talks today.

In 1964, Richard Hoggart founded the Center for Contemporary Cultural Studies (CCCS) at the University of Birmingham to examine the relationship between cultural forms, practices, institutions, and social change (Turner, 2002). In response to the "conceptual bankruptcy of youth cultural theory" (Murdock & McCron, 1976: 24), founded on conceptions of classlessness among youth, the CCCS constructed a paradigm that placed socioeconomic class at the heart of any understanding of youth culture. The CCCS theorists abandoned the term "youth culture" in favor of "youth subculture" and left the assumption that "age and generation were most significant, or that youth culture was classless" (Clarke et al., 1976: 15).

Subculture will be introduced later. Not all youth are members of subcultures. We may claim that subcultures aid individuals in addressing structural and personal concerns. Some of these are only short-term fixes for particular problems, particularly among the working-class youth subcultures. Others have a more prolonged impact and bring about societal transformation. Subcultures address systemic issues and carry a societal critique, although one that is usually inarticulate and tangential. This has been explained as adolescent transitional concerns, particularly in neo-functional theories.

3.1.1.2 Generation Z

However, who is the best bridge to spread youth culture? The answer is that **Generation Z**, born with the Internet, is the ideal bridge between people and technology. Not like previous generations, millennials grew up with social media, smartphones, and instant access to information. In contrast to previous generations, they were not required to learn or adapt to technology. This also benefits them from never having experienced a non-digital situation, enabling them to have a more developed human character.

> **Generation Z**
> People born during the mid to late-1990s and the 2010s.

Generation Z is currently maturing with significantly increased access to globalized media, which they use to establish and maintain transnational connections. They have increasingly experienced global migration and cultural integration. The world's expanding young population has been at the forefront of technological advances that transformed all aspects of social life. Their voice and influence are global because they continue to fuel social media. It is sent instantly to their cellphones, becoming as usual to them as breathing, and is absorbed effectively by the artificially intelligent, tailored, platform-based, exponential models servicing them (Scopelliti, 2018).

In the dissemination of youth culture, Generation Z is crucial. Youth has become a significant supply of new information and entertainment through the Internet age. Despite this, they have been at the forefront of utilizing these technologies for new forms of cultural expression and self-representation (Osgerby, 2020). Furthermore, the symbolic configurations of youth have inevitably played a part in how the media has perceived these shifts, with young people depicted as the embodiment of the societal advantages of technological progress and its pernicious effects. So, what happens when a highly expressive micro-video meets a young person eager to express themselves?

3.1.1.3 Youth Studies

Youth is a transitional period between childhood and adulthood determined by the division of labor. Youth were initially connected with delinquency, notably in the Chicago School. Whyte's (1943) depiction of gang culture established a link between youth and juvenile criminality or gang formation. In early ideas, subculture creation was linked to youth-related unlawful acts, deviance, and delinquency. However, the "natural" relationship between "lost" youth and subculture is entirely incorrect. Despite this, it remains a prevalent notion in several debates today.

The notion of "youth" grew up with modernization and commercialization. Generations are fragmented by color, gender, class, ethnicity, nationality, urbanization levels, and education, even though we may consider them homogenous (Acland, 2004). In contemporary or in the process of modernization countries, the life course is designed to establish a separation between children and adults. On the one hand, youth experience hinges on the duality of young people as objects of commercial culture. In contrast, the same people are also the founders of consumer subcultures. This dichotomy underscores the field's historical reference point, notably the work initially linked with the British Cultural Studies tradition (Brake, 1985, 2013; Hall & Jefferson, 1976; Hebdige, 1979; Willis, 1977, 1978). This school of thought includes several eminent scholars (Raymond Williams, Stuart Hall, Richard Hoggart, and Edward P. Thompson) who have worked on various topics that occasionally touch on youth; however, Stuart Hall and his collaborators have provided significantly more youth-specific scholarship. In this study paradigm, young subcultures were first lauded as signs of resistance to capitalism—as a means for individuals to recover what commercialization removes. Their opposition, however, was primarily symbolic and devoid of tangible reality. Youthful defiance unwittingly enhanced societal systems. An additional study (Bennett, 2000; Bucholtz, 2002; Buford, 1993; Willis, 1990) indicates that consuming cultures may function, to varying degrees, regardless of a rigid class position or an exclusive link with youth. The coherence commonly attributed to generational cohorts may be an illusion created by media-generated effects or samples implicitly or openly constrained by class, gender, and other criteria.

3.1.2 The Creativity of Audio-Visual Communication

As the globe entered the digital era, there has been a discernible change in recent years from sector to sector, catching trends and effectively maintaining culture. This shift coincides with the advent of the digital age. Businesses, societies, and even lifestyles were all affected by technology's global change. Many people have asserted that this product is responsible for the outbreak, although this is not the case. On the other hand, Covid-19 sped up the process.

3.1.2.1 The Parallel Comparison of TikTok and Douyin

In 2016, TikTok was introduced in China under the name Douyin. In 2017, the app began entering international markets under the name TikTok. It is the worldwide version of the Douyin app, which is a Chinese version of the famous short video app that is used all over the world. Despite ByteDance's best efforts, Douyin and TikTok are two separate organizations, despite the company's marketing efforts to the contrary. Youth in the US is abandoning Instagram in favor of the video-sharing platform TikTok. To an American audience, TikTok can feel like a most excellent hits compilation, containing only its predecessors' most engaging elements and experiences. This is true to some extent.

Douyin (抖音, literally "shaking sound" in Chinese) belongs to ByteDance, a rising Chinese Internet powerhouse, and is a media application used to create and share short videos. The application allows users to make, edit, and share short films and live streaming, many of which contain background music. TikTok is the international name for the app that appears to be the same as Douyin. Despite ByteDance's efforts to brand the company, the two companies remain distinct.

In actuality, this signifies that if you are not a resident of China, you will be using the "international version", and you will have access to content exclusive to the international version. Users with Chinese telephone numbers are unable to view this content. The Chinese app has some functions absent from the international version's Wallet: two different applications and two different systems.

DOUYIN vs. TIKTOK

Douyin	TikTok
Only accessible in Chinese mainland	Accessible across the world except China
Advanced live streaming features—group livestreams, screen recording & voice comments	Basic live streaming features—stream chat, QnA and lives with only one co-host
About 75% of the users are below 35 years old making Douyin a Millennial & Gen Z-dominated application.	About 60% users are between the ages of 16–24 making TikTok a Gen-Z dominated platform.

Douyin vs. TikTok

3.1.2.2 Infrastructure

TikTok and Douyin's similar design elements, such as logos and aesthetics, and functionalities, like video recording and publishing, highlight their ownership by the same parent company. Both platforms share a consistent user interface, architecture, and design logic. The homepages also look strikingly similar, with the top left corner of videos on both platforms displaying an identical emblem—a red and blue musical chord. Furthermore, the graphical user interfaces of the two platforms are identical (Kathryn Read, 2023).

The onboarding procedure is the most glaring and evident distinction. With Douyin, users may start interacting with content as soon as they launch the app. Users are not required to register until they engage with elements outside the primary interface. On the other hand, TikTok requires an 8-step sign-up process for new users straight away.

While the interface and option names on Douyin and TikTok are identical, the default camera filter on Douyin renders users' skin tones substantially lighter than on TikTok. This shows a cultural divide among the intended audience. Meibai (lit. "beautify whitening") is a popular camera attachment in China (Li, 2019).

Exploring both apps' "effects" settings, which include visual effects, filters, and stickers, showed other cultural variances. Both apps incorporate references to aesthetics, popular entertainment, or online parodies uniquely related to their particular local, regional audiences, resulting in predictably diverse "effects". Given the importance of cultural proximity in mobile video consumption, the many cultural connections on Douyin and TikTok aid in bringing consumers to the two platforms.

3. 1. 2. 3 Markets

ByteDance looks to have been adhering to a gift market monetization model that is reliant heavily on live broadcasting and crypto currency exchange, which appears to be more effective in Chinese markets than in international markets.

On the one hand, regarding the platforms themselves, TikTok and Douyin rely significantly on venture financing and advertising for revenue (Zhang, 2020).

The only way for producers to earn money directly through both platforms, on the other hand, is through a virtual currency system. Douyin has a dedicated live streaming section. Compared to Western markets, this underlines the cultural significance of live streaming in China.

Douyin has much more advanced e-commerce features. Users can directly link to products on Taobao, Jingdong, and the like when publishing videos or hosting a live stream. Additionally, it offers a significantly more effective marketing platform for companies that wish to advertise their products. Brands can form partnerships with KOLs to increase direct sales of their products and brand recognition and consideration. In addition, Douyin has introduced mini-programs that allow businesses to establish their stores on the platform. This will enable consumers to finish their purchases within the Douyin app, increasing conversion rates. Because Douyin understands the importance of video sales, the company does not want users to go away from the app to finalize their transactions with a third-party vendor. However, because of the variations in the international e-commerce marketplaces, techniques analogous to those used on TikTok are less effective. Although content producers are increasingly subject to the political economy of platforms (Nieborg & Poell, 2018), emerging platforms are also subject to the political economy of the platform ecosystems in which they are embedded. This is true, even while content creators are more vulnerable to the political economy of platforms.

Douyin, in addition to virtual gifting, includes a "merchandising on behalf" (Daihuo, 带货) capability that permits live streams to have product-linking icons. Live stream viewers may purchase something by clicking on the symbol, bringing money to the streamer. However, the ability to link to Amazon and Shopify on TikTok is limited to certain users and locations, limiting its utility for e-commerce.

Additionally, users of Douyin are more likely to make purchases than those of TikTok. Consumers in Douyin are well-educated, from Chinese cities, have excellent purchasing power, and have had a lot of exposure to international consumer brands. Because of this, the app is effective for brand marketing.

As a result, the growth of China's social e-commerce business has helped Douyin. Chinese consumers' penchant for live streaming shopping (Yeung, 2019) and virtual gifts (Zhang et al., 2019) have enabled Douyin to implement profitable business strategies on its platform.

3.1.2.4 Governance

ByteDance's readiness to settle legal disputes and alter its platform governance principles to placate overseas authorities and critics demonstrates how difficult it is for the company to adjust to the increased scrutiny in international environments.

Governance of Douyin

In China, digital platforms are obligated to comply with the regulations that are set by the country. Even though the Chinese government only exercises indirect control over Chinese corporate platforms (Van Dijck et al., 2018), the regime decides which Chinese platforms should prioritize political ideas.

Governance of TikTok

The governance of TikTok has changed on multiple occasions in response to changes in national content. A critical regulatory issue has been the use of the platform by children and teenagers, which has led to prohibitions in countries like India and Indonesia and class-action lawsuits in nations like the United States.

3.1.2.5 User Content

Li et al. (2020) have specifically compared the cultural distinctions between these two well-known short video apps by scrutinizing their video content. It can support users from different social classes and cultures because it only needs a basic manufacturing technique to function as a social media platform.

First, compared to TikTok users, Douyin users have a more straightforward and consistent way of living. According to an analysis of similarity matrices, labels for stationary and often used objects are more likely to appear under the same category in TikTok. Users of TikTok frequently record a variety of topics; however, many videos on Douyin have a clear subject and purpose.

Second, family-related events dominate Douyin, whereas individual-related events dominate TikTok. Label statistical analysis has shown that TikTok and Douyin are dominant in separate categories. While TikTok offers more items in the technology and appliance categories, Douyin has more in the accessory and kitchen categories. The former deals with tools and necessities of life, but the latter transcends these. Additionally, this result is supported by the label-person distribution. Videos in Douyin have a disproportionately high concentration of indoor family-related topics. Users of TikTok simultaneously make movies by interacting with friends and passersby outside. The theory is supported further by a study of how people behave—TikTok emphasizes sports more than Douyin does. On Douyin, as opposed to TikTok, relaxing activities are more common.

3. 1. 2. 6 Critical Elements of Youth Culture in TikTok

Each key component of TikTok's youth culture is described here.

A significant portion of the platform is music. TikTok permits music usage, but it's also a fantastic venue for up-and-coming musicians to submit their songs and gain exposure to listeners. Additionally, users can remix, do dances, and make memes.

Fashion videos are prominent on the app. However, the style aspect of TikTok is not limited to users displaying their favorite outfits. Due to the app's visual nature, we can see what young people wear in each video.

Vocabulary and language are critical parts of the app. In various circumstances, a variety of terms and idioms are used. Although not all of them have roots in the app, their usage has proliferated into Generation Z's slang.

On the app, civic engagement is joint, especially when there is intense public discussion about a particular subject. TikTok has made the environment low-resistance. Users can engage in these chats creatively, already familiarly (Abidin, 2019). Participating in political movements and discussions has become a regular part of the app's user experience, as opposed to being confined to specific parts of the Internet (Abidin, 2019). This kind of content typically comes in two shapes. In the first, a user instructs other users on a subject, while in the second, films of protests, marches, and movements are shown how content is distributed, bringing it directly to the viewer, eliminating the need for them to search for it.

Although Chinese company ByteDance developed the video-sharing application TikTok, it is not available in China.

To be released on TikTok, specific Douyin viral videos will be picked, with one selection criterion being that the video must be appropriate for the region in which TikTok is based.

As a result, ByteDance can facilitate cultural connections between the two parallel universes of short videos, and TikTok can become more competitive in the global short video platform market.

3.2 Subculture

3.2.1 What Is Subculture?

In English-language texts, the term "subculture" first appeared in 1914. To put it another way, a subculture is a culture that develops from a small group of individuals who exist and set themselves apart from the parent culture. Initially, "subculture" referred to a specific demographic and civilization. For instance, the OED provides the following illustration of a "subculture":

Subculture

An identifiable subgroup within a society or group of people, especially one characterized by beliefs or interests at variance with those of the larger group (*Oxford English Dictionary*).

"This subculture, nicknamed hip hop, is about... status and competition, particularly among males." (*Time*, May 21, 1983)

Frequently, the subculture upholds the original tenets of the parent culture. It can also be described as a sizable group that differs from the more incredible culture regarding interests and beliefs. There are numerous subcultures, with punk serving as the foundation for many. Punk is the origin of multiple subcultures, including skinheads, hipsters, art punks, hardcore kids, and straight edge, among others. Others consider their subculture to be a stereotype...

3. 2. 2 Categories of Subculture

3. 2. 2. 1 Punk

Punk, or punk rock, is an aggressive subgenre of rock music that American rock reviewers first coined to define the mid-1960s garage bands in the early 1970s. Punk gained popularity as an ideology and aesthetic movement, evolving into an ideal of adolescent alienation and rebellion that is often politicized and bursting with vitality beneath a hostile, sardonic exterior. Short, punk rockers often produce shortened songs with yelled anti-establishment political lyrics, and hard-edged melodies and singing styles are of rock's subset known as "Art Punk", which features musicians who go beyond the garage rock limitations of the genre and are thought to be more sophisticated than their peers. In contrast to pub rock's furious, working-class audience, these bands developed the punk style, which is straightforward, provocative, and free-spirited.

Science fiction's "combination of lowlife and high tech" is the focus of the cyberpunk subgenre, which contrasts a certain level of social breakdown or radical change with cutting-edge technological and scientific advancements like artificial intelligence and cybernetics. Cyberpunk is set in a dystopian future.

Punk Hairstyle

Science fiction author K. W. Jeter is credited with coining the term "steampunk", which was first used in 1987 to describe a flurry of fantasy novels that were largely steam-powered and set in the Victorian era. The cyberpunk genre generally has automated, future, or cyberpunk genres, which is the reverse of steampunk.

3. 2. 2. 2 Goth

Initially, the term "Goths" referred to the Germanic peoples who lived in Western Europe and were known as

Nancy Downs is one of the main characters of *The Craft*, eventually becoming the film's main antagonist and a minor character of *The Craft*: Legacy. She is a troubled girl who practices witchcraft to try and improve her life.

Person of the Year 2021—Elon Musk.

the Goths. Additionally, the Goth fashion style is widely followed in the areas of clothing, font, and various other regions of the visual arts. The utilization of towering, dark, weird, mysterious, and scary components is the primary characteristic that sets it apart from other works. The attributes of gothic art include being exaggerated, asymmetrical, odd, light, detailed, and decorative. It is easily distinguishable due to the extensive use of longitudinal lines. Important symbolic objects include black clothing, bats, roses, solitary castles, ravens, crosses, blood, and black cats, among other things.

3. 2. 2. 3 Techies

Techies are experts in or enthusiastic about technology, especially computing.

Elon Musk is a prime example of a tech entrepreneur. He built a fortune that made him a multimillionaire after founding X.com in 1999, which later became PayPal, SpaceX in 2002, and Tesla Motors in 2003.

Musk gained public recognition in 2012 after his business SpaceX successfully launched the first commercial spaceship to the International Space Station. He increased his assets in 2016 by adding SolarCity to his portfolio. He worked as a consultant during the early phases of President Donald Trump's administration, solidifying his standing as a pioneer in his area.

3. 2. 2. 4 Beatnik

A beatnik is a person who participated in the 1950s and early 1960s social movements that emphasized artistic self-expression and the rejection of traditional social mores. It also describes a person who opposes the conventions of traditional society and is typically young and imaginative.

Auasey Hepburn also immortalized the beatnik style in *Funny Face* (1957).

Jimmy Savile belongs to the beatnik subculture. This British radio and television personality was as well-known for his offbeat, humorous style as his platinum-dyed hair, flashy tracksuits, and a big cigar. His comedy approach was also considered to be unconventional.

3. 2. 2. 5 Hippies

Hippies were a component of a counter-cultural movement that opposed traditional American values in the 1960s and 1970s. Even though the campaign started on American college campuses, it quickly expanded to countries like Canada and the UK. The bulk of hippies was white, middle-class, baby boom generation twenty-somethings. They regarded middle-class culture as harsh and materialistic and felt alienated from it. Hippies created a sense of marginalization by developing their distinctive way of life.

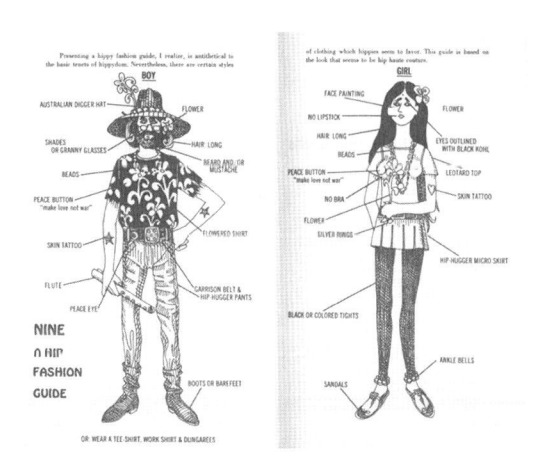

A Hip Fashion Guide

In addition, hippies were known for their unique sense of style, liking long hair and informal, usually bizarre clothing, occasionally in "psychedelic" colors. Both men and women wore sandals and beads, and many males sported beards. Women liked wearing long, flowing "grandma" clothes, while both sexes preferred rimless "grandma" spectacles.

The Beatles, a British musical quartet and a global cynosure for the hopes and dreams of a generation in the 1960s, are also a representative group of hippies.

3. 2. 2. 6　Metalheads

Metalheads are fans or performers of heavy metal music. As with the fashion of other fashions, heavy metal fashion is used to identify the styles of members of that subculture. A metalhead typically has long hair, is bald, or has short hair, and is generally attired in band T-shirts, denim jeans, or army pants. Metalheads may also wear leather jackets, gloves, or wristbands with spikes, denim jackets, etc.

3. 2. 2. 7　Urban Primitives

Urban primitives, or modern primitives, adorn their bodies in ways typically associated with tribal societies, such as tattooing, piercing, and scarification. They engage in body alteration rituals and activities inspired by ceremonies, rites of passage, or bodily decoration in "primitive societies".

3. 2. 2. 8　Furries

The furry subculture is a community of enthusiasts who are interested in anthropomorphic animals, or animals that have human characteristics and qualities. These characteristics can include walking on two legs, talking, and wearing clothes. Members of the furry community, known as "furries", often express their interest through various forms of art, such as drawings, stories, and costume-wearing. One of the most visible aspects of the furry subculture is the creation and wearing of "fursuits", which are elaborate animal costumes. These suits allow individuals to adopt their "fursona", an animal alter ego, which can be a fully original creation or inspired by characters from cartoons, myths, or other sources.

Youth Culture, Audio-Visual Communication, and Platformalization LECTURE & SEMINAR 3

Some furry fans create and wear costumes called "fursuits" depicting their characters.

3. 2. 2. 9 Hipsters

A hipster follows the most recent trends and styles, especially those deemed to be outside of the cultural mainstream. This subculture represents a consumer ethic that seeks to commercialize the concept of revolt or counterculture. Hipster identity can be significantly predicted by one's sense of style.

Vintage attire, alternative fashion, or style clothing, such as slim trousers, checkered shirts, knit beanies, a full beard or purposely attention-grabbing mustache, and thick-rimmed or lensless glasses, are all stereotypical.

The Hipster Kit (Wartena, 2013)

59

3.2.2.10 Straight Edge

Straight edge is derived from the 1981 song *Straight Edge* by the hardcore punk band Minor Threat, which is sometimes abbreviated as sXe or denoted by XXX, X, xXx, S. E., or SxE. In response to the excesse S. E. the punk subculture, members of the straight edge subculture refrain from using alcohol, tobacco, and recreational drugs. For some, this means giving up coffee and prescription drugs, going vegetarian or vegan, and refraining from promiscuous sexual conduct.

3.2.3 Subculture and Digital Platforms

Such adolescent subcultures and trends have only begun to form compared to the world. It is related to China's form in a but rapid economic and technological development. Unlike Western children, Chinese youths forge connections and create virtual social relationships on cutting-edge online platforms. However, this may cause them to follow trends without knowing how long they will last. Youth subcultures and movements frequently have unclear and overlapping objectives. Young people's need to identify with others and distinguish themselves from the masses also contributes to this phenomenon.

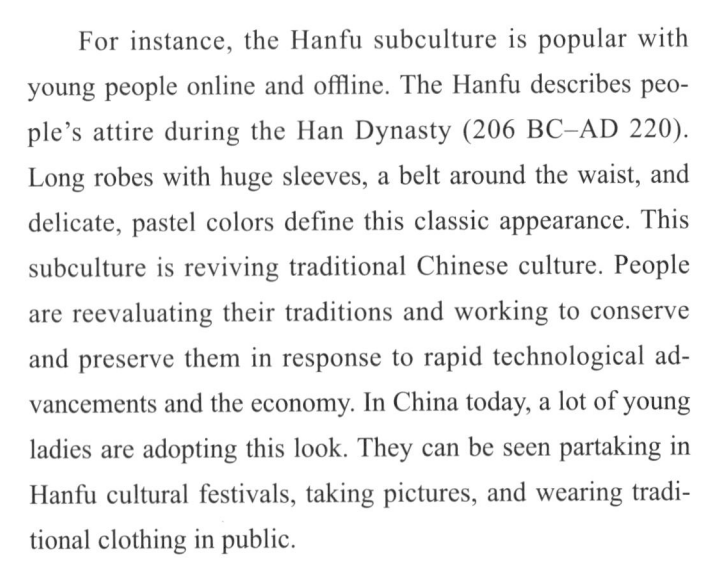

Traditional Chinese Hanfu

For instance, the Hanfu subculture is popular with young people online and offline. The Hanfu describes people's attire during the Han Dynasty (206 BC–AD 220). Long robes with huge sleeves, a belt around the waist, and delicate, pastel colors define this classic appearance. This subculture is reviving traditional Chinese culture. People are reevaluating their traditions and working to conserve and preserve them in response to rapid technological advancements and the economy. In China today, a lot of young ladies are adopting this look. They can be seen partaking in Hanfu cultural festivals, taking pictures, and wearing traditional clothing in public.

3.3 Case Study

3.3.1 Case 1: An Example of Popular Revenge

Since its debut in 1993, the series *Beavis and Butt-Head*, has gained a varied audience of ardent fans while sparking heated debate regarding its meanings and effects. In a run-down home, the two main protagonists spend the majority of the day watching television, mainly music videos, which they criticize (either "cool" or "suck"). When kids leave the house for school, a job at a fast food restaurant, or an adventure, they frequently perform disruptive and criminal behaviors. Here's an example of one of their conversations:

Butt-Head: "These guys remind me of Danzig and my butt."

Beavis: "That's not very nice, Butt-Head."

Butt-Head: "Yeah, it is. My butt rules!"

They said while watching a **Type O Negative** video.

Beavis and Butt-Head

Type O Negative

An American gothic metal band formed in Brooklyn, New York City in 1989.

In the series, young people and those at the bottom of the social scale are shown taking revenge on older, middle-class adults who are portrayed as tyrannical authorities. They rebel against more privileged classes and authority figures, including conservative men and liberal traditional hippies.

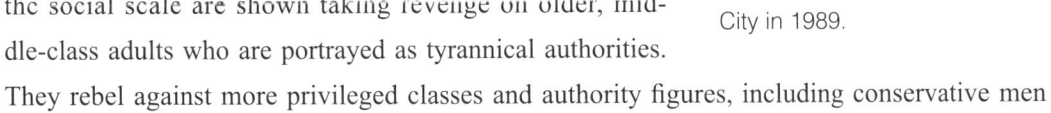

From this angle, Beavis and Butt-Head serve as an example of media culture as popular vengeance. The male authority figures may symbolize the authoritarian guys Judge (the author) nurtured during his adolescence in San Diego, New Mexico, and Texas because most conservative men have a slightly Texan or southern accent.

Butt-acute and Beavis Head's estrangement, love of heavy metal music culture, media portrayals of sex and violence, and violent cartoon conduct sparked a heated debate. As soon as the show first aired, the media was intensely focused on it and strongly opposed opinions. *Rolling Stone* labeled the group "the Voice of a New Generation" (August 19, 1993). "Hey, Beavis, let's

61

walk over to Stuart's house and fire a cigarette in his cat's butt" is the thought that Butt-Head has as his concept of a plan. This is where the downward spiral of the living white guy undoubtedly comes to an end. On its front cover, *Newsweek* lauded and denounced them (October 11, 1993). The media has also referred to the characters and series as being "stupid, lazy, vicious; devoid of objectives, ideals, and futures" (*Dallas Morning News*, August 29, 1993). Numerous requests to prohibit the show have been made.

Nonetheless, *Beavis and Butt-Head* were so popular in the mid-1990s that it spawned a best-seller heavy metal album, a popular book, and countless consumer products.

3.3.2 Case 2: Urban Entertainment Subculture and Black Music: Blues, Ragtime and Jazz

In the late 1800s, "the blues" originated in the south of the United States. It combines the African-American community's work songs, spirituals, chants, and ballads. Along with the explicit depiction of melancholy and grief, the blues also popularized stylized scales, chords, and original formations. The boundaries of conventional harmony are often ambiguous since "blue notes" are frequently interpreted as flattened thirds or occasionally as pitches between notes. The 12-bar blues is a kind of music that is now widely used in popular music worldwide.

In the 1890s, African-American neighborhoods in St. Louis gave birth to "Ragtime". Like John Philip Sousa's music, African music's syncopated or "ragged" rhythms are added to a classic march structure. The genre's popularity declined in the early 20th century as jazz gained popularity. However, many people liken the American rag to waltzes, mazurkas, and minutes from Europe. The ragtime rhythm has affected composers like Satie, Debussy, and Stravinsky.

Scan the QR code to read the article "Timeline Blues, Ragtime and Jazz" to know more about the history of black music.

"Jazz" means pep or energy. This genre was influenced by the blues and Ragtime, which also developed in the taverns of New Orleans. But jazz also had elements of the Cuban and Spanish cultures. Habanera rhythms, blues patterns, and Ragtime thrust formed something new. The rigid patterns of the beat eventually relaxed to produce the sensation we call "swing". Swing is challenging to define and notate. Louis Armstrong once stated, "If you don't feel it, you won't know it." The Jazz Age began to emerge in the United States during the 1920s Prohibition, firmly establishing this fashion and sound in American culture.

Let's use the urban sub-cultural theory to analyze the black music.

When the number of members of a given social group achieves a "critical mass" to "have a visible and confirmed identity", a thriving urban subculture will emerge (Fischer, 1984: 37).

The vitality of a subculture will be reflected in rates of "unconventionality"—for example, in the propensity of members of the group to express beliefs or exhibit behaviors that are regarded as "deviant" or "innovative" by the larger society (see also Ogburn & Duncan, 1964: 141-142).

Robert L. Boyd (2005) contends that a critical mass of blacks is responsible for the correlation between the rate at which blacks are hired as professional musicians and the size of the black population.

Use linear and quadratic regressions on the dependent variable, the dependent variable on ln-(black population), the natural log of the black population, and the dependent variable on ln-(black percentage), the natural log of the black percentage. The equation depicts the relationship between the proportion of blacks who work as professional musicians (Y) and the black population (X).

$$Y = \alpha - \beta_1 X + \beta_2 X^2$$

According to the study, without a critical mass of blacks, the best opportunities for blacks to become professional musicians were located in cities with the smallest black populations. Nonetheless, when the black population of towns expanded to a critical number, these opportunities proliferated.

The critical mass concept explains the social vitality of black musicians in the United States urban north in the early 20th century.

3.3.3 Case 3: China's Cultural Evolution: Egao, Digital Parody, and Politics

3.3.3.1 The Definition of Egao

Egao is a popular Internet approach that hilariously subverts and deconstructs the so-called normal in language, visuals, and animation, according to *Guangming Daily*.

Digital Culture and Globalization

Egao is a well-known subculture that deconstructs serious topics for humorous effect. According to *China Daily*, the characters E, which means "evil", and gao, which means "work", represent a subculture marked by comedy, revelry, subversion, grassroots spontaneity, defiance of authority, and mass participation in multimedia high-tech.

3.3.3.2 Egao in China

In early 2006, a 20-minute video entitled *The Bloody Case of a Steamed Bun* (《一个馒头引发的血案》), became one of the most popular online video clips in China.

In 2006, a greater number of Egao works appeared, and the population of Chinese netizens hit a new high of 137 million, with 63.8 percent of those aged 18 to 30 living in cities rather than the rural.

Scan the QR code to watch the video.

3.3.4 Case 4: Harajuku Culture in Japan

Harajuku is a district in Shibuya, Tokyo, Japan. Harajuku culture began during the occupation of Japan by the Allies when American soldiers and civilians lived there.

Harajuku style is a diverse and inclusive subculture. This is reflected in the following aspects.

Both Japanese and Western motifs are heavily present in Harajuku culture, whether in the West or Japan. Between man and woman, the blurring of this border is not only characteristic of Harajuku but all Japanese cultures. Creators and players can be interchangeable. Different motifs—when combined—allow players to express their outlook. Tradition and modernity become fused, traditional motifs inspire fashion designers (for example, Takuya Angel), and they appear in music videos or constitute players' images. Fantasy and reality overlap. The barrier between fantasy and reality is blurred by self-expression and freedom. Fashion, music, the West, Japan, tradition, modernism, women, men—owing to the abundance of potential sources of inspiration, the use of all accessible motifs is acceptable.

3.4 Conclusion

This lecture introduced the rapid development of network audio-visual platforms and then tried to find the connection between its popularity and youth culture. If we follow the progress of the age, we understand that Generation Z play a vital role in the kinds of Internet platform. Here we take TikTok and Douyin as examples.

The descriptions and lists of several subculture instances follow. By studying other cultures, you may learn about and understand how historical and sociological changes, such as political upheaval, armed warfare, technological advancements, and exploration that led to the discovery of new, distant civilizations, have altered cultural norms.

Five scenarios, spanning research approaches and well-known cases related to this subject, are provided in conclusion. The fashion trends forecaster must stay up to date on national and international events, technological advancements, economic fluctuations, and environmental changes, in addition to fashion-related arguments.

After finishing the reading, we hope you will conduct research on a culture of your choosing and explain how political and natural events have influenced it.

3.5 Extended Readings

Scan the QR code to get extended reading materials.

3.6 Post Questions and Discussion

(1) How do you define culture, subculture, and counterculture? What do you think are the similarities and differences between subcultures and countercultures? You can scan the QR code and watch the video.

(2) What subcultures are you exposed to or familiar with? Why did you become interested in and identify with this culture?

3.7 Bibliography

Acland, C. R. (2004). Fresh Contacts: Global Culture and the Concept of Generation. In N. Campbell(ed.), *American Youth Cultures* (pp. 31-52. Edinburgh: Edinburgh University Press.

Bainbridge, J., Norris, C. (2013). Posthuman Drag: Understanding Cosplay as Social Networking in a Material Culture. *Intersections: Gender & Sexuality in Asia & The Pacific*, 32: 6.

Beendtt, A. (2000). *Popular Music and Youth Culture: Music, Identity and Place*. London: Palgrave.

Berger, B. (1963), Adolescence and Beyond. *Social Problems*, 10: 294-408.

Brake, M. (1985). *Comparative Youth Culture: The Sociology of Youth Cultures and Youth Subcultures in America, Britain and Canada* (1st ed.). London: Routledge. https://doi.org/10.4324,/9780203408940.

Brake, M. (2013). *The Sociology of Youth Culture and Youth Subcultures*. London: Routledge.

Bucholtz, M. (2002). Youth and Cultural Practice. *Annual Review of Anthropology*, 31.

Buckingham, D., Kehily, M. J. (2014). Introduction: Rethinking Youth Cultures in the Age of Global Media. In D. Buckingham, S. Bragg & M. J. Kehily(eds.), *Youth Cultures in the Age of Global Media* (pp. 1-18). London: Palgrave.

Clarke, J., Critcher, C., & Johnson, R. (eds.). (1976). *Working Class Culture*. London: Hutchinson.

Gatewood, J., Cameron, C. (2009). Belonger Perceptions of Tourism and Its Importance in the Turks and Caicos Islands. Report of the Department of Sociology and Anthropology, Leigh University. http://www.lehigh.edu/~jbg1/perceptions-of-tourism.pdf.

Goodman, P. (1960). *Growing Up Absurd: Problems of Youth in the Organized System*. New York: Random House.

Gracious, M., Sibanda, Ethelia. (2013). Global Youth Culture. *Greener Journal of Social Sciences*, 3: 128-132. 10.15580/GJSS.2013.3.012213402.

Hall, S., Jefferson, T. (eds.). (1976). *Resistance through Rituals: Youth Subcultures in Post-War Britain*. London: Routledge.

Hebdige, D. (1979). *Subculture: The Meaning of Style*. London: Routledge.

Johnson, S., Chris M. (1993). *Beavis and Butt-Head: This Book Sucks*. New York: Pocket Books.

Katz, E., Paul F. L. (1955). *Personal Influence*. New York: Free Press.

Laura M. (2004). Those Naughty Teenage Girls: Japanese Kogals, Slang, and Media Assessments. *Journal of Linguistic Anthropology*, 14: 2.

Manifold, M. C. (2009). Fanart as Craft and the Creation of Culture. *International Journal of Education through Art*, 5. doi: 10.1386/eta.5.1.7/1.

Mascheroni, G. (2007). Global Nomads' Network and Mobile Sociality: Exploring New Media Uses on the Move. *Information, Communication, and Society*, 10(4): 527-546.

Merton, R. K. (1968). *Social Theory and Social Structure*. New York: Free Press. (Orig. pub. 1957).

Miller, L. (2003). Male Beauty Work in Japan. In J., Roberson, N., Suzuki (eds.), *Men and Masculinities in Contemporary Japan: Dislocating the Salaryman Doxa* (pp. 27-58). New York: Routledge.

Murdock, G., McCron, R. (1976). Youth and Class: The Career of Confusion. In G., Mungham, G., Pearson (eds.), *Working Class Youth Cultures* (pp. 10-26). London: Routledge.

Nagy, P., Neff, G. (2015). Imagined Affordance: Reconstructing a Keyword for Communication Theory. *Social Media + Society*. 1. 10.1177/2056305115603385.

Osgerby, B. (2020). *Youth Culture and the Media: Global Perspectives* (2nd ed.). London: Routledge. https://doi.org/10.4324/9781351065269.

Paris, C., Musa, G., & Thirumoorthi, T. (2010). Comparing Backpackers from Australia/New Zealand and SE Asia: A Cultural Consensus Approach. Paper presented at the 4th backpacker research group meeting of an expert conference in Hermanus, South Africa.

Ribeiro, N. (2011). Do Tourists Do What They Say They Do? An Application of the Cultural Consensus and Cultural Consonance Models to Tourism Research. Proceedings of the 42nd Travel and Tourism Research Association (TTRA) Annual Conference, London.

Romney, A., Boyd, J., Moore, C., Batchelder, W., & Brazill, T. (1996). Culture as Shared Cognitive Representations. Proceedings of the National Academy of Sciences, 93(9): 4699-4705.

Scopelliti, R. (2018). *Youthquake 4.0: A Whole Generation and the Industrial Revolution*. Tarrytown: Marshall Cavendish Business.

Sun, L., Zhang, H. Q., Zhang, S. Y., & Luo, J. B. (2020). Content-Based Analysis of the Cultural Differences between TikTok and Douyin. 4779-4786. 10.1109/BigData50022.2020.9378032.

Turner, G. (1992). *British Cultural Studies*. London: Routledge.

Wartena J. (2013). Hipster before It Was Cool. *The UVU Review*. http://www.uvureview.com/2013/02/18/hipster-before-it-was-cool/.

Whyte, W. F. (1943). *Street Corner Society: The Social Structure of an Italian Slum*. Chicago: University of Chicago Press.

Willis, P. (1977). *Learning to Labour: How Working-Class Kids Get Working Class Jobs*. London: Routledge.

Willis, P. (1978). *Profane Culture*. London: Routledge.

Willis, P. (1990). *Common Culture: Symbolic Work at Play in the Everyday Cultures of the Young.* London: Open University Press.

LECTURE & SEMINAR 4
ESport, Platform Economy Career Development and Wellbeing

Electronic sports (eSports) has performed an increasingly crucial role in China's globalization and digitalization since the government announced its ambition to be a global sporting power. This lecture will give a brief introduction to the development of China's eSports industry in the context of neoliberalism and throw light on its socio-cultural concerns. By introducing several key concepts with two case studies, the platformization of Tencent, one of China's largest media conglomerates, and the challenges faced by Chinese eSports professional players, we aim to offer you a general picture of eSports development in China and its academic research. The concepts/theories include platformization and infrastructralization as well as stigma power.

Framework

4.1 Background

4.2 Theory

    4.2.1 Platformization and Infrastructuralization

    4.2.2 Stigma Power

4.3 Case Study

4.3.1 Case 1: Tencent—The Platformizing ESports Conglomerate

4.3.2 Case 2: Challenges Faced by Chinese ESports Professional Players

4.3 Conclusion

4.4 Extended Readings

4.5 Post Questions and Discussion

4.6 Bibliography

Terms

eSports of China, videogame, platformization infrastructuralization, stigma power, neoliberalism, meritocracy, precarity, mental wellbeing, Tencent

Pre-lecture Discussion

(1) Why is it controversial to define eSports as a sport?

(2) What role does Tencent play in the development of eSports industry in China?

(3) How does the Chinese government exert influence on eSports industry?

(4) What challenges are eSports athletes facing in their career?

4.1 Background

ESports, also known as electronic sports or **e-Sports**, thrives as a promising industry in competitions using digital games. It is the name given to competitive videogame playing

> eSports = Sports + Industry

or professional gaming (Seo, 2016). This cyber-athletic competition cannot be thought of in terms of media, sport or computer gaming. The institutional and material boundaries separating them have imploded, leading to creating a new social form, "e-sport". Within this broader picture, eSports indicates a form of meta-change, a largescale transformation in our society (Hutchins, 2008). Academically, Hemphill (2005) first defined it as alternative sports realities for electronically extended athletes in digitally represented sporting worlds. Later, he expanded the definition to include electronically extended human actions in computer-mediated or -generated sporting worlds (Hemphill, 2015), significantly broadening the understanding of eSports within a more complex socio-cultural context.

As the world's largest digital gaming market since 2016, China boasted revenue of online and offline PC and mobile eSports and games exceeding 91.2 billion RMB (13.63 billion USD) in 2018. And the over 350 million gamers comprised 52.9% of this revenue (iResearch, 2018). The nexus among the state, the platforms, the professional athletes, and other professional sectors in eSports is deeply embedded in the digitalization and globalization process. As one of the most rapidly expanding videogame and eSports marketplaces, China has witnessed a significant development in the eSports industry and may serve as a specific changing context for the study of the culture of eSports.

2003 marks a turning point of eSports' development in China. The General Administration of Sports approved eSports as the country's 99th official sport (modified as 78th in 2008), which is part of a drive to establish China as a leader in the digital arena. Since then, the eSports industry has soared rapidly. ESports also emerges as an essential component of contemporary digital youth culture, producing a vast cohort of videogame players whose peak age ranges between 16 and 22(HRSS, 2019). As we can see, the Chinese government is like an "umbrella cloth" of the infrastructure of digital platforms because it determines both the life cycle and the expansion of Chinese eSports and videogames.

The industrial growth echoes with the expansion of Chinese digital platforms—or digital media intermediaries—in the Asia-Pacific region and eSports' expanding popularity. The rise of digital platforms with emerging digital technologies, competing tools and services in China's eSports industry illustrate two major trends, academically named platformization and infrastructralization.

These platforms are developed by media conglomerates, which can be described as an "umbrella stand" corresponding to the government as an "umbrella cloth". Among all the companies running the gaming business, Tencent is one of the leading enterprises domestically and worldwide. In terms of the scale of earnings in the gaming market, Tencent held the No.1 position among the global top 10 companies[1] for the second consecutive year in 2020, earning $52 million, or approximately RMB 348 million, in the third quarter of 2019, an increase of 13.04% compared to the same period last year (Newzoo, 2020). In the Chinese eSports industry, the coexistence of the state and government, or the "umbrella cloth" and "umbrella stand" composes a business ecosystem as coevolution, closing the loop between the platform owners and the government.

Despite the increasing economic importance of eSports, relatively little is known about the mental wellbeing of professional players. ESports players competing in top-level tournaments face similar pressure and stress to professional athletes due to the stigma power from the society and the government. In China, eSports players tend to be stigmatized as game addicts, and gaming is associated with so-called spiritual opium. In 2004, the State Administration of Press, Publication, Radio, Film, and Television of China [SAPPRFT, now renamed National Radio and Television Administration (NRTA)] even banned the mainstream media, including digital TV channels, from broadcasting eSports related content. Mianzi, a Chinese term symbolizing social status, is closely linked with stigma power. Such negative circumstances have changed since 2011, for three main factors—political support, private investment, and introduction of foreign training systems—drove China's eSports industry's fascinating development and helped eSports players develop confidence and self-actualization. In spite of having been recognized as professional athletes, these players still face a tough decision on whether choosing athletes as a lifelong career. On the one hand, it is surely a meritorious discourse both for the national glory and personal achievements if the player succeeds to be an eSports star; on the other hand, the chances of that are extremely slim and the future for most eSports players remains disposable accordingly. The game among meritocracy and precarity of eSports players is highly embedded in the eSports industry in China.

---

1 The top 10 companies by game revenue are Tencent, Sony, Apple, Microsoft, Google, NetEase, EA, Nintendo, Activision Blizzard, and Take Two, according to a report releasd by newzoo.com/global-games-market-report.

4.2 Theory

4.2.1 Platformization and Infrastructuralization

Over the past decade, digital platforms developed by media conglomerates such as Tencent, ByteDance, and Alibaba have pioneered a new mode of content production, distribution, and monetization.

While debuting as the leading producer of videogame content in the eSports industry, Tencent has become a fully-fledged eSports platform and an integrated services provider. From accelerating game content production and distribution to organizing tournaments, coordinating with governments, becoming a hub for eSports in China, offering live streaming services, and inviting more actors to the eSports ecology, there is little that Tencent cannot do. Understanding the eSports industry in China from the perspective of platformization helps with explicating boundaryless infrastructural power and platform capitalism in the context of globalization and digitization.

The surrounding environment of the digital industry is described by Plantin et al. (2018) as widely accessible systems and services, often provided or regulated by governments in the public interest. However, this is also an environment where various dominant Internet enterprises have broken the boundaries of their platforms by restructuring their business activities or their platform community or societies—concepts familiar to platform studies. The concept of **platforms** can be exemplified as an assemblage of the following three main types:

(1) a layered structure often based on hardware;

(2) support for content most associated with social media or user-generated content sites;

(3) a mediation-type platform that enables financial transactions to take place.

Platform

A media concept.

Basic definition: a software-based platform as an architectural construct or as an online marketplace. It usually serves as the extensible code-base of a software-based system.

Media & communication definition: digital infrastructures that enable two or more groups to interact (Srnicek, 2016).

Categories: advertising, product, lean, industrial, and cloud (Srnicek, 2016).

Furthermore, the "-ization" in "platformization" implies a before and after, including a pre-platform period subject to platformization and a post-platform period wherein cultural production has effectively become platformized.

The term platformization was first introduced by Helmond (2015) to conceptualize the rise of digital platforms as the dominant infrastructural and economic model of the social web and its consequences. Therefore, platformization can be defined as how various sectors within an industry are transforming due to the mutual shaping between digital platforms and entities using platform infrastructures to provide products and services to end-users. In economic terms, platformization implies replacing two-sided market structures with multisided and complementary platform configurations dominated by big platform corporations. Cultural content producers must continuously grapple with seemingly serendipitous changes in platform governance, ranging from content curation to pricing strategies. Simultaneously, these producers are enticed by new platform services and infrastructural changes. In the process, cultural commodities become fundamentally "contingent", which is increasingly modular in design and continuously reworked and repackaged, informed by data-driven user feedback.

The first substantial body of research on platformization is generated by a prolific and di verse collective of business scholars, who primarily focus on for-profit companies operating as intermediaries in platform markets. Focusing on digital videogames as "contingent cultural commodities", Nieborg and Poell (2018) introduced platformization as a theoretical lens to investigate how economic, governmental, and infrastructural extensions of digital platforms are reshaping modes of production in the cultural industries. Therefore, a platform company acts as an intermediary between the providers and consumers, facilitates its development in a more communicative way than older offline analogues (McKee, 2017), and is associated with the sharing business model, which is supported by access rather than ownership (Gansky, 2010). Theories of platformization continue to develop and call attention to how cultural products and society are influenced by the penetration of platform logic or "the norms, strategies, mechanisms, and economies" of platforms (Van Dijck & Poell, 2013).

Infrastructure is generally defined as something that runs on things substrate to events and movements—railroads, highways, electricity, and more recently, the information superhighway (Star, 2002). This concept was eventually regarded as too shallow and absolute, thus evolving into three categories of infrastructure—corporate information, business sectors (such as an infrastructure supporting a manufacturing supply chain), and universal services (such as the Internet) (Hanseth & Lyytinen,

Infrastructure

An informational and sci-tech concept.

Basic definition: something that runs on things substrate to events and movements—railroads, highways, electricity and more recently, the information superhighway (Star, 2002).

Expanded definition: three categories—corporate information, business sectors, and universal services (Hanseth & Lyytinen, 2004).

2004). It was then expanded to include information and data infrastructures. Hanseth and Lyytinen (2004) described information infrastructure as a shared, open (and unbounded), heterogeneous, and evolving socio-technical system (installed base) consisting of a set of IT capabilities and their user, operations, and design communities. Data infrastructure is defined as socio-technical systems implicated in the creation, processing, and distribution of data, hosting a variety of platform instances, including app and website instances.

Infrastructure and platforms are evolving and growing. Both concepts examine structures that underlie something more salient and share the features of invisibility, extensibility, and broad coverage (Plantin et al., 2018). Both help theorists frame and understand the expansion of digital media. The emerging digital technologies and competing tools and services provide the potential for infrastructuralization of platforms—thus, Plantin et al.'s (2018) theoretical bifocal platform-as-infrastructure and infrastructure-as-platform concepts. Nieborg and Helmond (2019) likewise developed an analytical framework for understanding digital companies' economic growth and technical expansion, and examined how Facebook Messenger's platformization evolved to have infrastructural properties—in particular, how it emerged as a data infrastructure that operates dynamic platform instances through data interactivity and connectivity.

Both Plantin et al. (2018) and Nieborg and Helmond's (2019) research suggest the benefits of studying the evolution of infrastructralized platforms in the digital age as they are platformized on capital-intensive infrastructures through information technology. Hence the concept of the platform economy and relevant business literature clarifies the insights into the economic and managerial mechanisms of platform markets and the process of platformization.

4.2.2 Stigma Power

By 2016, China has overtaken the United States, becoming the world's largest digital gaming market by revenue and number of consumers, with the Chinese company Tencent becoming the world's largest gaming firm. Tencent has developed and published many popular games, and it owns and operates eSports leagues in China that are popular among the younger generation. Despite the increasing economic importance of eSports, relatively little is known about the mental wellbeing of professional players. Actually, eSports players competing in top-level tournaments face similar pressure and stress to professional athletes.

In China, the public, including parents, educators, and medical professionals, is more concerned with videogame addiction as a negative consequence of eSports development. In contrast, the popularity of videogame playing is seen negatively compared to pursuing academic success, a much-preferred cultural value for Chinese youth. Hence, videogamers are often stigmatized in China as gaming addicts. **Stigma power** in China is closely linked with the Chinese cultural norm of Mianzi.

Stigma is not a self-evident phenomenon but, like all concepts, has a history. The conceptual understanding of stigma, which underpins most sociological research, has roots in the ground-breaking account Erving Goffman (1963) penned in his best-selling book *Stigma: Notes on the Management of Spoiled Identity*. Concerning stigma, Goffman famously defined the term as an "attribute that is deeply discrediting", and that reduces the bearer "from a whole and usual person to a tainted, discounted one" (Goffman, 1963). Stigma highlights the differences between normalized and stigmatized individuals and pivots on the established social consensus of "what is normal" (Goffman, 1986/1963). As a result of stigma, individuals may suffer from reduced status, prejudice, discrimination, stereotyping, or social exclusion.

Stigma Power

It roots in social identities as perspectives produced in the interactional setting and the situation of the individual who is disqualified from full social acceptance (Goffman, 1986).

In the 50 years since its publication, Goffman's account of stigma has proved a productive concept in further research on social stigma and its effects, widening public understandings of stigma, and developing anti-stigma campaigns. Stigma power was then defined as "the capacity to keep people down, in and away by using stigma-related processes" (Link & Phelan, 2014), which helped ground the construction of stigma operated through a social structure. This was because stigma's "social, political function is an instrument of social policy and a component of the state's coercive apparatus" (Davis, 2004). Richman and Lattanner (2014) employed stigma power—whether social, economic, or political—as a central ingredient to critically understand how both structural and interpersonal stigmas influenced health and wellbeing. Video-gamers, for example, as stigmatized individuals, might refuse to stay within normative boundaries or accept these devaluations because of stigma power. For instance, Norton et al. (2012) demonstrated that stigmatized individuals might challenge stigma power by delivering a persuasive "power" during face-to-face interactions and negotiation with non-stigmatized individuals.

The concept of **Mianzi** ("face"), which is a symbol of social status in China, may be helpful in understanding stigma formation and may play an operative role in the creation of stigma power (Yang & Kleinman, 2008). These structural components might lead stigmatized individuals to internalized stereotypes, causing them to suffer a reduction in their self-esteem and sense of self-worth (Vogel

Mianzi

" 面子 " in Chinese. It symbolizes social status, perceived as a consciousness of glory and shame, representing one's reputation and social status in others' minds and perceptions (Hu, 1944).

et al., 2013). Thus, Mianzi is understood to be the relationship between "normal" and stigma in China, in that it creates power relationships either at the macro-level (e.g., structural power) or the micro-level (e.g., everyday interactions) (Tyler, 2018).

In other words, the significance of political and economic components affecting the extent of Mianzi might drive the establishment of social control, a consequence that has been largely ignored. In our specific area of investigation, Mianzi in Chinese culture is positively associated with academic success, such as attending universities and negatively associated with gaming addiction. ESports players' socio-cultural conceptions might have self-stigmatized or internalized (Corrigan, 2004; Corrigan & Watson, 2002) when considering the degree of loss of face due to "cognitive and evaluative beliefs", and continue to bolster current digital-sociological concerns. However, "stigma consciousness" (Pinel, 1999), related to the concept of self-stigma, has been under-explored in this new digital field. In particular, there is a need to identify the kinds of psychological predicaments further that eSports professionals experience between the self and others (Link & Phelan, 2014). Mianzi is very important for Chinese eSports players when it comes to winning competitions against other nations (Ismangil, 2018). However, Mianzi is more than winning games. And it is deeply embedded in the everyday lives of Chinese people. Attending university is seen as the path to success in China; for young eSports players to compensate for not attending university, they may earn Mianzi by succeeding in competitions or becoming rich through successful live streaming engagements.

4.3 Case Study

4.3.1 Case 1: Tencent—The Platformizing ESports Conglomerate

The rise of Chinese eSports has taken place alongside the expansion of digital platforms via a state-centered approach to regulatory platformization and the digital economy. In other words, the relationship between the state and booming industries run by the private enterprises in China—such as artificial intelligence or eSports—is inextricably embedded in its own character of governance. In particular, Schneider (1993) asserts the significance of the state's role in setting the parameters of discourse but allowing diverse actors to negotiate its exact meanings.

4.3.1.1 Umbrella Cloth: Regulatory Platformization of Infrastructures

Chinese eSports has the attributes of entertainment, media, and sport, thus significantly in-

Umbrella Cloth

In the umbrella-like structure of the Chinese eSports industry, the Chinese government is analogous for the umbrella cloth due to its leading role.

fluenced by various policies (Dai, 2019). However, its rise has not been smooth. The Chinese government can be described as the "umbrella cloth" of the infrastructure of digital platforms because it determines both the life cycle and the expansion of Chinese eSports and videogames. Six government departments1 have launched a series of regulations and policies to cover game content, game licensing, game competitions, education, coaches, and professional players.

The most significant policy relates to eSports broadcasting. In 2003, *ESports World* began broadcasting on Channel 5 of China Central Television (CCTV-5). However, the State Administration of Press, Publication, Radio, Film and Television of China (SAPPRFT) issued a ban on online games, and CCTV-5's *ESports World* program was suspended. Consequently, eSports broadcasting had been limited to the Internet since 2004. This resulted in significant changes to the market's value chain and made the Chinese eSports model significantly different from Korea's, which offered game completion TV broadcasting. In the following challenging decade (2004–2015), eSports' growth and development in China had embarked on a meandering path and generated a complicated environment (see the table below). 2008 marked a turning point of the eSports development, for China's General Administration of Sports reviewed the existing sports and redefined eSports as the 78th officially recognized sport.

An Overview of Major Policy Events in the Chinese ESports Industry from 2003 to 2015

Time	Events
November 2003	ESports became the 99th formal sports event recognized by the General Administration of Sports of China.
February 2004	The first China eSports Games took place, supported by the General Administration of Sports of China and organized by the China eSports League with Sports.
February 2007	CCTV was accused by netizens of "under-the-table dealing" as the World of Warcraft player Li Xiaofeng (Sky) failed to be selected as one of the most influential figures in sports.
October 2007	ESports appeared in the 2nd Asian Indoor Games; this was the first time that eSports had been included in a comprehensive international sporting tournament.
2008	Chengdu, China, successfully bid for the WCG 2009 Global finals.
August 2010	The Ministry of Culture's prohibiting the launch of game products without official permission served as a useful "catch-all" to limit content.
2012–2013	The WCG were successfully held twice in Kunshan, Jiangsu Province (eastern China).
2013	A 17-member eSports national team organized by the Ministry of Sport represented China at the 4th Asian Indoor Games.
January 2013	*Sports World*, on CCTV 5, produced and broadcast a program named *Running on the Road of Chasing the eSports Dream*.

---

1 Ministry of Culture (now renamed Ministry of Culture and Tourism), Ministry of Education, State Development and Reform Commission, Ministry of Public Security, General Administration of Sport, and State Administration of Press, Publication, Radio, Film and Television (now renamed National Radio and Television Administration)

Continued

Time	Events
2014	Yinchuan, a city in northwest China, became the permanent host of the World Cyber Arena and its advertising was broadcast on CCTV-5.
February 2015	Perfect World Games announced a strategic partnership with Huayi Culture Co. Ltd. They launched the first domestic game program to be broadcast on a populat TV channel. It was broadcast simultaneously during prime time in 20 large provincial capitals in China.

In 2016, eSports in China entered a new stage—the Chinese government reacted to eSports' global popularity (Lu, 2017) by signalling a newfound willingness to actively solve problems within the eSports industry. China's six administrative bodies launched four regulations which:

(1) covered support for importing digital technology from other provinces;

(2) encouraged the industry to improve the development of mobile games, live-streaming services, and virtual reality technology;

(3) founded initiatives to organize international and national professional eSports tournaments;

(4) encouraged Chinese colleges and universities to offer professional eSports courses.

However, two SAPPRFT regulations[1] issued in March and May 2016 prohibited game content that subverted state power and disturbed the social order. These regulations temporarily halted the licensing of imports of gaming products to China, particularly those judged unhealthy and with poor taste content. Thus, these regulations only serve to support the launch of domestic games. For instance, *Player Unknown's Battlegrounds* was banned in 2018 due to its gory animation. Shaped by techno-nationalist media laws and regulations (Qiu, 2010), such regulations represent a multifaceted, strategic signal and an ambiguous attitude from the government toward the eSports industry. Therefore, these policies and regulations gave rise to a significant practical concern: The government's regulatory infrastructural synergies serve the techno-nationalist eSports industry.

Consequently, eSports clubs have criticized these policies to enhance the government's political performance rather than increase its political efficiency. These stakeholder critiques indicate that Chinese eSports regulations and policies are shaped by techno-nationalist architectures and affordances of the governed platforms. However, these regulations and policies function ambiguously—even though the government's politically driven attempts to attract industrial synergies are apparent. When considering the perceptions of user practices (Nieborg

---

1 "Internet Publication and Service Management" and "Online Mobile Games Publication and Service Management".

& Poell, 2018), this ambiguity results in a decline of authorities' political influence on users, which is often considered a hallmark of authoritarian society. Moreover, the political economy of platforms should be considered in further explorations—do Tencent ESports and the Chinese government roles in managing eSports' platformization and their own infrastructural ambitions complement, oppose, or compete with each other?

4. 3. 1. 2 Umbrella Stand: The Growth of the Value Chain and Multisided Platforms

Tencent has worked diligently to develop its platforms by operating with the Chinese government. Tencent ESports acts as an "umbrella stand" for the growth of the value chain and multisided media, thereby driving Tencent's model of capitalism and maintaining its enormous economic power in the eSports platforms in China.

Umbrella Stand

In the umbrella-like structure of Chinese eSports industry, the multisided platforms like Tencent are analogous for the umbrella stand due to its market power complemented for the state control.

Given the development of the upper stream of the eSports value chain, Tencent facilitates its business infrastructure as the leading producer of videogame content in China, including popular games such as *League of Legends, Arena of Valor, CrossFire* (distributor), and *Survival of the Last Jedi*. However, the Chinese government's support of eSports changed in 2016. In December 2016, Tencent ESports was established and soon became the largest of Tencent's four business matrices[1] of pan-entertainment.

Therefore, Tencent has moved, consolidated, and built up its platformized infrastructure internationally through part or complete ownership of the world's leading games publishers and developers of popular games (see the table below).

Tencent's Major Investments in External Gaming Companies (2006–2018)

Year	Mergers and Acquisition Target	Shareholding Ratio	Value	Games
2006	GoPets (the ROK)	16.9%	CNY 32.813 million	
2007	PvP (Shenzhen, China)	100.0%	CNY 452.9 billion	
	Horizon 3D (Beijing, China)	63.9%	Unknown	X5.qq.com
	Vina Games (the ROK)	30.2%	Unknown	*BnB (Bubble and Bubbke)*
2008	Outspark (the USA)	Unknown	USD 11 million	*Lord of the Century*
2010	Youxigu (Beijing, China)	68.0%	CNY 168 million	7.QQ.com
	Eyedentity Games (the ROK)	Unknown	KRW 3.999 billion	*Dragon Nest*

---

1 Tencent Animation, Tencent Literature, Tencent Film, and Tencent ESports

Continued

Year	Mergers and Acquisition Target	Shareholding Ratio	Value	Games
2011	Roit (the USA)	100.0%	CNY 1,679 billion	*League of Legends*
	Epic Games (the USA)	48.4%	CNY 2.087 billion	*Gears of War*, *Fortnite*
2013	Activision Blizzard (the USA)	24.7%	USD 1.4 billion	*Call of Duty*, *World of Warcraft*, *Starcraft*, *Diablo*, *Hearthstone*, *Overwatch*
	iDreamsky games (Shenzhen, China)	20.4%	USD 15 million	*Fruit Ninja*, *Temple Run*, *Subway Surfers*, *Monument Valley*
2014	CJ Games (the ROK)	28.0%	USD 500 million	TBC
2016	Paradox Interactive (Sweden)	5.0%	CNY 138 million	*Mount & Blade*
	Supercell (Finland)	Unknown	USD 9 billion	*Clash Royale*, *Boom Beach*
2017	Xishanju (Zhuhai, China)	9.9%	USD 143 million	*Sword Net*, *World of Sword*
2018	Shengda Games (Shanghai, China)	Unknown	CNY 3 billion	*Legend*, *Million Arthur*
	Bluehole (the ROK)	10.0%	KRW 588.2 billion	*Player Unknown's Battlegrounds*
	Ubisoft (France)	5.0%	EUR 370 million	*Assassin's Creed*, *Rainbow Six*, *Rayman*

Tenccent's "Expansion" in ESports Industry

Tencent bought 100% of shares in the American frontier developer Riot Games and 10% of the American company Activision Blizzard's eSports branch. In 2016, it bought Finland's Supercell, whose *Clash of Clans* was a mobile gaming hit. Between 2010 and 2013, online PC games contributed 57.2%, 71.3%, 45.7%, and 55.1% of Tencent's annual revenue. However, between 2014 and 2017, mobile games emerged as a major source of revenue. Mobile games represented 55.6%, 38.5%, 34.9%, and 28.4% of Tencent's annual revenue in those years. In 2017, Tencent's total revenue from online games approached 97.88 billion RMB, and 64.2% (62.8 billion RMB) of this revenue stemmed from mobile games—Tencent has grown to become the world's largest gaming company.

Regarding the middle streams of the eSports value chain, tournament operations represent the industry's core resources. Tournaments' importance is best exemplified by the World Cyber Games (WCG), which demonstrates the material integration of media, sport, and participants (e.g., the audience and professional players). Tencent values organized competitive gaming and has radically expanded its platformalized infrastructures to capitalize organized gaming's potential profitability.

First, Tencent has become a major executive of gaming leagues (including the KPL, KCC, and KOC) and runs many significant tournaments, such as LPL (LoL Pro League) and LSPL (LoL Secondary Pro League). Second, the Tencent Games Arena (TGA) Grand Prix, founded in 2010, covers various gaming genres and integrates organizational physical, and interactive digital technologies into tournaments. The total prize pool of the Grand Prix is approximately RMB 18 million. Third, the top clubs of China's LPL are supported by Tencent, which aims to build up its physical infrastructures by locating these clubs in six of the top so-called first- and second-tier cities in China.

Tencent ESports Industry Domination

· Main producer of game content:

League of Legends

Arena of Valor, *CrossFire* (distributor)

Survival of the Last Jedi

· Major executive of gaming leagues:

LPL (LoL Pro League)

LSPL (LoL Secondary Pro League)

Tencent Games Arena (TGA)

· Establisher of the live broadcasting industry chain:

Live broadcasting platforms

Live broadcast products

Tencent Live Broadcasting Industry

In 2016, Tencent deployed domestic live broadcasting platforms (the first table below) and launched numerous live broadcasting products (the second table below), which established the live broadcasting industry chain in China.

Tencent's Deployment of Domestic Live Broadcasting Platforms (2012–2018)

Year	Mergers and Acquisition Target	Shareholding Ratio	Value	Financing Round
2012	guagua.cn	16.03%	CNY 75 million	A
2014			Unknown	B
	longzhu.com	20%	CNY 300 million	A
2015			CNY 278 million	B
2016	ingkee.com	0.99%	CNY 310 million	B
	douyu.com	18.98%	USD 100 million	B
			USD 1.5 billion	C
2018			USD 630 million	Strategic investment
	huya.com	Unknown	CNY 460 million	B

Tencent's Major Launches of Live Broadcasting Products in 2016

Name	Orientation
egame.com	Tencent's official live gaming platform
live.qq.com	Video and live broadcasting of sports events
now.qq.com	National social broadcasting platform for live videos
v.qq.com	Concert live broadcasting
qzone.live.com	Social live entertainment
huayang.qq.com	Interactive live entertainment broadcasting platform

Livestreaming is among the bottom streams of the eSports value chain. Livestreaming is the critical means of reviewing and distributing games and expanding and engaging game audiences and experts (Johnson & Woodcock, 2019). Between 2012 and 2018, Tencent deployed domestic live stream broadcasting platformalized infrastructures to capitalize organized gaming's potential profitability.

In 2018, Tencent set up a mobile eSports brand (Penguin ESports) and invested in Douyu and Huya, two leading livestream broadcasting platforms. In the first half of 2018, live broadcastsing of professional events in the LPL tournament area generated 7.09 billion views and over 1.38 billion hours of viewing time. The finals of the 2018 Mid-Season Invitational had more unique viewers than the Season Seven final, and in 2017 the King Pro League (KPL) attracted more than 10 billion views. The spring 2018 regular season saw a year-on-year increase of 100% to 34 million LPL spectators. Thus, Tencent's livestreaming responded well to the expanding role and needs of eSport audiences and embodied the new interactivity between production and consumption in its gaming platforms.

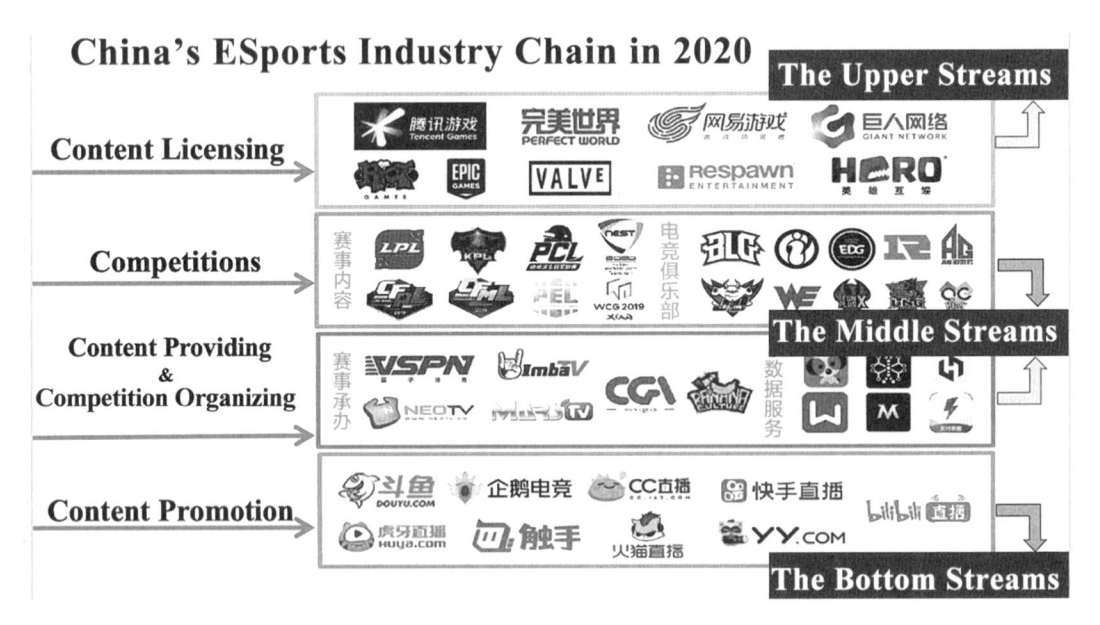

4.3.1.3 Digital Properties and Technological Expansion of Infrastructuralization of Platforms

To better understand how the rapid development of Tencent's eSports capitalized on digital platforms and influenced significant changes in its platformization, it is crucial to analyze its archived data sources and digital properties. Technical information illustrates how Tencent has broadened the scope of digital platforms and highlights the diversity of Tencent eSports in three key ways. First, by introducing new technical resources and frameworks, such as a content delivery network, digital acceleration, and networking options. Second, through a variety of products, functionalities, and development opportunities that Tencent provides. Third, with Tencent's guidelines for the technical implementation of its eSports initiatives.

The following table provides in-depth insights into Tencent's technical infrastructural and eSports platform-based expansions—starting up social media platforms instances such as QQ, encoding eSports online and social-related activities into data for further processing, cross-articulating digital media properties, functions and its business extensions to promote the interests.

Summary of Tencent's ESports Infrastructure and Platform Properties

	Infrastructure	Platform	Examples	Scope
Architecture	Client end and service systems; network speed up using dynamic CDN (content delivery network) systems; voice and video media systems	Reliable and elastic loud computing system; portal servers for user authorzation; runing game on block servers which divide players into different blocks; dynamic CDN systems based on hundreds of data centers in every province of China	Qtalk product; CDN product: DSA	Technical bussiness
Relation between components	Users reach out and lock in	Customer relationship management analysis	Tencent Video, Tencent Comic, Tecent Online Literature	Technical bussiness
Market structures	A close loop that consists of game production, account systems, social media platform, payment systems advertisement system and live stream	Game studios produce and operate games; WeChat and QQ provide account systems for authorization; cross promotion through different games; social promotion using virus-like spreading model through WeChat friend cireles and Q-Zone; Douyu live stream	QQ, WeChat, QQ-Zone, Douyu	Technical business
Focal interest	Company revenue and activeness of users	Company revenue by in-game purchasing and advertisemens; promote adhesiveness of users by MOBA games and social media	*League of Legends*	Business
Temporality	Decided by the lifetime of games and the popularity of online social ecology	3–5 years popular time for each top games; sustainable output of new games by entertainment business group; online game ecology based on IM apps such as QQ and WeChat	DNF	Business
Scale	Large to very large; widely accessible	May grow to become ubiquitous	The greatest global game vender/agency/opera or and the second largest social media company	Business
Funding	Revenue from games, advertisements, and game broadcasting	Company revenue by in-game purchasing; advertisement income from other game venders, and commission fee received from game broadcasting	*CrossFire*	Business
Agency of users	None	None	None	None

We can conclude that Tencent ESports, strategy of implicitly striking against the traditional markers of the infrastructure of platforms (e.g., authoritarian governance) and eventually challenging the state-led Internet management itself—this not only illustrates the problem of conceiving platforms in monolithic terms, but also illustrates how we can reconceive supposedly monumental entities as not-so-monumental by breaking down digital boundaries from the inside out. These findings clarify how Tencent facilitates its evolving umbrella platforms through technical interactivity and the digital properties associated with the data infrastructuralization of platforms, including architecture, relationships between components, market structures, focal interests, temporality, scale funding, and the agency of users.

The following infographic illustrating the conceptual metaphor of umbrella platforms is explanatory not only for documenting eSports capitalist platforms growth, state-managed infrastructure, and multisided platform integration in the eSport industry, but for understanding the rapid development of the Chinese eSports industry from its initial state of disorder and confusion. It also normalizes the ambitions of platform capitalism, tracking the digital platforms' expanding boundaries. The concept of platformization offers a critical perspective for examining the "umbrella cloth"—regulatory platformization of infrastructures governed by Chinese authorities and examining how the "umbrella stand"—Tencent's value chain, multisided platforms, as well as technical dimensions have empowered themselves. Even though this umbrella is initially supported from and entangled with the umbrella cloth, it is not an intrusive role in the process of rapid development. Hence the Chinese government only takes direct control on bottom-line sensitive issues and provides more space to invite other stakeholders like Tencent to act as a strong umbrella stand to support and negotiate the exact meanings of the industry.

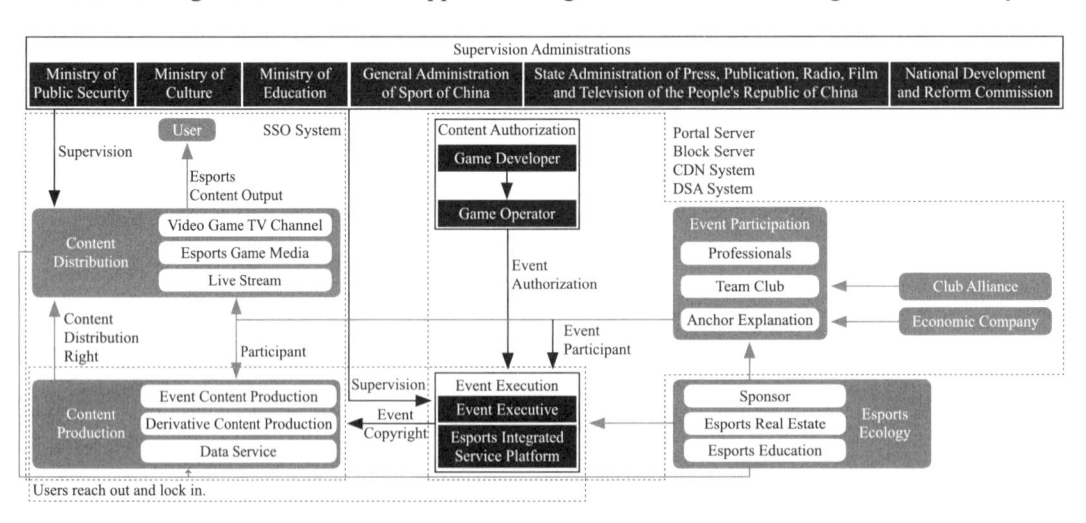

A combination of technical expansion and value chains of the Chinese eSport umbrella platforms.
CDN: content delivery network; DSA: dynamic site accelerator; SSO: single sign-on

Tencent's eSports industry has played multiple roles simultaneously to proactively establish its multisided platforms, including authorizing, producing, and distributing content, acting as the executive body of many leagues, and posing as a monopoly power enterprise and dominant market player in the Chinese eSports industry. Most eSports clubs and athletes see Tencent as the industry leader and see the industry as driven by platformization. On the one hand, this implies (for some) that government works hand in hand with market power within an era of techno-nationalism. On the other hand, Tencent eSports, through its multisided platforms (data infrastructures), has successfully operationalized its infrastructural agendas.

4.3.2　Case 2: Challenges Faced by Chinese ESports Professional Players

There is no doubt that video and computer gaming is a matrix of eSports, from which eSports initially emerged; eSports have their roots in video or computer gaming. Therefore, the most basic definition of eSports is that they are competitive (professional) video or computer gaming, combining the gaming essence of video and computer games with the competitive features of sports. In other words, eSports are a competitive and organized way of playing video and computer games within a professional setting. In this sense, eSport is in itself video and computer gaming, but it distinguishes itself from casual gaming by its sense of skill-based rivalry coordinated by a unique set of competencies.

4.3.2.1　"Spiritual Opium"

In the late 1990s, personal computers (PCs) became affordable for the Chinese public, and the 2000s witnessed a market growth in the popularity of console and PC games in China. Since this time, the expanding eSports culture has produced a vast cohort of videogame players in China whose peak age ranges between 16 and 22 years. With the first unofficial online StarCraft championship in 1999, eSports gained official recognition in China, and China's General Administration of Sports approved it as the country's 99th official sport in November 2003. On June 19 of 2004, the General Administration of Sports, together with the All-China Sports Federation (ACSF), launched the First China ESports Games (CEG). In 2003, the sports channel of CCTV-5 launched a show called *ESports World*, which became very popular with young audiences. However, the show also received complaints from concerned parents who feared their children might develop Internet addiction disorder (IAD), which resulted in the show being canceled in 2004. Online gaming has been subject to negative stereotypes in the Chinese media following an incident in which 24 young men were killed in a fire in an illegal Internet café in Beijing on June 17, 2002, which resulted in the government consistently treating Internet cafés and online gaming as a cause for concern.

Indeed, the China Internet Network Information Center (CNNIC) reported that the majority of online game consumers are adolescents between the ages of 10 and 19 years, who spend a significant amount of time playing either at home or in Internet cafés (CNNIC, 2019). Rehabilitation facilities for Internet addiction were established in various cities and towns to treat adolescents whose parents volunteered to commit their children in the hopes of turning a person regarded as an Internet addict into a person that would "firmly grasp his studies". Meanwhile, mass media in China have consistently associated online gaming with Internet gaming disorder (IGD) and branded gaming addiction unhealthy and in contradiction to the Chinese cultural value of academic success as the norm for Chinese youth.

The prominent stigma associated with eSports is the stereotype of the gaming hobby as "spiritual opium", a term used to condemn the rapid and vigorous development of the gaming industry, which has caused young people to become addicted to playing games rather than attending school. This "addiction" includes those players who either steal money from their families or lie to their parents and teachers, to skip school to play games. This reputation creates dim, unhealthy, or sullied impressions with the public. Since the peak age of a professional eSports player is between the ages of 16 and 22 years (only 20% or less have a college degree), after secondary school, young players must choose whether to attend university or become a professional player. In Chinese culture, Mianzi is positively associated with achieving a higher education degree; by selecting the eSports career and skipping university, young eSports players bring "shame" to their parents, thus causing them to lose Mianzi.

4.3.2.2 Sportsmanship and Meritocracy

Although **eSports** have already become recognized institutionally, for example, being included as an official sport at the 2022 Asian Games, controversy about whether they are a sport has never stopped. In 1999, the Sports Academy refused to acknowledge the United Kingdom Professional Computer Game Championships as a sport (Wagner, 2006). Scholars argued that eSports, thus far, cannot be considered a sport concerning five key traits: physical activity, competitive elements, recreation, organizational structures, and acceptance. However, sports science scholars Jonasson and Thiborg (2010) defined eSports within the framework of traditional sports as individual or team competitions and challenges, where the goal of each athlete and team is to win against competitors; here, eSports are categorized in the framework of traditional sports. Meanwhile, "professional", as understood

> eSports = Sports?

in eSports, was associated with professional salaries, which have reached or even substantially exceeded the level of traditional professional sports, or have the same skills and capacities required by conventional professional sports, such as physical prowess, agility, and quick reflexes.

This controversy is particularly complex because of the industry's novelty and the unique convergence of culture, digital technology, and sport encompassed in eSports.

Three main factors have driven China's eSports industry since 2003, particularly in 2011. These have been recognized as the key "powers" that have helped eSports players to develop confidence and self-actualization.

First, the Chinese government has facilitated numerous policies and events to support the eSports industry, including game content, licensing, tournaments, education, coaches, and professional players. Additionally, regional-level governing bodies, for example in Xi'an, Chengdu, Shanghai, and Taicang, have launched a series of regulations and policies to attract eSports clubs and investment (e.g., Taicang ESports Town) to stimulate the local market and gain tax revenue. The most significant is that official news agencies have started to refer to eSports professionals as athletes (Jenny et al., 2017) rather than addicts, and that they have been legitimized as national heroes by winning international eSports championships.

Second, Mr. Wang Sicong, a well-known second-generation Chinese billionaire and entrepreneur of Wanda Co. Ltd, has invested RMB 500 million (equivalent to 70.62 million USD) in Prometheus Capital to facilitate a strong entry into the field of eSports since 2011, thereby contributing to the eSports industry boom in China. This remarkable event has wholly shifted the entire value chain of the eSports industry and has improved the quality of the whole ecology.

Third, the training programs and daily operation system in eSports clubs significantly draw on the United States' National Basketball Association's (NBA) training systems and value chain. In most clubs, these include constant cycles of intense training, (informal) psychological counselling, team management, strategic skills development, and a six-round recruitment system (e.g., 94% to 97% elimination rate).

Therefore, meritocracy is typically salient for eSports athletes; it has formed a doctrine in practice for the regulation of players by the government and capitalized marketing. There used to be a substantial amount of social stigma attached to video and computer gaming, which was regarded as "e-heroin" due to public concern over video game addiction in China. Such under-represented groups affected by social stigma may be especially attached to meritocratic principles to validate and motivate themselves. More importantly, managers also use the meritocratic discourse to evaluate, regulate, and govern players, which finally become internalized through self-evaluation, self-regulation, and self-governing practices.

Notable events in this regard included, as early as 2016, the Chinese team's victory in the DOTA International Invitational Championship. Furthermore, on November 3, 2018, IG gained its first championship victory in the LPL S8. At the end of July of that same year, the Chinese OMG team won the FPP (First Person Perspective) final in the PUBG Global Invitational (PGI) Tournament. The momentum of the Jakarta Asian Games, which was won by the Chinese team at the end of August, played a positive role in re-labelling eSports players from video gaming players to professional athletes. In this way, players employ a meritocratic discourse, embodied in sports practice and internalizing their work as a professional pursuit, to destigmatize themselves from being seen as "gaming addicts" and earn more Mianzi.

Once eSports were professionalized as a career, eSports players could further fulfil their stigmatization and self-legitimization needs by pursuing meritocracy in gaming. However, the salaries of ordinary players are usually low, while the bonus for the championships is generally in the millions, forcing the players to focus solely on the championships. More importantly, this meritocratic discourse has gone beyond personal interests and has been associated with national glory. Again, eSports' strong connection with national glory and pride may not be specific to eSports, as many other sports have this characteristic. However, as explained above, this characteristic is especially salient for Chinese eSports because the Chinese government used to regard video and computer gaming as harmful to healthy Internet culture and, for a long time, downplayed eSports, such that Chinese eSports players are eager for official legitimization and recognition by winning honor for the country. Especially since 2003, when eSports were recognized as a sport in China, eSports have become a platform to "display carefully crafted nationalism and China's soft power" (Yu, 2018).

4.3.2.3 Precarious Jobs and Disposable Future

In addition to the meritocracy described above, eSports have also witnessed **precarity**. Except for scarce star players, most eSports players have severely precarious working and living conditions, resonating with the concept of precarity widely and frequently used in academia. The concept of precarity is used to explain the transformation of working and living conditions toward existential, financial, and social uncertainty, vulnerability, and insecurity that many workers are currently experiencing.

Precarity

Existential, financial, and social uncertainty, vulnerability, and insecurity that many eSports workers are currently experiencing.

Although there is a comprehensive base of leisure, amateur, and recreational players, eSports are played at a highly professional and competitive level. And there is only an extremely narrow apex of professional players in this field. Therefore, eSports can only become a career for a tiny minority of players. In this sense, choosing eSports as a job creates uncertainty, vulnerability, and insecurity at the beginning and throughout the career path. To some extent, precarity has become the structural condition and an "existential truth" for eSports players in China (Berlant, 2011). The eSports industry is ballooning and has become fragmented and subsequent at the same time. It has outpaced regulation, so common regulations are amiss (Green, 2016). This precarious condition affects players' protections, including entry drafts, standardized contract terms, guaranteed salaries, and protection from arbitrary dismissal.

However, precarity is not just "material and concrete" realities (Arvidsson et al., 2010) and practices experienced in working conditions. Instead, it is also "an affective atmosphere" in daily life (Berlant, 2011). For example, eSports players, in this case, are not even allowed to be in a relationship, for this is regarded as a "distraction" during their training and career as professional players. In this sense, the precarity penetrates not only their work life but also their personal life, exerting effects "on all the dimensions of life" (Lodovici & Semenza, 2012). Within such an atmosphere, players usually face severe mental and psychological pressure.

In this sense, eSports players are just a new set of disposable and losable people. While precarity refers to different dimensions of precariousness and its detrimental effects on people's lives, this kind of **disposability** refers directly to people's bare lives, which means disposable lives with no protection or value. The majority of eSports players are doomed to be nameless pawns in the industry.

Disposability

Lack of protection or value in eSports players' lives.

4.3.2.4 Professionalism and Commercialism

The most effective policy related to the eSports industry came into effect in 2004 when the SAPPRFT banned the mainstream media, including digital TV channels, from broadcasting eSports-related content. Thus, the famous *ESports World* program on CCTV-5 was suspended in April 2004. Further, in February 2007, CCTV was accused by eSports players of "under-the-table dealing", as the *World of Warcraft*'s champion Li Xiaofeng (Sky) failed to be selected as one of the most influential figures in sports.

This policy of banning eSports from televised broadcasts brought about essential changes in the eSports industry chain in China, which differed from Korea's model of game-competition broadcasting, in which eSports can be broadcast through digital TV. In China, livestreaming broadcast platforms, as the main bottom stream of the eSports value chain, have played a vital role as the most crucial distribution channel (Johnson & Woodcock, 2019). In late 2015, livestreaming became a burgeoning media industry in China, with diverse livestreaming applications receiving significant investment (iiMedia, 2016). ESports players may participate in livestreaming (e.g., playing and commenting on a live gaming show) to showcase professional skills, maintain a close and interactive relationship with their fans, earn virtual gifts or sell gaming products.

However, this model has propelled some players into an economic-driven career path—or even forced some players to take this option—because of the vast gap in the annual income of official players, which can vary between 80,000 RMB and 20 million RMB (equivalent to 11,299 USD and 2.82 million USD). Those who receive significantly higher incomes often benefit from livestream bonuses and may lose focus on actual tournaments.

The perception of eSports as non-secure, casual, and irregular work has been internalized by the public in China. ESports players have experienced two specific types of stigma over the past twenty years. First, adults simply associate eSports with gaming addiction, leading young people to miss out on higher education, potentially leading to promising careers. Second, these youth may be perceived, somewhat naively, as celebrating their gaming addiction by engaging in eSports as a professional pursuit to cover up the fact that they are losers, causing them to lose Mianzi. Both cases require unpacking insights into the relationship between stigma power and perceptions of career chances among eSports professionals in China. Otherwise, there is a potential risk that eSports will continue to be perceived as occupying a thin line between a sports hobby and an addiction.

4.3.2.5 Implications

Since "stigma processes have a dramatic and probably a highly underestimated impact on such life chances" (Link & Phelan, 2001), the stigma associated with power flows over cognitive cultural beliefs (e.g., Mianzi), economic stimulation (e.g., income), and authority attributions (policy support) should be deconstructed. As social control processes (Trammell & Morris, 2012), the stigma power flows represent the three stages of mental change in eSports career development. First, eSports players are easily self-stigmatized and engage in "cultural value control" to navigate their own identity through daily social interactions, particularly based on the reciprocation of Mianzi. Second, the Chinese government reinforces socio-cultural norms by labelling eSports players as athletes and has legitimized these professionals as engaging in techno-nationalist pursuits, which provide a social and political environment for them to overcome their discredited identity.

Moreover, the financial support of the famous young entrepreneur Wang Sicong is not perceived solely as capital; instead, it is perceived as legitimizing eSports as a business, providing not only symbolic access to mobilize eSports professionals' network resources, but also to the fast-track evolution of the eSports industry in China. Third, the stigmatized players are still defined by the discredit and greed associated with the digital economy, which eventually causes them to engage in impression management by becoming eSports professionals. This implies that stigma jeopardizes eSports players' ability and desire to obtain income to attain essential social statuses. In combination, the three stages show how eSports players navigate "stigma consciousness" between the self and the power of social control embodied through Mianzi in China. This enables them to change their professional performance, which, in turn, is interwoven into their professional practices as a way to transform social identity and reduce stigma.

In conclusion, young eSports players risk developing self-stigma, and their mental changes throughout their careers are influenced by a more sophisticated form of state power as part of proactive stigma management. These young people may lack guidance regarding mental and emotional growth when facing intense pressure in a fast-growing digital economy. Therefore, policies and regulations should be completed to support young players' physical and mental wellbeing, destigmatize eSports, and unlink professional eSports from gaming addiction. Policymakers might consider strategies involving the de-stigmatization of eSports via mainstream media and standardized education.

4.4 Conclusion

In the context of globalization, eSports are far beyond merely videogames or sports, but have more complex socio-cultural implications with various attributes of entertainment, media, culture, sport, etc. With a global expansion of eSports audience and gamers, the eSports industry steps in and keeps growing dramatically. China, the world's largest eSports marketplace, boasts a no.1 gaming company, Tencent, forming a Chinese character-loaded eSports industrial system and, amid a unique cultural system, generates a distinct nexus among the governments, enterprises, platforms, professional athletes and other professional sectors in eSports. It also holds a specific cultural phenomenon in Chinese society. According to the level of relevant entities in the whole industrial chain, the Chinese eSports industry can be described in three aspects as follows.

At a macro level, the relation between the state and the platforms developed by media conglomerates is taken analogous to an umbrella platform. The umbrella cloth refers to the Chinese government that is responsible for the regulatory platformization of infrastructures; the umbrella stand is the enterprises, Tencent in particular, who drive the growth of the value chain whereas manage their own infrastructural ambitions. State-led as China's eSports industry is, the government works hand in hand with market power and the two are in need of each other.

At a medium level, multisided platforms are the main bodies in China's eSports industry chain. These platforms are most developed by media conglomerates like Tencent to play multiple roles simultaneously including content licensing, distributing and promoting, competition organizing, and posing as the major executive of gaming leagues. The platformization in China's eSports industry are closely linked with its infrastructuralization and moreover, the two tend to be mutually constitutive. The emerging digital technologies, tools and services provide the potential for the infrastructuralization of platforms, whereas the platformization facilitates the replacement of monopolistic government infrastructure, fostering the platformization of infrastructures.

At a micro level, the major entity of the self-enterprising eSports is eSports players, particularly the professional athletes. It is the stigma power deeply rooted in the Chinese cultural context that has kept the stigmatization of the eSports and eSports players for a long time. Although things have taken a turn for the better since 2011, the game between sportsmanship & meritocracy and professionalism & commercialism take turns as a conundrum for the players. What's more, the tiny possibility to survive in the competitive industry and the short career lifecycle make professional eSports a precarious job and the players' future disposable.

4.5　Extended Readings

Scan the QR code to get extended reading materials.

4.6　Post Questions and Discussion

(1) If you are extremely good at playing videogames, will you consider being a profession-

al eSports athlete? Why or why not? Please answer this question from the perspective of your career planning, parents' opinions, working conditions, and the potential of this job.

(2) If you are the manager of one eSports club, how will you prolong the athletes' careers, and how will you deal with their conservative parents?

(3) What's the relationship between commercialization and professionalization of the eSports industry? Do they complement, oppose, or compete with each other?

4.7 Bibliography

Arvidsson, A., Malossi, G., & Naro, S. (2010). Passionate Work? Labour Conditions in the Milan Fashion Industry. *Journal for Cultural Research,* 14(3): 295-309. https://doi.org/10.1080/14797581003791503.

Berlant, L. (2011). *Cruel Optimism*. Durham: Duke University Press. https://doi.org/10.1515/9780822394716.

CNNIC. (2011). China Internet Network Information Center Research Report on Chinese Online Game Users in 2010. http://www.cnnic.cn/hlwfzyj/hlwfzzx/qwfb/201106/t20110620_31145.htm.

Corrigan, P. (2004). How Stigma Interferes with Mental Health Care. *American Psychologist,* 59(7): 614-625.

Corrigan, P. W., Watson, A. C. (2002). Understanding the Impact of Stigma on People with Mental Illness. *World Psychiatry*, 1(1): 16-20.

Dai, Y. (2019). *A Brief History of Esports*. Shanghai: Shanghai Renmin Press.

Davis, A. (2004). Political Prisoners, Prisons, and Black Revolution. In Zinn H, Arnove A. (eds.), *Voices of a People's History of the United States*. New York: Seven Stories Press.

Dyer-Witheford, N., De, P. G. (2009). *Games of Empire: Global Capitalism and Video Games*. Twin Cities: University of Minnesota Press.

Erving, G. (1963). Stigma: Notes on the Management of Spoiled Identity. New York: Simon & Schuster Inc.

Fan, R. (2013). Confucian Meritocracy for Contemporary China. In *The East Asian Challenge for Democracy: Political Meritocracy in Comparative Perspective* (pp. 88-115). Cambridge: Cambridge University Press.

Gansky, L. (2010). The Mesh: Why the Future of Business Is Sharing. New York: Penguin.

Goffman, E. (1986 [1963]). *Stigma: Notes on the Management of Spoiled Identity*. New

York: Touchstone.

Helmond, A. (2015). The Platformization of the Web: Making Web Data Platform Ready. *Social Media + Society*. https://doi.org/10.1177/2056305115603080.

Hemphill, D. (2005). Cybersport. *Journal of the Philosophy of Sport*, 32(2): 195-207.

Hemphill, D. (2015). Cybersport. In C. R. Torres(ed.), *The Bloomsbury Companion to the Philosophy of Sport* (pp. 346-348). London: Bloomsbury.

Hu, H. C. (1944). The Chinese Concepts of "Face". *American Anthropologist*, 46: 45-64.

Hutchins, B. (2008). Signs of Meta-Change in Second Modernity: The Growth of E-sport and the World Cyber Games. *New Media & Society*, 10(6): 851-869.

iiMedia. (2016). Chinese Livestreaming Industry Encounters Setback in 2016. https://www.iimedia.cn/c400/42373.html.

Ismangil, M. (2018). (Re) creating the Nation Online: Nationalism in Chinese Dota 2 Fandom. *Asiascape: Digital Asia*, 5(3): 198-224.

Jenny, S. E., Manning, R. D., Keiper, M. C., & Olrich, T. W. (2017). Virtual (ly) Athletes: Where ESports Fit within the Definition of "Sport". *Quest*, 69(1): 1-18.

Johnson, M. R., Woodcock, J. (2019). The Impacts of Livestreaming and Twitch. tv on the Video Game Industry. *Media, Culture & Society*, 41(5): 670-688.

Jonasson, K., Thiborg, J. (2010). Electronic Sport and Its Impact on Future Sport. *Sport in Society*, 13(2): 287-299. https://doi.org/10.1080/17430430903522996.

Link, B. G., Phelan, J. C. (2001). Conceptualizing Stigma. *Annual Review of Sociology*, 27(1): 363-385.

Link, B. G., Phelan, J. C. (2014). Stigma Power. *Social Science & Medicine*, 103: 24-32. https://doi.org/10.1016/j.socscimed.2013.07.035.

Lu, Z. (2017). From E-heroin to E-sports: The Development of Competitive Gaming in China. *International Journal of the History of Sport*, 33 (18): 2186-2206.

McKee, D. (2017). The Platform Economy: Natural, Neutral, Consensual and Efficient? Transnational Legal Theory. https://doi.org/10.1080/20414005.2017.1416516.

Nieborg, D. B., Helmond, A. (2019). The Political Economy of Facebook's Platformization in the Mobile Ecosystem: Facebook Messenger as a Platform Instance. *Media, Culture & Society*, 41(2): 196-218.

Nieborg, D. B., Poell, T. (2018). The Platformization of Cultural Production: Theorizing the Contingent Cultural Commodity. *New Media & Society*, 20(11): 4275-4292.

Norton, M. I., Dunn, E. W., Carney, D. R., & Ariely, D. (2012). The Persuasive "Power" of Stigma? *Organizational Behavior and Human Decision Processes*, 117(2): 261-268.

Pinel, E. C. (1999). Stigma Consciousness: The Psychological Legacy of Social Stereotypes. *Journal of Personality and Social Psychology*, 76(1): 114-128.

Plantin, J. C., Lagoze, C., Edwards, P. N., & Sandvig, C. (2018). Infrastructure Studies Meet Platform Studies in the Age of Google and Facebook. *New Media & Society*, 20(1): 293-310.

Qiu, J. L. (2010). Chinese Techno-Nationalism and Global WiFi Policy. In M. Curtin, & H. Shah (eds.), *Reorienting Global Communication: Indian and Chinese Media beyond Orders* (pp. 284-304). Urbana: University of Illinois Press.

Richman, L. S., Lattanner, M. R. (2014). Self-Regulatory Processes Underlying Structural Stigma and Health. *Social Science & Medicine*, 103: 94-100.

Rofel, L., Halberstam, J., & Lowe, L. (2007). *Desiring China: Experiments in Neoliberalism, Sexuality, and Public Culture*. Durham: Duke University Press. https://doi.org/10.1515/9780822389903.

Srnicek, N. (2016). *Platform Capitalism*. Cambridge: Polity Press.

Star, S. L. (2002). Infrastructure and Ethnographic Practice: Working on the Fringes. *Scandinavian Journal of Information Systems*, 14 (2).

Trammell, R., Morris, T. (2012). The Connection between Stigma, Power, and Life Chances: A Qualitative Examination of Gender and Sex Crime in Yemen. *Sociological Focus*, 45(2): 159-175.

Tyler, I. (2018). Resituating Erving Goffman: From Stigma Power to Black Power. *The Sociological Review*, 66(4): 744-765.

Vogel, D. L., Bitman, R. L., Hammer, J. H., & Wade, N. G. (2013). Is Stigma Internalized? The Longitudinal Impact of Public Stigma on Self-Stigma. *Journal of Counseling Psychology*, 60(2): 311.

Yu, H. (2018). Game On: The Rise of the Esports Middle Kingdom. *Media Industries Journal*, 5(1). https://doi.org/10.3998/mij.15031809.0005.106.

LECTURE & SEMINAR 5
Hip-Pop, Music and Technological Power

  This lecture of the course focuses on hip-hop music and technological power. With the development of communication technologies, hip-hop music has disseminated and been localized in different civilization globally. It's scarcely been mentioned that hip-hop as cultural forms were rooted in African-American culture in the United States. In this lecture we'll learn to clarify this phenomenon. Through cultural syncretism, cultural hybridization and critical transculturalism, we will talk about localization and mainstream emergence of hip-hop music in China, and explore how Chinese rappers navigate the twin demands of authenticity ("keeping it real") and major social values ("peace and love") becomes a vehicle to investigate the processes of localization in a context where culture, globalization and politics are closely intertwined.

Framework

5.1 Theory: Critical Transculturalism

5.1.1 Cultural Syncretism

5.1.2 Cultural Hybridization

5.1.3 Cultural Imperialism vs. Cultural Pluralism

5.3 Conclusion

5.5 Post Questions and Discussion

5.2 Case Study: Hip-Hop in China

5.2.1 Background: Keywords that Help to Understand Hip-Hop

5.2.2 Globalization of Hip-Hop

5.2.3 Chinese Hip-Hop Music

5.4 Extended Readings

5.6 Bibliography

Terms

hip-hop, technological power, cultural syncretism, cultural hybridization, critical transculturalism, cultural imperialism, cultural pluralism

Pre-lecture Discussion

  (1) What happens when a subculture crosses over into politically circumscribed mainstream culture?

  (2) How do artists strive for authenticity and make a meaningful cultural contribution when their music is decried as being at odds with local norms and tastes?

5.1 Theory: Critical Transculturalism

To make a deep description of the courses on hip-hop music and technological power, we could start with one question: What's the relationship between culture and communication?

The views below may provide you with some references.

"Culture is mediated and enacted through communication [and] cultures themselves… become fundamentally transformed, and will be more so over time, by new technological systems" (Castells, 1996: 328).

James Carey proposed a "cultural" approach to communication, arguing that "the original or highest manifestation of communication is not in the transmission of intelligent information but in the construction and maintenance of an ordered, meaningful cultural world that can serve as a control and container for human action" (Carey, 1989: 18 19).

Nowadays, rap and hip-hop music with roots in African-American culture have disseminated globally and rolled over a global trend. In the process of its evolution, hip-hop has been localized in different civilization and cultural forms, which has attracted scholars to reserch on. So in this lecture we may have a deeper understanding of the process in multiculture phenomena and localization in different societies. Theories based on the studies on hip-hop will be introduced as well.

5.1.1 Cultural Syncretism

The first theoretical utilized framework is **cultural syncretism**. It focuses precisely on accommodation, contest, appropriation, indigenization, and a host of other dynamic intercultural and intracultural transactions (Stewart, 1999: 55).

Cultural Syncretism

Cultural syncretism is a phenomenon that occurs as a product of the mixture between two or more cultures, producing a new one from this event.

Have you ever experienced cultural syncretism? It may be hard to answer. Let's switch the question. Have you ever opened a fortune cookie (or eaten a fortune dumpling) in McDonald's, or celebrated Christmas in December or the Spring Festival?

The term syncretism was properly coined in the 17th century, used to define a cultural movement that occurred in ancient Greece. Syncretism is a joint process to combine separate concepts into one brand new idea. Cultural syncretism is a phenomenon that occurs as a product of the mixture between two or more cultures, producing a new one from this event.

Culture is a set of values, customs, social practices that social groups adopt and shared characteristics of certain communities to identify their members from the other.

Cultural syncretism usually involves various schools of thought. This phenomenon occurs when different cultures encounter and create new thoughts, practices, artefacts, art, architecture, and cultural traditions. There are various ways in which cultural syncretism can manifest itself, but all are related to the development of a society and the cultural traditions that define it.

Cultural syncretism can occur for many reasons, from immigration to military conquest to the marriages between groups, and results in a culture finding ways to blend new customs into their own. A contemporary example of cultural syncretism is the popularity of hip-hop, which was originated in the Bronx in the early 1980s. The dissemination of hip-hop is a remixture of different cultures that was propelled by the mediated imagery and international travel. Mediated imagery is a collective of media-mediated information usually applying advanced communication technologies, for example, TV shows, podcasts and vlogs/plogs/blogs. Later in this lecture, we'll show you how the mediated imagery and international travel have encouraged the cultural syncretism.

5.1.2 Cultural Hybridization

Cultural Hybridization

The process by which a cultural element blends into another culture by modifying the element to fit cultural norms.

The term hybridization refers in science basically to a fusion or mixture. **Cultural hybridization** was introduced by the Argentine anthropologist Néstor García Canclini in 1990. It appeared for the first time in his work entitled *Hybrid Cultures: Strategies for Entering and Exiting Modernity*. Canclini takes up this term and applies it to social studies. Using cultural hybridization refers to the culture developing process that occurs after the mixture of two different cultures.

Different scholars have defined cultural hybridization differently. According to Pieterse (2015), cultural hybridization forms become separated from existing practices and recombine with new forms in new practices. While Kraidy proposed that "attention ought to be paid to hybridity's ability or inability to empower social groups to have influence over the course of their lives… the value of a theory of hybridity resides in the extent to which it emphasizes human agency" (Kraidy, 2005: 151).

"Transculturalism" conveys a synthetic notion of culture and a dynamic understanding of relations between cultures (Kraidy, 2005). Kraidy (2005) conceives that **critical transculturalism** is at once an engagement with hybridity as a discursive formation, a framework for international communica-

Critical Transculturalism

Critical transculturalism was proposed by Kraidy in 2005 to solve theoretical

tion theory, and an agenda for research. He mentioned three general observations that underlie critical transculturalism. Here are the observations that might help you to understand the concept.

problems involving two dominant theoretical frameworks in international communication: cultural imperialism and pluralism.

General Observations of the Critical Transculturalism

Hybridity must be understood historically in a triple context:
- The development of vocabularies of racial and cultural mixture from the mid-nineteenth century onward;
- The historical basis of contemporary hybrid identities;
- The juncture at which the language of hybridity entered the study of international communication.

Hybridity must be understood as a rhetorical notion:
- Uses of hybridity in mainstream public discourse;
- The analysis of the advent of hybridity in international communication studies for its rhetorical aspects.

The concept of hybridity must be "operationalized" in case studies.

5. 1. 3 Cultural Imperialism vs. Cultural Pluralism

Cultural imperialism is the cultural domination and manipulation of one "advanced" or mighty culture over another. Despite the cultural factor, economic, political and technological factors play a role in the whole process by policy (including military action), commerce and culture export. Cultural imperialism can take various measures to immerse and manipulate the target culture. It reveals that empires with greater power will make up the value of culture and construct an international culture through global media to control the world, leading to inequality among different cultures (Schiller, 1971).

Cultural Imperialism

It is the domination of one culture over another. Cultural imperialism can take the form of a general attitude or an active, formal and deliberate policy, including (or resulting from) military action. Economic or technological factors may also play a role.

Cultural pluralism treats culture as a battlefield of ideology. It considers the resistance or adaptation of external cultures as the activeness and autonomy of its internal cultures' own identity (Wallerstein, 1990; Kraidy, 2005). However, according to Kraidy (2005), cultural imperialism thesis is giving way to a benign vision of global cultural diversity, local cultural resistance, and cross-cultural fusion. Hence, cultural pluralism is an in-

Cultural Pluralism

A condition in which minority groups participate fully in the dominant society, yet maintain their cultural differences (Dictionary. com).

adequate vision for international communication and culture for its ignorance of power.

While both cultural imperialism and cultural pluralism adopt bipolar views on the conception of culture, global culture, agency, media effects, and relations between structure and agency in the understanding of cultural hybridity, critical transculturalism considers these issues from a lopsided perspective. Critical transculturalism considers all cultures to be essentially hybrid rather than globally holistic. The key concepts of critical transculturalism rely on power and agency; it explores power relations between cultures from translocal ("local-to-local") and intertextual perspectives (Lin & Zhao, 2022).

5. 2 Case Study: Hip-Hop in China

Here are some topics widely mentioned in hip-hop:
- All men are created equal…
- With certain unalienable rights…
- Whenever any form of government becomes destructive of these ends, it is the right of the people to alter or to abolish it.
- Declaration of Independence 1776

What is hip-hop? How do we identify the real hip-hop and fake hip hop? Here is a video that may help you understand hip-hop. Scan the QR code to watch the video.

As you can see, the Declaration of Independence guarantees the right of free expression for all people. What's the relationship between the Declaration of Independence and hip-hop? Learning about the origins of hip-hop and rap, you'll find the answer.

In the theory section, we have introduced critical transculturalism. So next let's analyze the localization and mainstream emergence of hip-hop music in China from a critical transculturalism perspective.

Here are two key points:
(1) What role does power and agency play in the hybridization and mainstream emergence process of Chinese hip-hop music?
(2) How do the news media portray that power and agency?

With these two questions in mind, let's begin the following study. When we talk about hip-hop culture, there are two keywords: (1) self expression; (2) a multilayered culture.

5.2.1　Background: Keywords that Help to Understand Hip-Hop

Hip-Hop & Rap: Poetry & Spoken Word

Long before records were spun at park jams and parties across New York City, spoken-word artists paired the natural rhythm of their words with music from the Harlem Renaissance through the 1960s. It was when the artists relied on the spoken word for powerful political and social commentary. The style and messages of poets and artists such as Wanda Coleman, Jayne Cortez, The Last Poets, and Gil Scott-Heron created a platform for generations of slam poets, MCs, and rappers.

Written poetry and spoken word express the rich and dynamic range of African American culture and bear witness to the many ways African Americans speak. Mastery of the written word also communicated education and elevation to those who regarded blacks as neither.

American traditions, blues, jazz, hip-hop, and many other sources all echo through the work of African American poets. Written or spoken, some black poetry also protests the oppressive conditions that African Americans have experienced over time.

In a TV program *Rap in China*, Ouyang Jing performed *Fight for Hip-Hop* telling a story about the rise of hip-hop as a musical genre and cultural movement. The story is about Kool Herc, a Jamaican-born DJ who once lived in the Bronx and who is considered to be the godfather and originator of hip-hop.

Creativity

During a hot summer night in the Bronx in 1973, Clive "DJ Kool Herc" Campbell took two turntables and a microphone and mixed beats that moved the crowd. The "hip-hop" beat came to represent an essential component of this growing youth movement-creative expression. From the unique ways people rhyme and tell stories to the borrowing of other music and rhythms to form new sounds, hip-hop is about adaption and innovation, and reflects the intrinsic importance of creativity to this long-standing art form.

1970s' Hip-Hop in New York

Poets

Bradley and Dubois (2010: 29) argueed in *The Anthology of Rap* that hip-hop music is a vogue mediated form mainly depending on the use of language and technology of composing musical rhythms, creating beats and the street vernacular by a rapper or MC. Rappers are, therefore "the poets and rap is the poetry of hip-hop".

Identity

Hip-hop was established in the Bronx in the 1970s and provided voice for a youth culture that felt abandoned by the city and the nation. The Bronx lost 300,000 people between 1967 and 1977, and by the 1980s it even had surpassed rural Mississippi as the poorest area in the country. Despite its struggles, the Bronx emerged as an artistic powerhouse, ushering in a new era of music, photography, dance and public art in a community-rooted independence movement. Hip-hop consists of four indispensable elements: The first three elements are related to music and dance, DJ-ing, rapping and breakdancing, and graffiti or aerosol art is the last and only visual art element. Between 1973 and 1977, these four elements were spontaneously put together in block parties and improvisation.

As MC Afrika Bambaataa, founder of rap group Universal Zulu Nation, says, the art form made up of these four elements is meant to convey hip-hop's fifth element: knowledge, the culture's basic tenets which are peace, love, unity and having a good time. What's more, the original expressions of rhyming over breakbeats, the graffiti and breakdancing were lustered by fancy styles of dress that reflected the creativity and resilience of the community.

All these elements represented the aspirations of the artists who embraced this art form to tell personal stories and universal truths.

Community

Community is an important part of hip-hop culture and highlights the value of collective memory and shared identity. Hip-hop started as a grassroots community effort in the Bronx, New York. As the hip-hop phenomenon gained momentum, large numbers of people would often gather in a circle, known as a cipher, to witness dance-offs or rap battles. Community reaction during these gatherings was immediate, celebrating the most talented, clever, or inventive of the performers.

Getting the Music Heard: African Americans & the Music Industry

In the 1900s, the unparalleled development of technology had profound implications for the music industry.

Development of communication technologies such as the photograph, radio, jukeboxes, television, and the Internet resulted in a cultural interplay that spread African American music around the world and greatly enriched the musical traditions in the US.

As hip-hop spread from the United States to the rest of the world, China rightfully became influenced as well. Emerging from an underground cultural form, hip-hop culture has deep roots in rebellion and negotiates marginalization.

The ideological content of rap often includes opposition, resistance, confrontation, and social critique that empowers subaltern communities to establish their explicit and/or implicit counter-hegemonic discourse (Rose, 1991; Martinez, 1997; Zou, 2019).

5. 2. 2 Globalization of Hip-Hop

Hip-hop culture, which originated from African American culture half a century ago, has now evolved into a global phenomenon.

Its globalization has been considered a new type of universality, because its development is rooted in "the local and the temporal" and is about "where I'm from".

And in its globalization process, there are four important factors:

(1) the influence of material structure;

(2) political economic power;

(3) consumers' agency;

(4) the influence of communication technologies.

Because cultural pluralism neglects the influence of material structures related to politics and economy on the hybridization of hip-hop, and consumerism assumes rational action and human agency and does not consider the influence of media communication on cultural hybridity, so we need to use critical transculturalism to analyze Chinese hip-hop music. It focuses on "power in intercultural relations by integrating both agency and structure" in analysis (Kraidy, 2005: 149). This theory, considers that culture is essentially hybrid with agency located in social practice, that is, the reproduction of material structure.

Chinese hip-hop music has developed into cultural hybridity distinct from African American hip-hop music (Flew et al., 2019). Now, let's review its development.

5.2.3 Chinese Hip-Hop Music

Critical transculturalism sheds light on the localization and mainstream emergence of Chinese hip-hop music from both longitudinal and comparative perspectives. We suggest that while cultural factors (e.g., social norms) and political factors (e.g., regulations) were influential on both localization and mainstream processes of emergence, the factor of capital (e.g., Wilber Pan) played a major role in the mainstream emergence of hip-hop in China. The processes of localization of Chinese hip-hop music included imitation, the exploration of Chinese grassroots and place-based local culture, adaptation to social norms and cultural regulations, and promotion of hip-hop music through.

5.2.3.1 The History and Characteristics of Chinese Hip-Hop

The development of Chinese hip-hop music began after Dana Burton (a.k.a. Shotyme), an American rapper and one of the "godfathers of Chinese hip-hop" (Barrett, 2012: 251), traveled to Shanghai in 1999.

Members of the BBS hip-hop communities gained hip-hop knowledge from the Original Gangsters (OG) who owned CDs of foreign hip-hop music or lived abroad.

In the mid-2000s, the first generation of Chinese rappers or pioneers in Chinese hip-hop development became wealthier and more famous nationwide.

2008 was the first significant year for Chinese hip-hop mainly because of the emergence of Myspace (the first social networking website in the world) and Hiphop.cn (one of the earliest hip-hop websites in China), which helped increase communication among rappers.

Hiphop.cn was founded by a Swiss businessman, Martin Spinnler, who had worked in China for nine years. He believed hip-hop could be a superb form of self-expression for young Chinese people gradually creating their own views and styles.

Hiphop.cn employed rappers and actively provided professional information in various formats including news, music, interviews, and performances (Song, 2007; UDIG, 2017).

However, Hiphop.cn shut down after it lost funding in the 2008 financial break. Some former team members established their own websites to continue contributing to the development of Chinese hip-hop.

In 2010, Keyso (Shou Junchao), a rapper from Shanghai, participated in the first series of *China's Got Talent*. People began to learn about hip-hop music as a cool and fashionable musical type through television programs, but they had no professional knowledge about it.

"Got Talent" franchise was one of the first instances when the Chinese public was exposed to hip-hop (UDIG, 2017). In the first-round competition, Keyso performed not only his prepared hip-hop but also freestyle rapping, that is, improvisational rapping without prepared lyrics. He sang hip-hop using the Shanghai dialect as well.

After that, record labels in China featuring both Chinese hip-hop at the national level and place-based hip-hop at the local level proliferated, although they were underground and not industrialized.

Hip-hop was still considered a marginalized culture without potential or a profitable market (Shao & Meng, 2017).

The third golden year and final mainstream emergence of Chinese hip-hop was in 2017 when the competition-based reality show *The Rap of China* aired.

The show was not expected to succeed, but it tremendously increased national attention and discussion about hip-hop music (Shao & Meng, 2017; Flew et al., 2019).

Opening of *The Rap of China*

Hip-hop music successfully became part of mainstream culture and appeared in all kinds of social and cultural activities.

Although the show was a mediator between underground hip-hop and mainstream culture, it was also a cultural product of the two-decade hybridization process.

So as you can see, Chinese hip-hop music was marginalized for nearly two decades until *The Rap of China* emerged in 2017. When the show gained popularity, hip-hop culture successfully entered the mainstream (Flew et al., 2019), but it is interesting why that did not occur over the previous two decades.

From the perspective of critical transculturalism, hip-hop music in China cannot be oversimplified into a discursive and textual combination of African American and Chinese cultures. It is a form of hybridity that deals with power relations between African American, place-based local, and Chinese underground and mainstream hip-hop. And it was influenced by mediated material power that selectively empowered certain human agencies to dominate others.

The findings can be divided into the following four parts.

(1) The Unacclimatized

Two socio-cultural powers, the African American traditions of hip-hop and Chinese culture, were found to be in tension during the evolvement of Chinese hip-hop music.

In the early days of Chinese hip-hop music development, Chinese rappers tended to superficially adopt African American hip-hop traditions in their own music, and regarded stylistic elements only as the semiotics of hip-hop music. As suggested by news articles, "hip-hop is not just a pair of fat-leg pants and a cap, but a diverse culture originating from a social environment and cultural background. However, in many cases, we only superficially 'learn' from it" (Liu, 2008).

MC Jin (Jin Au-Yeung)

Besides, the significant difference between this newly introduced musical style and the musical style to which the Chinese public was accustomed led to a controversy in mainstream Chinese society.

The stylistic elements of African American tradition, the Chinese language, and the place-based local culture in China have acted as important semiotics of Chinese hip-hop music during the collision of the two cultures.

(2) Cursing and "Positive Energy": Bottom-Up Social Norms and Top-Down Regulations

The deprecation of cursing and swear words is an important element of social cognition in the hybridization of Chinese hip-hop music, driven both by bottom-up social norms rooted in the etiquette of traditional Chinese culture and by top-down regulations.

The following is a statement from an interview with Ayal Komod (Zhang Zhenyue), and we can feel his attitude.

Ayal Komod: "Now I'm old, and I don't want to be angry anymore. It's so tiring. When you're young, it doesn't matter if you say swear words; but now if I say swear words, I will look naive. Now celebrities in the entire entertainment industry pay attention to public image. Fortunately, we know where the boundary is. We try not to make others feel uncomfortable, but we are not that kind of seriousness, like sitting seriously in front of interviewers and saying: Hello. Shall we start now? We don't have that kind of personality. Casualness is a double-sided thing. Some people like it, bur some don't." (Zhang, 2017)

Ayal Komod (Zhang Zhenyue)

(3) Authenticity: Public Resonance and Grassroots Struggles

The localization of Chinese hip-hop music involves combining the ideology of authenticity with everyday struggles at the grassroots level.

Chinese hip-hop culture emphasizes the catchphrase "**Keep it real**". Some people say that China does not have the cultural foundation of hip-hop. Hip-hop was invented by black Americans. It used to be an art form of black Americans to express demands for ordinary people. But now the times have changed and hip-hop is no longer combative. It can be a kaleidoscope that has many facets. Today's hip-hop is just a part of the entertainment industry. Of course, Chinese hip-hop music does not sound like the African American one. "The hip-hop spirit helps us express our experiences, emotions, and feelings through words and music." (*China Business News*, 2017) This may also explain why young people in this era need hip-hop music more than 20 years ago .

Keep It Real

A condition in which minority groups participate fully in the dominant society, yet maintain their cultural differences (Dictionary. com). In this era, the "real" that the younger generation in China believes in is the self. "This is a view of consumerism, the pursuit of material, and the yearning for materialized life."

(4) The Mainstream: Symbolic Hybridity and Public Hip-Hop Literacy

Beginning in the early 2000s, Chinese hip-hop underwent a hybridization of many elements, including rhythmic imitation, the deprecation of swear words, an ideology of authenticity, the focus on everyday struggles, the generation of positive energy, the integration of place-based local culture, and the exposure to television audiences. However, hip-hop remained a marginalized artform.

Two contrasting agencies significantly contributed to the mainstream emergence of Chinese hip-hop and also accelerated and inosculated a great hybridity in hip-hop culture: celebrity Wilber Pan as an agent of capital, and public hip-hop literacy as an agent of socio-cultural power.

5.2.3.2 Successful Case: *The Rap of China*

As a model of success, *The Rap of China* is a localization of hip-hop music in China. It firstly shows the acceptance of hip-hop in the mainstream television industry. Besides, "Hip-hop cannot be simply regarded as an expression of African America culture; it has become a vehicle for global youth affiliations and a tool for reworking local identity all over the world" (Mitchell, 2001: 1). "It's an international language, a style that connects and defines the self-image of countless teenagers" (Bozza, 2003: 130).

Today, hip-hop has become one of the most popular and lucrative subculture genres worldwide. Through the analysis of the globalization of hip-hop, we can understand how the cultural hybridization works and influences the global culture, whereby "forms become separated from existing practices and recombine with new forms in new practices" (Pieterse, 2015: 61).

So now we are going to study *The Rap of China* and discuss on the cultural syncretism and resonance of Chinese hip-hop to identify how it reflects the transformation of Chinese youth culture in the digital era.

The reason why *The Rap of China* is so special is that it shows both rebellion and submission. *The Rap of China* has brought the desolated hip-hop culture to the formal stage and made it ingrained in Chinese popular culture since 2017. However, later in 2018, hip-hop was restricted by the State Administration of Press, Publication, Radio, Film and Television. As a result, the later seasons had to make numerous changes to the content and design: The word "rap" was hidden from the title; performers were requested to create more active and positive works. More specifically, "Chinese characteristics" were also stressed. That's how "Jianghu Flow" has emerged. It meets the authenticity in the mainstreaming of Chinese rap, and reflects globally resonant hip-hop themes of masculinity, fraternity, and loyalty as depicted in the self-narrated struggles of knights-errant navigating Jianghu (Sullivan & Zhao, 2019: 2).

These constructions positioned rap as possessing the "positive energy", while retaining the notion of authenticity central to hip-hop's self-narrative. And they also marked the boundaries where the show's producers and contestants were required to negotiate.

As we all know, the Chinese entertainment industry is structured by multilayered institutions. So there exists "imposing positivity".

From a national perspective, it has many necessities:

(1) to protect the country's youth from exposure to content in poor taste;

(2) to safeguard the moral health of the nation;

(3) to curb the excesses of entertainment programming;

(4) to ward against threats to national cultural security.

Constrained by multifacet factors, *The Rap of China*'s contestants were thus faced with multiple challenges to their "authenticity".

But the co-winner GAI meanwhile continued to project an image more palatable to mainstream media, appearing on the CCTV show *I Want to Go to the Spring Gala* and leading the studio audience in a rendition of *Long Live the Motherland*.

GAI participated in the recording of *I Want to Go to the Spring Festival Gala*.

Comparing generic styles and localization styles, we can find many changes in Chinese hip-hop music in *The Rap of China*.

Generic Styles

(1) Baggy T-shirts, low hanging pants, baseball caps, old-school sportswear, chains, tattoos, and even the gun-toting mime.
(2) Homage to the US and American hip-hop culture.
(3) Hedonistic.
(4) Materialism.

Localization Styles

(1) Contestants demonstrated their pride in place, whether province, city, or neighborhood.
(2) Assertions of local identity were cemented using local languages alongside Putonghua.

There are some main themes and elements in *The Rap of China*, which show the unique characteristics of Chinese music.

Solidarity

Nearly all contestants invoked escapades with their brothers, honor codes, reciprocal loyalty, and described the way solidarity emboldens and empowers them.

Struggle

The themes of struggle, striving, and enduring hardship recurred frequently.

Classical Chinese Inflections: Jianghu Flow

In *The Rap of China*, for his lyrical allusions and incorporation of traditional bowed, plucked, wind, and percussion instruments, GAI developed a style which has been described as "Jianghu Flow" (江湖流).

Female Knights-Errant

The first season of *The Rap of China* featured just two women contestants. Establishing authenticity is complicated for Chinese women rappers, for whom associations with the vulgarity and lawlessness of "the underground" are incompatible with mainstream gendered cultural expectations. They have also had to struggle to gain respect from male counterparts within the hip-hop community.

TV Screen Shot from *The Rap of China*

Outside of Season 1 of *The Rap of China*, women rappers have tapped into the cultural resources of the "Jianghu" imaginary. The tradition embraces both the feminine (symbolized by the chaste, filial, domestic woman) and the masculine (the physically imposing military man). And it legitimizes and celebrates a woman's equal participation in "Jianghu".

5.3 Conclusion

This lecture focuses on hip-hop music and the technological power.

In the first section, by clarifying the definition of cultural syncretism, cultural hybridization and critical transculturalism, we sort out the literature and the cultural logic of globalization. We introduced the theory of critical transculturalism which benefits the description of how hip-hop music as a cultural form with roots in African-American culture in the United States could prosper in different forms globally with the development of communication technologies.

In the second section, from the case of *The Rap of China*, we can clearly see that hip-hop is thus localized as a medium of cultural communication.

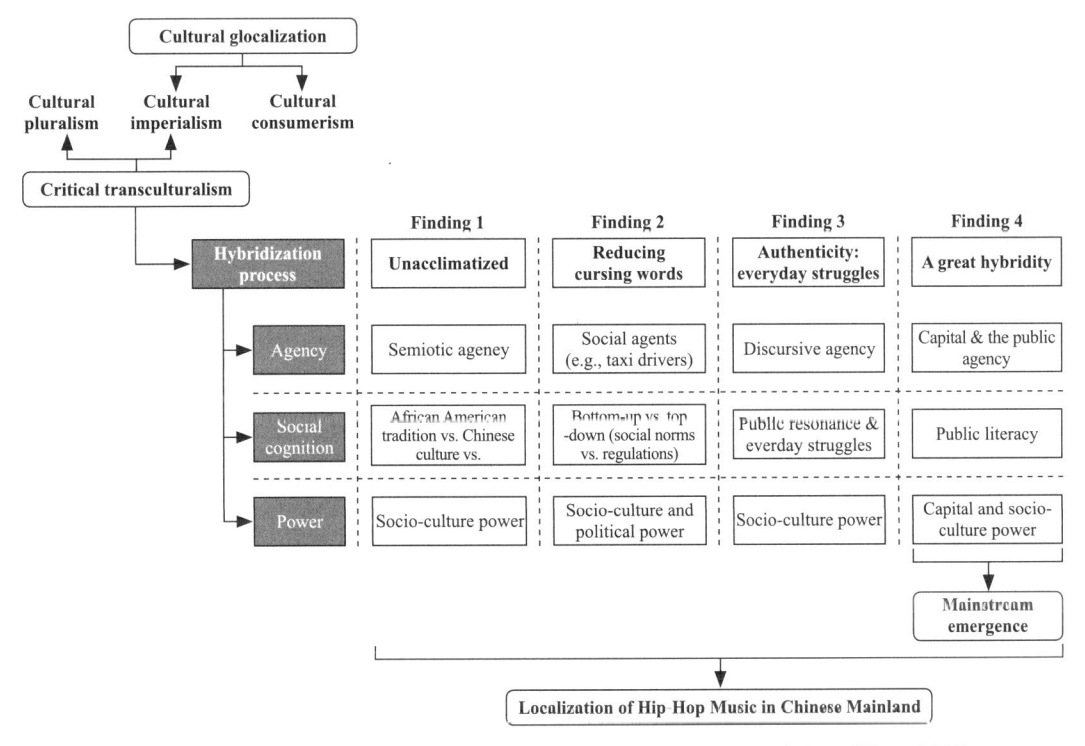

Conceptual Framework of Critical Transculturalism in Chinese Hip-Hop Culture (Zhao, 2020)

5.4 Extended Readings

Scan the QR code to get extended reading materials.

5.5 Post Questions and Discussion

(1) How could hip-hop survive in China in the future?

(2) How do Chinese rappers associate with the media and become the mainstream?

5.6 Bibliography

Barrett, C. (2012). Hip-Hopping across China: Intercultural Formulations of Local Identities. *Journal of Language, Identity & Education*, 11(4): 247-260.

Bozza, A. (2003). *Whatever You Say I Am: The Life and Times of Eminem*. London: Bantam Press.

Bradley, A., Dubois, A. (2010). *The Anthology of Rap*. New Haven: Yale University Press.

Kraidy, M. M. (2005). *Hybridity, or the Cultural Logic of Globalization*. Philadelphia: Temple University Press.

Martinez, T. A. (1997). Popular Culture as Oppositional Culture: Rap as Resistance. *Sociological Perspectives*, 40 (2): 265-286.

Miranda, D., Claes, M. (2004). Rap Music Genres and Deviant Behaviors in French-Canadian Adolescents. *Journal of Youth and Adolescence*, 33(2): 113-122.

Mitchell, T. (2001). *Global Noise: Rap and Hip-Hop Outside the USA*. Middletown: Wesleyan University Press.

Morgan, M. (2016). "The World Is Yours": The Globalization of Hip-Hop Language. *Social Identities*, 22(2): 133-149.

Pieterse, J. N. (2015). *Globalization and Culture: Cultural Mélange* (3rd ed.). Lanham,: Rowman & Littlefield.

Rose, T. (1991). "Fear of a Black Planet": Rap Music and Black Cultural Politics in the 1990s. *The Journal of Negro Education*, 60 (3): 276-290.

Schiller, H. (1971/1992). *Mass Communication and American Empire* (2rd ed.). Boulder:

Westview.

Stewart, C. (1999). Syncretism and Its Synonyms: Reflections on Cultural Mixture. *Diacritics*, 29(3): 40-62.

Zhang, N., Tang, J. Y. (2019). Business Logic and Youth Subculture Production: Critical Discourse Analysis of Internet Reality Show. *Contemporary Communication*, 2: 138-142.

LECTURE & SEMINAR 6
Chinese Cinema History and Globalization

This lecture focuses on Chinese cinema history and transnational Chinese film studies. Under the background of globalization, the film industry in China has been facing a strong revolution. This lecture will be divided into two parts. Firstly, we will learn about Chinese cinema history following a chronological order from an earlier age to the Fifth Generation, the Sixth Generation, and the current Chinese cinema. Secondly, we will focus on the discussion about transnational Chinese film academic studies.

Framework

6.1 Background

6.2 Chinese Cinema History

    6.2.1 Beginning of Chinese Cinema

    6.2.2 Early Communist Era: 1949–1960s

    6.2.3 Cultural Revolution: 1967–1977

    6.2.4 The Fifth Generation: Mid-Late 1980s and 1990s

    6.2.5 The Sixth Generation: 1990s–

    6.2.6 Current Cinema Culture in China

6.3 Transnational Chinese Film Studies

6.3.1 Transnationalism of Transnational Chinese Films

6.3.2 Challenges of Transnational Chinese Film Studies

6.4 Conclusion   6.5 Extended Readings

6.6 Post Questions and Discussion   6.7 Bibliography

Terms

Chinese cinema, Chinese film, Chinese-language film, cinema history, transnationalism

Pre-lecture Discussion

(1) Do you know about Chinese film history? When was it started?

(2) In your opinion, what is the relationship between the history of Chinese film and globalization?

6.1 Background

Over twenty years has passed since the chivalrous martial arts film *Hero* (《英雄》, 2002) unveiled the curtain of China's blockbuster era towards the end of 2002. Over the next decades, China's film industry has witnessed unprecedented changes, which can be divided into the following three aspects.

(1) The Fifth Generation directors have followed the steps of Zhang Yimou closely, producing commercial films but gaining a mixed reception.

(2) Privately-owned film companies have sprung up while many old previously successful state-owned film production companies, such as Beijing Film Studio (北京电影制片厂), Xi'an Film Studio (西安电影制片厂, 1958—2000), and China Western Film Group (西部电影集团, 2009—), have been facing very challenging times.

(3) Box office income has soared dramatically since 2009, multiplying by the dozen year on year.

By 2012, China had surpassed Japan with a box office of 17 billion RMB, becoming the second-largest film market globally after North America (Sun, 2016). All large Chinese and foreign film production companies strive openly and discreetly for success and dominance in the increasingly competitive industry. The film box office battle in China is now growing ferociously like a raging fire and it shows no sign of slowing down in the near future.

6.2 Chinese Cinema History

6.2.1 Beginning of Chinese Cinema

6.2.1.1 The Beginnings: 1896–1920s

The first Chinese film was a recording of the Beijing Opera, *Dingjunshan* (《定军山》), which was made in Beijing in 1905.

For the following decade, the production companies were mainly foreign businesses, and the main domestic film industry was centered in Shanghai (Xin & Mossig, 2017). Pathé[1] (百代电影公司) was the primary enterprise in that period.

---
1 Pathé is a French film company founded in 1896 by Frenchman Charles Pathé and his brother Emile Pathé.

A Still of *Dingjunshan*

The first Chinese-owned film production company was set up in 1916 by Zhang Shichuan (张石川). After that, more Chinese-owned companies opened during the 1920s and 1930s. Most notably were Mingxing Studio (明星电影公司), and the Shaw brothers' Tianyi Film Company (天一影片公司, 1925—1937) or Shaw Brothers Studio (邵氏电影公司, 1958—2011).

6.2.1.2 The Leftist Movement: 1930s

This period is known as the first "golden age" of Chinese cinema (Berra & Ju, 2014). The "golden age" refers to the hybrid film exhibition mostly available in Shanghai. Although there are no physical records, we can learn this from watching films of this period and reading filmmakers' diaries.

In general, films in the 1930s have two main characteristics. One typical feature is that these films mix artistic expression, experiment, and political involvement. The other is that the Nationalists and the Communists struggled for power and control over the major studios (Xiao, 2013). Their influence can be seen in the films produced by these studios during this period.

The Leftist Movement

The progressive film movement in the 1930s under the leadership of the Chinese Communist Party. After the "September 18th Incident", the operators of the film companies began to "turn to the left" to get rid of the difficulties and attract patriotic audiences.

The Leftist Movement is a controversial historical film movement. In the 1930s, China was facing a severe national crisis. Many Chinese intellectuals in the literature field transformed to the film industry, who might more or less contain a radical tendency, and the number of them kept growing. These literary and art workers with progressive ideology tended to arouse public awareness of anti-imperialism and anti-feudalism through films. The leftist directors expressed their thoughts on social issues through the images, thus changing Chinese film production.

These movies are always described as "progressive" or "left-wing". Their emphasis was on class struggle and external threats, as well as the ordinary people that were mede known to the public. The most common themes included modern women, prostitutes' struggles, and criticism against wealth and power. *Street Angel* (《马路天使》), produced by Mingxing Studio, one of the three leading studios[1] in this period, is one of the examples of so-called "progressive" movies.

Case Study I: *Street Angel* (《马路天使》, 1937)

Profile
Directed by Yuan Muzhi
Produced by Mingxing Studio
Adapted from *Street Angel* which was directed by Frank Borzage
Leading actors: Zhao Dan, Zhou Xuan

Background

A spirited young woman (Gaynor) struggles earning money to pay for her ill mother's medicine bills. In the process, she finds herself embroiled in an illegal act. She is caught in the act, but runs away from punishment. However, she then finds her mother dead. Destitute and deprived, she joins a traveling carnival where she meets a vagabond painter...

As the last film released by Mingxing Studio, *Street Angel* is considered to be one of the representatives of the "left" films. The theme of the movie is to do with new realism. In addition, it can be seen as an experiment of sound, since plenty of sound experiments could be found in the movie. The most classic one is *Wandering Songtress* (《天涯歌女》).

Discussion

(1) What do you think about the film *Street Angel*?
(2) Do you think the title is accurate for the film?

Scan the QR code to watch the movie.

6. 2. 1. 3 The Second Golden Age: 1940s before 1949

Many filmmakers or producers fled to Hong Kong during these years, including the Shaw brothers, but some returned to Shanghai. Under tough circumstances sometimes, they made

---
1 Three main studios in this period: Mingxing, Lianhua (联华影业公司) and Tianyi.

some classics such as *Crows and Sparrows* (《乌鸦与麻雀》, 1949). In this period, some early left-wing filmmakers became more closely linked to the CPC (Communist Party of China) and more integrated into its structures and modes of operation.

6.2.2 Early Communist Era: 1949–1960s

With the communist victory in China in 1949, the government saw motion pictures as a critical form of mass artistic production and a propaganda tool. Starting from 1951, the government banned pre-1949 films, from both Chinese mainland and Hong Kong as welll as Hollywood productions. Instead, films centering on farmers, soldiers and workers were produced in large numbers, such as *Bridge* (《桥》, 1949) and *The White Haired Girl* (《白毛女》, 1950). *Crows and Sparrows* which we discussed above is an essential film that marks such a transition.

In the years between the founding of the People's Republic of China (PRC) and the Cultural Revolution, 1213 films were released. More than 600 featured films[1] were sponsored primarily by the government. The content and themes of these films were pretty similar, and they all tended to share one agenda, that is, to help reinforce the governance of the country. In addition, filmmakers were sent to Moscow to study the Soviet socialist realism style of filmmaking, which significantly affected the type of Chinese films in the era.

The most eminent filmmaker of this era was Xie Jin. In particular, with three films, Xie Jin exemplifies China's increased expertise in filmmaking. During this period of time, most films were polished and presented a high quality of production and elaboration. As long as the content was on the right track, there woule be sources to support any experiments for creativity.

Case Study II: *Crows and Sparrows* (《乌鸦与麻雀》, 1949)

Profile
Directed by Zheng Junli
Produced by Kunlun Studio
Leading actors: Zhao Dan, Zhou Xuan

Background
The film was made and set in Shanghai in 1949. It was a consequence of the collaboration between a dedicated group of left-wing filmmakers at Kunlun Studio.

---

1 Quoted from an interview with Zhang Jianyong, Deputy Director of China Film Archive and China Film Art Research Center, in 2013.

The film tells the story of a group of poor tenants in a Shanghai house exploited by their landlord.

Scan the QR code to watch the movie.

Case Study III: Xie Jin (谢晋, 1923—2008)
Profile

Xie Jin was born in Shangyu City, Zhejiang Province. He spent his childhood there and attended elementary school for one year. In the 1930s, he moved to Shanghai with his parents and continued his education there. In 1938, he followed his father to Hong Kong, where he studied for a year. After returning to Shanghai in 1939, he attended several drama courses and eventually became interested in screenplay and cinema. He made 20 films in total.

Significance of His Films

(1) Aesthetically (artistically) similar to Yuan Muzhi's works;

(2) Continued to experiment different techniques in constructing narrative, from the Soviet to Hollywood;

(3) A witness of the transition of political power;

(4) Considered as the first example of the propaganda model.

Representative Works

Woman Basketball Player No.5 (《女篮五号》)
The Red Detachment of Women (《红色娘子军》)
Two Stage Sisters (《舞台姐妹》)
Legend of Tianyun Mountain (《天云山传奇》)

***Two Stage Sisters* (1964)**

Two Stage Sisters is a 1964 Chinese drama film produced by Shanghai Tianma Film Studio and directed by Xie Jin. Unlike most Chinese films of its period, which were adaptations of accepted and well-known dramatic and literary works, it was made from an original screenplay.

Discussion

(1) What are the main characteristics of this film?

(2) How can the film ending be different?

Scan the QR code to watch *Two Stage Sisters*.

6.2.3 Cultural Revolution: 1967–1977

During the Cultural Revolution, especially during the early years from 1967 to 1972, the development of the film industry almost came to a halt. Almost all previous films were banned, with only a very few new ones made, the so-called "revolutionary model operas". The most notable of these was a ballet version of the revolutionary opera, *The Red Detachment of Women* (《红色娘子军》, 1970).

6.2.4 The Fifth Generation: Mid-Late 1980s and 1990s

"The Fifth Generation" refers to those directors who were active between the mid-late 1980s and 1990s. Most of the FifthGeneration directors graduated from **Beijing Film Academy** in 1982. Their rise to prominence led to the growing popularity of Chinese cinema abroad from the mid-late 1980s onwards. The 1990s was when Chinese films were highly exported and consumed by the art circuit in the West.

Beijing Film Academy

Beijing Film Academy (BFA) is an art college jointly established by the Beijing Municipal People's Government, the State Administration of Radio and Television of the People's Republic of China and the Ministry of Education of the People's Republic of China.

Chen Kaige
陈凯歌

Zhang Yimou
张艺谋

Jiang Wen
姜文

Tian Zhuangzhuang
田壮壮

There were several representative directors during this period, like Zhang Yimou, Chen Kaige, Jiang Wen, Tian Zhuangzhuang, etc. Here are several representative works of them. The works of the Fifth Generation directors exhibit a strong "image aesthetics" characterized by intensity, realism, subjectivity, and the beauty of strength. This is evident in four main aspects.

Questions:

(1) The Fifth Generation is the "most exciting generation". In your opinion, why is that?

(2) What elements have enabled such unique cinematic exploration by the Fifth Generation?

First, the image aesthetics of the Fifth Generation highlights the enhancement of image expression and the dilution of plot expression. Film styling is no longer merely a form but becomes the content itself, deepening the drama and achieving the integration of form and content, which is also a primary characteristic of modern art. Second, the Fifth Generation's cinematic aesthetics displays a commitment to the realism of life's details. Directors strive for the texture of life, seeking to preserve the original state of life in their visual and sound styling. Third, the Fifth Generation's image aesthetics shows a strong sense of subjectivity in their reflections and evaluations of history and culture. This is manifested in the symbolic and metaphorical film styling and the widespread use of surreal film styling among these directors. Finally, the Fifth Generation's image aesthetics reveals the beauty of strength in film styling. The rise of the Fifth Generation films represents a rebellion against traditional cinematic language, with a film styling that pursues the texture of life and aesthetic intensity, blending representational and expressive styling in a system that has brought Chinese film styling art and cinematic aesthetics to an unprecedented height.

Farewell My Concubine
《霸王别姬》(1993)
Directed by Chen Kaige
Leading actors: Leslie Cheung, Zhang Fengyi, Gong Li

Reception Abroad
Palme d'Or at the 46th Festival De Cannes; Nominated as the Best Foreign Language Film at the 66th Oscars.

Raise the Red Lantern
《大红灯笼高高挂》(1992)
Directed by Zhang Yimou
Leading Actress: Gong Li

Reception Abroad
Silver Lion Award at the 48th Venice International Film Festival; Nominated as the Best Foreign Language Film at the 64th Oscars.

Case Study IV: *In the Heat of the Sun* (《阳光灿烂的日子》, 1994)

Profile
Directed by Jiang Wen
Adapted from Wang Shuo's novel *Wild Beast*
Leading actor: Xia Yu

Background

In the Heat of the Sun has its story unfold from the perspective of a teenage boy, in whose memories the revolution always takes place in summertime and "in the heat of the sun". To match and represent his reflective impression, the rhythm of the film carries out in a sprightly and unrestrained, passionate and dynamic way as indicated in the opening sequence, which makes of a montage collage of statue, portrait, dancing adults, dashing boys, moving vehicles (including tanks), operating aircrew, and charming trees.

Reception Abroad

The film was well-received in China and the Chinese-speaking world, but very obscure in the US. It won the 51st Venice International Film Festival's Best Actor Award for its young leading actor Xia Yu.

Words from the Director

"Wang Shuo's novel was like a needle into my skin, with blood to take out. I cannot judge his literary value. I always put texts into picture. I always consciously or unconsciously translate novels into movies. I saw the novel, and smelled, and smelled, and it appeared in the music. In *Wild Beast* I found my own time was real, either real or subjective…" (Jiang, 2013)

Scan the QR code to watch the movie.

Case Study V: *Ju Dou* (《菊豆》, 1990)

Profile

Directed by Zhang Yimou

Leading actors: Gong Li, Li Baotian

Reception Abroad

Ju Dou was nominated as the Best Foreign Language Film at the 63rd Oscars, Palme d'Or at the 43rd Festival De Cannes, winning the Luis Bunuel Special Award, Valladolid International Film Festival's Golden Spike, Chicago International Film Festival's Gold Hugo, and Norwegian International Film Festival's Best Foreign Feature Film.

Reviews on *Ju Dou*

Ju Dou was seen by Cui (1997) from as a gendered perspective: the construction and representation of subjectivity and sexuality.

Since its release in 1990, Zhang Yimou's *Ju Dou* has drawn intense interests from film critics, academic scholars, and general audience. Reading Ju Dou against the difficulties and errors that often occur in cross-cultural interpretations of non-Western texts, Lau (1994) finds qualities of "Chineseness" fundamental to the film's textual and conceptual meanings, especially as internet in the cultural notions of *yin* (excessive eroticism) and *xiao* (filial piety).

However, there are also some other opinions. Callahan (1994), by contrast, reads *Ju Dou* as an allegory invoking Confucianism. These systems of patriarchal domination, he argues, define the film narrative as a "woman's struggle against her social placement" and as a father-son embodiment of Confucian ideology. Chow (1995), in her book *Primitive Passions*, describes *Ju Dou* as "the sign of a cross-cultural commodity fetishism", and indeed, the appetite for viewing and writing about new Chinese cinema is strong.

One can, as Chow does, see the director in the role of an exhibitionist, displaying his "exotic female protagonist", and thus engaging the "oriental's orientalist" (Lu, 1997a).

Scan the QR code to watch the mocie.

Discussion

How is *Ju Dou* different from *In the Heat of the Sun*, and what are their similarities and differences?

6.2.5　The Sixth Generation: 1990s–

The Sixth Generation is later film school graduates who rejected conventional themes and styles. Their films demonstrate a "disengagement from the official political discourse", therefore were considered "illegal" by the Chinese Film Bureau. Their works prefer to show urban, contemporary stories, focusing on ordinary characters.

6.2.5.1　Directors from the Sixth Generation

The Sixth Generation is a general term for a group of directors in the 1990s of China. They were mostly born in the 1960s to the 1970s. Representative directors include Zhang Yuan, Lu Chuan, Wang Xiaoshuai, Lou Ye, Wang Chao, Jia Zhangke. Their works often link to "independent movies" and "underground movies".

6.2.5.2　Characteristics of the Sixth Generation

Generally, the Sixth Generation directors have no nostalgia for the recent Chinese past, so we cannot tell the same primitive passion as the Fifth Generation in their movies. With the impact of **subculture and globalization**, these directors always consider themselves modernist or even postmodernist. That is why their films prefer to express more about personal feelings under the background of the changing society of China.

Based on their life experiences, the Sixth changed Chinese film from sacred art into ordinary life as a cultural product. Their films are down-to-earth products with a realistic spirit of creation, and surely offer a raw and unprecedented look at the attitudes and lifestyles of the people (Lau, 2003).

Their films' themes focus on the current city, the edge of the characters, and the unemployed youth. In terms of film language, they emphasize the true light, color, and sound, often with a long lens to form a documentary style.

> **Question:**
> What artistic improvements can you identify from the Fifth Generation to the Sixth ones?

6.2.5.3　Globalization and Youthful Subculture

We can analyze the reason why the Sixth Generation directors have the characteristics above from these aspects below (Lau, 2003):

(1) employing elegant craft in subversive narrative folklore, enjoying the last moments of the state-supported studio system;

(2) caught in a transitional period with significant changes in the cultural world and film-

making industry;

(3) the first group growing up during the full-fledged implementation of China's opening-up policy;

(4) the film industry transitioning from a socialist to a semi-market-driven business;

(5) losing a stable production environment, working within a still-forming system;

(6) no channels deemed proper or improper, legal or illegal;

(7) a confused stage with unclear funding, distribution, and exhibition methods for films;

(8) receiving money from outside China.

A Summary of Chinese Cinema History

Pioneers: around 1920s
Zhang Shichuan (张石川), Zheng Zhengqiu (郑正秋)

The Second Generation, the disciples of the pioneers: around 1930s–1940s
Cai Chusheng (蔡楚生), Fei Mu (费穆)

The Third Generation: around 1960s
Xie Jin (谢晋), Cheng Yin (成荫), Xie Tieli (谢铁骊)

The Fourth Generation: 1949–1960s
Zhang Aixin (张暖忻), Wu Yigong (吴贻弓), Teng Wenji (滕文骥), Wu Tianming (吴天明), Xie Fei (谢飞), Zheng Dongtian (郑洞天), Huang Jianzhong (黄建中), Huang Shuqin (黄蜀芹)

The Fifth Generation: 1980s–1990s
Chen Kaige (陈凯歌), Zhang Yimou (张艺谋), Jiang Wen (姜文), Tian Zhuangzhuang (田壮壮), Huang Jianxin (黄建新)

The Sixth Generation (the new generation): 1990s–
Zhang Yuan (张元), Lu Chuan (陆川), Wang Xiaoshuai (王小帅), Lou Ye (娄烨), Wang Chao (王超), Jia Zhangke (贾樟柯)

6.2.6　Current Cinema Culture in China

From the late 1990s onwards, the significance of current cinema culture in China has been marked by *Hero*.

A successful film cannot be produced without creative ideas and innovative selling points. One person's inspiration can initiate a creative planning. Still, any experienced film production company would have a whole professional planning team who can allow feasible proposals to be completed and fast-track the brainstorming of ideas. Each film proposal should include, at the fundamental level, the market positioning, the prospect analysis and the shooting purpose. In today's Chinese film market, to attract audiences and succeed at the box office, it could be argued that companies should produce genre films, particularly science fiction, comedy and romance—all of which are current favorites for the Chinese audience.

Sorry Baby (《没完没了》, 1999) marks the beginning of the partnership between the director Feng Xiaogang and the movie company **Huayi Brothers**. Wang Zhongjun and Wang Zhonglei at Huayi Brothers had visionary sights and ideas regarding Feng Xiaogang's comedy, which was tailored for the CCTV Spring Festival Gala—as early as 1997 after watching *The Dream Factory* (《甲方乙方》, 1997). They firmly believed that Feng's comedy style, which was full of unique characteristics, would be a massive success in the future. For this reason, soon after the company was established, their investments spanned for the next decade. From *Big Shot's Funeral* (《大腕》, 2002), *A World Without Thieves* (《天下无贼》, 2004) to *If You Are the One* (《非诚勿扰》) series, comedies by Feng had begun to bring significant success to Huayi Brothers, giving them a substantial competitive advantage in China's box office.

Huayi Brothers

Huayi Brothers Media Co., Ltd. is a well-known comprehensive private entertainment group in China, founded by brothers Wang Zhongjun and Wang Zhonglei in 1994.

Huayi Brothers has done business with prestigious film directors and producers such as Feng Xiaogang and Zhang Jizhong, turning their studios into subsidiaries. These celebrities and super filmmakers all but guarantee the quality of a film, giving the company complete confidence in developing themes and allowing it to invest in various film genres confidently. Aside from romantic comedies, Huayi Brothers has also had success in many other film genres, such as the war movie *Assembly* (《集结号》, 2007), the traditional costume drama film *The Banquet* (《夜宴》, 2006), the suspense film *Detective Dee and the Mystery of the Phantom Flame* (《狄仁杰之通天帝国》, 2010), and the historical feature film *After Shock* (《唐山大地震》, 2010), all of which returned huge revenues at the box office.

In the contemporary Chinese film industry, directors must navigate both business principles and artistic pursuits during film production. This suggests that while artistic setbacks might be overlooked, business failures can have severe consequences. Over time, in the competitive box office environment, the success of a director or a company tends to be measured more by income generated than by the quality of their films. Thus, artistic value does not always align with commercial success, with the latter often taking precedence.

There has never been a lack of examples of failed investments in the history of world motion pictures. At present, film companies are confronted with a large number of problems. Which kind of cost is necessary, and which is not? Starting as an advertising company, Huayi Brothers has developed into one of China's most influential media groups, focusing not on saving money but rather on making money.

Another significant advantage for Huayi Brothers is its artists. *The Message* (《风声》), released in 2009, enjoyed both strong recognition and a high gross at the box office. The personal charisma of the celebrities and superstars in the film can all but guarantee at least a certain level of success, even before the film's release. However, this is something that is far beyond the investment capacity of most small and medium-sized companies, as the price alone of inviting two top stars to be involved in the film may already take up half of their entire budget before even accounting for the necessary "agency fees" for connecting with and persuading actors to participate.

Therefore, an "all-star cast" can be an actual trump card in the box office battle, but it can only be played by the more powerful, wealthy companies such as Huayi Brothers and Beijing Bu Yi Le Hu Film Corporation (北京不亦乐乎电影文化发展有限公司). So, are films that lack well-known celebrities destined to lose money from the offset? Not necessarily. As far as *Assembly* goes, the main actors Zhang Hanyu, Wang Baoqiang and Deng Chao were not considered top stars at that time. Yet, the film still managed to top China's box office that year owing to its extraordinary public reception. However, its production cost only 80 million RMB, which was extremely low compared to many other war

The poster of The *Message*

Scan the QR code to watch the movie.

films. Hence, the key to success is to ensure that the right talent is selected and to invest in a good film genre.

The comprehensive digitization that has taken place in recent years will be an irreversible trend for the film industry. What is the reason behind Hollywood movies occupying a 52% market share in China, even though there are different policies and restrictions on imported films? The answer is obvious: science fiction films. There are only three domestic films that ranked among the top 10 in China's box office in 2012: *Lost in Thailand* (《人在囧途之泰囧》), *Painted Skin: The Resurrection* (《画皮2》) and *Chinese Zodiac 12* (《十二生肖》), with Hollywood science fiction films achieving a landslide victory. These productions will continue to dominate the film market in the next decade or two. Actors will spend more time in front of the green screen in the studio than on shooting locations. Directors will no longer need to learn mise-en-scène techniques from masters such as Miklós Jancsó and Béla Tarr, because no matter how complicated the planning of a full-length shot, computers are almost certainly able to make it happen. Comprehensive digitization gives us a strong signal that post-production qualities and advanced technologies are of paramount importance for China's film production.

Huayi Brothers is more aggressive and assertive in film release than most other companies. First of all, the company has its cinemas in major cities so that it can guarantee the optimal release of its films. Before the release of *Back to 1942* (《一九四二》), the big news spread on the Internet that Huayi Brothers had stopped issuing secret copy keys to 362 cinemas, leaving the cinemas very anxious. Huayi Brothers designated a special representative to explain that this was a warning to certain cinemas to stop stealing or concealing box office revenue.

6.3 Transnational Chinese Film Studies

It is proposed that 1896–1996 is the periodization of Chinese film history, predetermined by far-reaching global and national events (Lu, 1997b). From 1896 onwards, the consumption and circulation of Chinese cinemas began to take on a transnational characteristic.

Transnational Chinese language films are financed from a variety of external sources and circulate mainly in the international film market. Consequently, "Chinese-language cinema", instead of "Chinese cinema", is a more suitable term covering all the local, national, regional, transnational, diasporic, and global cinemas relating to the Chinese language (Lu & Yeh, 2005). The nonequivalence and asymmetry between languages and ethnic groups signify the continuity and unity of the political body and cultural belonging, as well as the fracture and division of the Chinese people in the modern world.

6.3.1 Transnationalism of Transnational Chinese Films

The plural form of the term "transnational Chinese films" demonstrates its prominent feature, transnationalism, in the context of the ongoing process of image-making throughout the twentieth century. In the Chinese case, the transnationalism of the Chinese-language films can be observed at the following levels (Li, 2010).

First, the globalization of Chinese films' production, marketing, and consumption in the age of transnational capitalism in the 1990s.

Second, the questioning of "China" and "Chineseness" in film discourse, which concerns the intersection of ethnic, cultural, political, racial and gender identities.

Third, a revising and revisiting of the history of China's "national cinemas", as if reciting the "prehistory" of transnational filmic discourse (Lu, 1997a).

6.3.1.1 Chinese Film Industry: Transnational Production, Marketing and Consumption

As we mentioned, the film *Hero* has unveiled the curtain of China's blockbuster era since 2002 and is perceived as a counterpoint of Chinese cinema history. One of the main reasons is the transnational nature of the film. As the first cinema which proved the significance of marketization, internationalization, and professionalization in the Chinese film industry, it had a profound impact on the following Chinese films in terms of the transnational production, marketing and consumption, such as *The Promise* (《无极》, 2005), *Curse of the Golden Flower* (《满城尽带黄金甲》, 2006), and *Assembly* (《集结号》, 2007). These Chinese films are all featured by transnationalism, which specifically refers to: (1) the multiresource investment; (2) presales of film intellectual property rights owing to the desperation of market; (3) foreign personnel involved in the film production; (4) overseas distribution.

The globalization of film has changed the existing film distribution order and the traditional film industry. For example, Hollywood, with its dominant initiative in the film industry, has the advantage in international film production and distribution. It has been interested in making Asia, especially the Chinese language region, the next "dream destination" of the cinema (Zhu, 2008). Most of the Chinese-language films acclaimed by the world involve Hollywood in production and distribution. Facing the so-called "hegemony" by Hollywood, Chinese films are encouraged to substitute resistance with dialogue and exchange to promote the Chinese films and Chinese culture in order to play a more important role in the world film landscape. As a powerful cross-cultural medium, the cinema needs to rely on its own culture and absorb wider human civilization, especially by sharing the fruits of other cultures. Only by embracing all rivers can Chinese cinema break through geographical boundaries and be accepted by audiences around the world.

6.3.1.2 Development of National Culture and Image

As an important medium, cinema should be included in the category of **soft power** (Yang, 2011). In today's information-rich age, soft power relies not only on the universality of culture and ideas, but also on the channels of communication. Since the globalization has extended to the field of culture, the national culture is seen as a representative category of a country's soft power. Cinema, with convincing and vivid expressions of through images, carries the state of development in culture, value, custom, economy, etc. In the process, cultural transmission through films can expand artistic choices of global audience, open their eyes in the importing countries and enable them to know more about the exporting countries.

Soft Power

"…the richest country in the world could afford both better education at home and the international influence that comes from an effective aid and information program abroad. What is needed is increased investment in 'soft power', the complex machinery of interdependence, rather than in 'hard power'—that is, expensive new weapons systems." (Nye, 1990)

In the context of globalization, Chinese cinema is also trying to take on the world. With the rise of the Fifth Generation directors since the mid-1980s, China has witnessed a dramatic growth of international cinema rewards and has gained much more attention in international film festivals. In the mid-1980s, Chen Kaige's *The Yellow Land* (《黄土地》) won prizes at the Nantes International Film Festival in France and the Nogaro International Film Festival in Switzerland for the first time. At the Berlin International Film Festival, *The Golden Bear Award* (《红高粱》) directed by Zhang Yimou won the highest award. The international film festival awards as a breakthrough, the Fifth Generation opened the internationalization of Chinese cinema. After that, the Sixth Generation, and even younger directors, continued to make the global influence of Chinese cinema at major international film festivals with their individual and realistic works. The international power of Chinese cinema has been drawing increasing attention of the international community and, more importantly, arousing their interest in China's cinema history and Chinese culture. It also gives eloquent proof of the international recognition of the Chinese aesthetic value and artistic creation demonstrated in the Chinese transnational films.

To present the "transnational" feature of Chinese films in a more specific way, there follows a case study in terms of *Crouching Tiger, Hidden Dragon* (《卧虎藏龙》), a swordsman movie directed by Ang Lee and published in 2000.

Case Study VI: *Crouching Tiger, Hidden Dragan* (《卧虎藏龙》, 2000)

Profile
Directed by Ang Lee
Produced by China Film Co-Production Corporation
Adapted from the novel of the same name by Wang Dulu
Leading actors: Chou Yun-Fat, Michelle Yeoh,
Zhang Ziyi

Background

A famous warrior Li Mubai has the intention of retreating from the Jianghu, entrusting his confidante Yu Xiulian to bring his blue meditation sword to the capital, as a gift to the collection of Baylor. However, Li's move actually causes more Jianghu feud.

This film obtained magnificent echo in the world community and won ten Oscars including the "Best Foreign Language Film" at the 73rd Academy Awards, and it was the first film in Chinese film history to win the Academy Award for Best Foreign Language Film. In September 2019, the film was ranked 51st in the "100 Best Films of the 21st Century" by the British newspaper *The Guardian*.

Transnational Features

The screenplay and the subtitle of the film were co-produced by Chinese scriptwriter Wang Huiling and American Hollywood writer James Schamus with translation, re-translation, writing, and rewriting time and time again. This made the film synthesis of Oriental and Western cultures, and therefore easier for Western audiences to understand without any elements featured by Chinese culture missing.

Besides, Chow Yun-Fat, Zhang Ziyi, Michelle Yeoh, Chang Chen and Zheng Peipei, the five stars from different regions and representing different humanistic values, have to a certain extent helped the film expand its potential overseas market and create an international image for the film.

The transnationalism of this film is also owing to the cross-cultural context of Ang Lee. He was born and grew up in Taiwan, and migrated to the US at 24, studying and living there for many years. The multicultural background of Ang Lee is naturally reflected in his film.

6.3.2 Challenges of Transnational Chinese Film Studies[1]

(1) The "national imaginary" is unquestionably a central subject of the foreign scholarship of Chinese-language film studies.

(2) A cultural and national identity problem—questions such as "whose films" "whose nation" and "whose identity"—naturally appears. "Who produces for what audiences" is also a question.

(3) Can dialects constitute a vital perspective in Chinese-language film studies? Can the study of this issue lead to a "heteroglossic" situation? Is subjectivity-formation still possible?

> **As for the third point, there are two tips for you to consider:**
> (1) A dialect is not equivalent to a provincial consciousness, e.g., Jia Zhangke's film. In Jia Zhangke's cases, although people speak local dialects, the spirit that they express is an all-China consciousness.
> (2) But what if there exists a dialect that entirely conveys the indigenous spirit of its region?

6.4 Conclusion

As the second-largest film market in the world, China has witnessed a tortuous film route. Yet, it undoubtedly boasts a bright and promising future with a long way to go. The current ecosystem of Chinese cinema is the combining result of political, economic, cultural, and technological factors domestically and worldwide, and is also deeply influenced by foreign films market, thus presenting a film culture with Chinese characteristics. As for the current Chinese film culture, games between art & business and actors & box office, urgent demands for promoting post-production quality and setting up a better-regulated system of film releasing, etc. require further exploration for academics and industrial folks.

From a broader perspective, Chinese film history is strongly bound up with globalization. The academic studies concerning transnational Chinese-language film are one of the typical examples. Prominently featured by transnationalism, some Chinese-language films are seen not only blending production, marketing and consumption home and abroad, but also assuming the political unconscious of filmic discourse. However, the "Chineseness" that such films question leads to problems in cultural and national identity. How to maintain a balance between subjec-

---
1 Extracted from Fengliang, L. (2010). New horizons of transnational Chinese-language film studies: An interview with Sheldon H. Lu. Journal of Chinese Cinemas, 4(3), 245-260.

tivity and transnationalism calls for further consideration.

6.5 Extended Readings

Scan the QR code to get extended reading materials.

6.6 Post Questions and Discussion

(1) If you were an investor, what type of movie would you produce to maximize the box office?

(2) If you were a director, what percentage of your budget would be spent on the artists, production, promotion, or other aspects that you think require money?

6.7 Bibliography

杨曙. (2011). 全球化时代的华语电影文化传播. 新闻界 (03)：33-35.

Berra, J., Ju, W. (eds.). (2014). *World Film Locations*. Shanghai: Intellect Books.

Callahan, W. A. (1994). Resisting the Norm: Ironic Images of Marx and Confucius. *Philosophy East and West*, 44(2): 279-301. https://doi.org/10.2307/1399595.

Chow, R. (1995). *Primitive Passions: Visuality, Sexuality, Ethnography, and Contemporary Chinese Cinema*. New York: Columbia University Press.

Kong, S. (2007). Genre Film, Media Corporations, and the Commercialisation of the Chinese Film Industry: The Case of "New Year Comedies". *Asian Studies Review*, 31(3): 227-242.

Lau, J. K. W. (ed.). (2003). *Multiple Modernities: Cinemas and Popular Media in Transcultural East Asia*. Philadelphia: Temple University Press.

Lau, J. K. W., Ehrlich, L. C., & Desser, D. (1994). *Ju Dou*: An Experiment in Color and Portraiture in Chinese Cinema. *Cinematic Landscapes: Observations on the Visual Arts and Cinema of China and Japan*: 127-145.

Lu, S. H. (1997a). *Transnational Chinese Cinemas: Identity, Nationhood, Gender*. Honolulu: University of Hawaii Press. https://doi.org/10.1515/9780824865290.

Lu, S. H. (1997b). *Transnational Chinese Cinemas*. Honolulu: University of Hawaii Press.

Nye, J. S. (1990). Soft Power. *Foreign Policy*, 80: 153-171.

Sun, S. (2016). *An Overview of the Chinese Film Industry.* London: Routledge.

Xiao, Z. (2013). Prohibition, Politics, and Nation-Building: A History of Film Censorship in China. *Silencing Cinema.* New York: Palgrave Macmillan.

Xin, X. R., Mossig, I. (2017). Co-evolution of Institutions, Culture and Industrial Organization in the Film Industry: The Case of Shanghai in China. *European Planning Studies*, 25(6): 923-940.

Zhu, Y. (2008). Transnational Chinese Language Cinema and Hollywood Blockbuster Films. *World Cinema*, 3: 48-61.

LECTURE & SEMINAR 7
Film Making, Communication, and Technical Skills

This lecture will introduce more about "cinematography", which is one of the most important and determinant parts of making a film. First, we will introduce theories and explain the views through many specific examples. Second, we will explore new technical skills and forms of films through the Internet and scientific development. After learning this lecture, students could have a general idea about cinematography and know some new film industry technologies. Besides, there are discussions about what challenges the digital age brings to film.

Framework

7.1 Visual Narration

7.1.1 Cinematography vs. Mise-en-Scène

7.1.2 Composition of the Frame

7.1.3 Aspect Ratio

7.1.4 Mobile Framing

7.1.5 Cinematography and Perspective

7.2 Technical Narration

7.2.1 New Style: Virtual Reality

7.3 Interactive Narration

7.3.1 Case Study: Netflix and Interactive Films

7.5 Extended Readings

7.7 Bibliography

7.4 Conclusion

7.6 Post Questions and Discussion

Terms

cinematography, mise-en-scène, camera angles, POV, aspect ratio

Pre-lecture Discussion

(1) In your opinion, can the image done by post-production be seen as a part of cinematography?

(2) In your opinion, what is the relationship between the history of Chinese film and globalization?

7.1 Visual Narration

7.1.1 Cinematography vs. Mise-en-Scène

Cinematography

A general conception which contains everything that has to do with cameras and lenses, for example, film, film stock (and its digital equivalents), exposure and processing of film or digital images.

Mise-en-Scène

The stage design and arrangement of actors in scenes for a theatre or film production.

Citizen Kane (Welles)

Digital cinematography and computer-generated imagery have brought changes in **cinematography**, which is traditionally based on chemical/photographic images and effects.

However, when discussing cinematography, we cannot avoid an essential concept: **mise-en-scène**. It is the design and arrangement of actors in scenes for a theatre or film production, which is developed from the stage area. Since the invention of film, the term has also been used to refer to individual scenes in visual arts representing a film through storyboarding, visual themes, cinematography, and narrative storytelling through the direction. The term has been referred to as film criticism's "grand undefined term".

Mise-en-scène in cinema refers to everything that appears in front of the camera and its arrangement. Composition, sets, props, actors, costumes, and lighting are included. Mise-en-scène, along with cinematography and editing, contributes to the realism or believability of a film in the eyes of its audience. Design contributes to the expression of a film's vision by creating a sense of time and space, establishing a mood, and sometimes suggesting a character's emotional state.

Cinematography can be compared with mise-en-scène (staging), which relates to "what is filmed" based on the customary link between the two concepts, while cinematography refers to "the process of filming".

Because of the differences between them, two questions can be raised:

(1) Visual special effects? Usually performed in post-production (esp. digital effects), are they cinematography?

An American Epic Science Fiction Film—*Avatar*

(2) Lighting? Typically, the cinematographer is in charge of effects such as exposure, lens setting, and focus (director of photography). However, because the lighting is part of "what is filmed", it can also be considered part of a film's mise-en-scène.

Black Swan (2010)

The conception of mise-en-scène can be seen as an answer to "what is filmed" and cinematography can be explained as "how it is filmed".

Main Elements of Cinematography

For the next part, we will further introduce the main elements of cinematography.

> 1. The Composition of the Frame and Mobile Framing
> - The frame shape (aspect ratios)
> - Camera distance (types of shots, e.g., CU, medium shot)
> - Angle, level, height
> - Mobile framing (camera movements and zooms)
> - Perspectives

> 2. Explanations and Discussions

- Specific camera, lens, & exposure choices & techniques (what used to be called "photographic elements")
- Camera choices (speed of motion, shutter speed)
- Lens types (e.g., telephoto, wide-angle)
- Lens settings (focus, aperture, depth of field, etc.)
- Exposure issues

7.1.2 Composition of the Frame

7.1.2.1 Camera Angles

Camera Angles

This term marks the specific location at which the movie camera is placed to take a shot.

High Angle

High angle is a cinematic technique in which the camera looks down at the subject from a high vantage point, and the focal point is frequently "swallowed up".

High-angle shots can make the subject appear vulnerable or powerless with the proper mood, setting, and effects. They can make the scene more dramatic in the film. This shot is frequently used when a person at a high elevation speaks to someone below them.

Psycho (Hitchcock)

Straight Angle or Straight On

Also known as the general shooting angle, the object is placed horizontally to the camera lens for shooting. The picture from this angle can easily make the audience feel a sense of identity and feel like they are in it. This is one of the most often used shooting angles.

Low Angle

A low angle, known as wide shooting, places the object on a horizontal line. The camera is lower than the horizon line, shooting from a low elevation upward. This angle will give the audience a tall, strong, and energetic image of the photographed object. This kind of picture is generally used to shoot people scenes that appear tall and heroic.

The Dirth of a Nation (1915)

Canted Frame (a.k.a. Dutch Angle)

The canted frame is created by tilting the camera on its axis, resulting in an obliquely framed shot. A canted frame typically depicts a crooked or asymmetrical world.

Man with a Movie Camera (Vertov) is one of the earliest films to employ canted angles. It has two primary characteristics:

(1) camera not level / not horizontal;

(2) often suggesting tension, trouble, distress, etc.

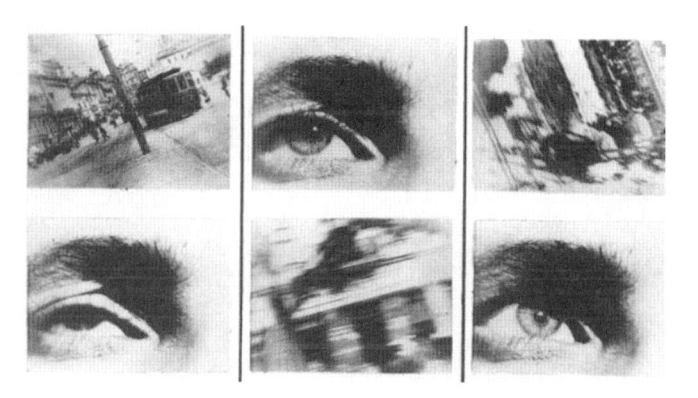

Scan the QR code and watch the movie.

Man with a Movie Camera (Vertov)

"Dutch angle" derives from the German word "Deutsch". In many German expressionist films, tilted angles convey madness and unease.

Question: Can you choose the right angle for the following pictures?

Other names include the Dutch tilt, oblique angle, and German angle, which mean "lens in the German style". This name originated from the 1930s and 1940s German films. Due to the extensive use of oblique lenses, this phrase was coined.

Typically, the scenes captured with this type of lens are dark, and the oblique angle can accentuate the erratic and unsettling mood of the image; thus, this type of shooting technique was developed. The image can become unbalanced when viewed from this perspective. Violence, excitement, and drunkenness can all be described with this word. Insanity, confusion, medication effects, and shifts in the weather are all examples of this term's versatility. German expressionism is associated with the pursuit of artistic origin.

Framing can become the signature of a director.

There are additional instances of framing, such as using the natural frame found in objects.

Tarantino's Low-Angle Trunk Shot

When shooting overhead shots, it is best to use a wide-angle lens with a larger angle. This backup shot conveys a sense of tension and empathy with the character's painful feelings. Many conventional film shootings mostly use mid-range shooting, while upward shooting often uses a broader angle. This type of lens is used in many of Quentin's films.

7. 1. 2. 2 Camera Distance

To some extent, camera distance can be seen as the type of shoot. There are mainly the following types:

- extreme long shot (els);
- long shot (ls);
- medium long shot (mls);
- medium shot (ms);

- medium close-up (mcu);

- close-up (cu);

- extreme close-up (ECU).

Extreme Long Shot (ELS)

An extreme long shot is a long shot that covers a greater region. It is also known as an extreme wide shot (EWS). The image frames the subject from a distance and concentrates on its surroundings. The character is frequently still apparent in the frame in a long shot.

Wide Shot in the Final Scene of *Fight Club* (1999)

Long Shot (LS)

A long shot is virtually identical to a wide shot. A long shot occupies nearly the entire frame height when referring to a person. It refers to a wide shot of the whole scene in other circumstances, which places the subjects in their context.

Nosferatu (1922)

Medium Long Shot (MLS)

The medium long shot demonstrates parity between the background and the subjects. It is frequently used in scenes with dialogue or a small cast of actors to give the audience a glimpse of the environment, like when the shot is "cutting the person in two".

It follows the initial shots of a new scene or location and is the most famous film shot.

Medium Shot (MS)

The line between what constitutes a long shot and a medium shot is not definitive, nor is the line between an MS and a close-up. Standard texts and professional references refer to a full-length view of a human subject as a medium shot.

Medium Close-up (MCU)

A medium close-up shot or MCU frames the subject from just above the subject's head to about midway down the torso. A medium close-up is frequently employed when a scene requires standard coverage that does not shock the viewer.

Close-up (CU)

This type of shot frames a person or object very closely. Close-ups are routinely employed alongside medium and long images (cinematic techniques). Close-ups feature a tremendous amount of detail but omit the wider scene. Ordinarily, zooming involves moving toward or away from a close-up. A close-up of the head and neck is captured. Therefore, it provides a clear image of the character's face.

Extreme Close-up (ECU)

As one of the CU, the shot is so tight that only a detail of the subject can be seen, such as someone's eyes.

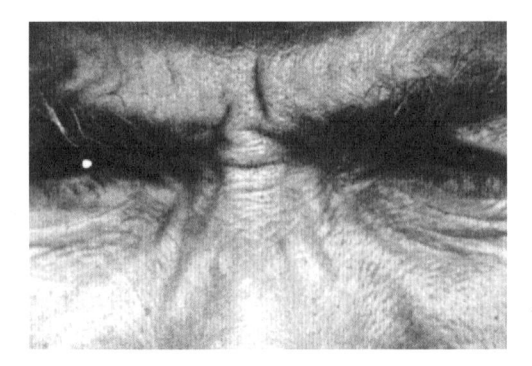

Clint Eastwood stars in *The Good, the Bad and the Ugly* (1966).

Other "shots" that aren't named for their shot distance:

- establishing shot;

- master shot;

- two and three-shot;

- reverse shot or reverse-angle shot;

- point-of-view (pov) shot (a.k.a. subjective shot).

7.1.3 Aspect Ratio

Mathematically, to be more precise, the **aspect ratio** can be calculated as follows:

$$aspect\ ratio\ (AR) = \frac{L}{W}$$

Aspect Ratio

The ratio of its width to its height and expressed with two numbers separated by a colon, such as 16 : 9, sixteen-to-nine.

Ratio Calculation

The Rules of the Game (Jean Renoir, 1939)
1.33 : 1 (4 to 3)

Aliens (James Cameron, 1986)
1.85 : 1

Rebel Without a Cause (Nicholas Ray, 1955)
2.35 : 1 (Cinemascope)

We should note how framing affects balance, visual information, and the relationship between on- and off-screen space.

2.2 : 1 Pan & Scan

1.33 : 1
Star Wars

16mm film has always been active in the field of film production. In particular, many TV commercials and TV programs were filmed in 16mm in the early stage, but 16mm copies are rarely shown in movie theatres.

The films in the picture on the previous page are called "film projection copies", to be precise. In other words, these films are used exclusively for projection on projectors. The most common 35mm film has 24 frames per second (1 frame is one frame), and each frame is projected 2 or 3 times. As a result, the screen has 48 or 72 frames per second. This makes the picture look smoother without feeling "flickering".

Different Ratios in Movies

The height of the three movies on the screen is the same, but the width is different. A significant concept, "aspect ratio", was introduced to define this distinction. The aspect ratio is the ratio of width to height. If the height is 1, the width will be X. The aspect ratio is then X : 1, which is very straightforward. In this way, the three types of pictures are 1.37 : 1, 1.85 : 1, and 2.35 : 1. We can abbreviate them as 1.37 pictures, 1.85 movies, and 2.35 movies. In short, these numbers represent the images of these movies on the screen. Remember, the aspect ratio of a film is defined by its final appearance on the screen, not by its appearance on the film. If we combine how they look on film, we can say:

1.37 = square screen = old movie 1.85 = blocked widescreen (standard widescreen) 2.35 = anamorphic widescreen. There are idioms (numbers or nicknames) in every industry, and for the film industry there is no exception, such as 1.85 and 2.35, meaning different copies.

The 1.37 movie has faded into obscurity for many years, and no one shoots such a square picture anymore. Movies displayed in the cinema today are either 2.35 or 1.85. And about 70%

of them are 2.35 movies. There is no inevitable rule with the release of 1.85 or 2.35 copies. Movie theatres can also be released. And most Hollywood movies don't think they are literary films, so they release 2.35.

Aspect Ratios (when shooting digital)

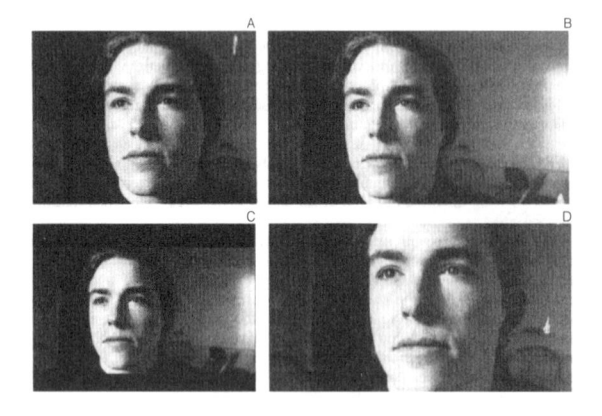

A. 4 : 3—composition well suited for a close-up

B. 16 : 9—loss of focus, i.e., the frame includes "extraneous" information

C. 16 : 9—letter boxed, i.e., the face is smaller

D. 16 : 9—to command attention, i.e., fill-up the frame—the face is cropped

7. 1. 4　Mobile Framing

Mobile framing involves the actual motions of the camera, including zooms, where the camera does not move, but the frame changes when the lens's focal length is altered: You can zoom in or out.

Examples of computer-generated photos include "fly-bys" and "rotations". As with conventional animation, computers have the potential to generate any movement.

Mobile framing: camera movements.

Pans: horizontally turns the camera ("camera revolves on vertical axis").

Tilts: vertical pivot/rotation, up and down.

(In pans & tilts, the camera does not change position, it pivots or rotates, usually tripod-mounted.)

Dolly shots: also named racking/traveling shots.

Mobile Framing

It refers to the effects in the framing of an object or scene by the motion of a camera with or without the help of a zoom lens and special effects and tricks. Thus, camera angle, height, level and distance can change which gives the illusion of a certain effect such as zooming in to show movement.

Dolly, tracking, and moving shots are identical. Sometimes "tracking shot" is used to mean "following shot". However, the term "tracking shot" originated from the "tracks" on which dollies moved. So, the terms dolly and tracking are interchangeable. A traveling shot is typically reserved for broader movements captured from a moving vehicle.

Dolly shots usually lead to long takes.

Dolly Shot, on Tracks

This interesting lens application technique is precise because the film master Hitchcock used it in movies. This technique is also known as "Hitchcock zoom" "vertigo effect" "the trombone shot", and "zoom in track out" in Hong Kong.

Hand-Held and Steadicam Shots

Hand-held and steadicam shots can tilt, pan, and track. Its "unsteady" movement was shot with a hand-held camera.

How does it work?

Steadicam is a patented device that reduces shakiness, resulting in a relatively smooth movement, even when walking or running. Operator training is required. Steadicam first appeared in *Rocky* (1976), with the first prominent appearance in Kubrick's *The Shining* (1980).

Children of Men (Alfonso Cuarón, 2006): an Example of Steadicam

A well-known shot from the 1975 film *Jaws* employed forward tracking and a zoom-out.

The opposite of Hitchcock's vertigo shot tracked out while zooming in. Both types are commonly referred to as "dolly zoom" shots.

Tracking vs. Zooming

- **Left**
Move the camera (track in);
Short focal length lens;
Relation of back/foreground, changed angles;
Distortion at edges.
- **Right**
Camera stationary;
Change of focal length (i.e., zoom in);
Closer relation of back/foreground (telephoto effect of flattening);
No distortion at edges;
Zooming is unnatural to the human eyes.

Emotional Framing

Like the Dutch angle, mobile framing can denote a specific psychological effect, and the motion signifies an abrupt rush. These framing techniques are cinematic depictions of a profoundly psychological emotion.

7.1.5 Cinematography and Perspective

Look at these two frames below, and discuss the questions:

(1) Who is the audience observing, and from which vantage point?

(2) From what angle does the camera place the audience?

M (Fritz Lang, 1931)

Black Swan (D. Aronofsky, 2010)

Film Making, Communication, and Technical Skills LECTURE & SEMINAR 7

Subjective Shot (or Point-of-View Shot)

Subjective shot/camera: From a character's position/point of view, as if viewing the world through that character's eyes. It was also known as a POV shot. Cinema corresponds to "first person" in writing.

Some people differentiate between subjective shots and point-of-view shots by using "POV shots" to include "over-the-shoulder" shots, which give the impression of POV without actually being from the character's position. However, it is simpler and more effective to treat POV and subjective as equivalent and over-the-shoulder as distinct.

Shot/reverse shots and eyeliner matching are based on the concept of seeing from the character's point of view. However, shot/reverse images display both "subjective" and "objective" perspectives.

One-Point Perspective

A positive (one-point) perspective generally highlights the theme and eliminates visual interference caused by changes in view. In contrast, asymmetrical composition based on a positive attitude is more memorable, profound, and indifferent, even in specific scenes. The down has a religious connotation.

Kubrick's One-Point Perspective

Kubrick is a passionate lover of punctual perspective. After graduating from high school, he became a photojournalist for the magazine *LOOK* in New York. Even based on his photographs from this period (1945–1950), positive perspective and symmetrical composition are among his typical compositional techniques. This demonstrates that Kubrick has observed and presented the objective world in a subjective manner that is individualized, cruel, and indifferent.

"Short films used to be ideal, but now they bloom everywhere in the film industry. With the advancement of technology, many ordinary people have become interested in short films, and everyone has made short films and uploaded them to the Internet. Suddenly, we no longer need to explain to people what a short film is because everyone has seen it."

7.2 Technical Narration

Films amalgamate scientific methods, literature, and arts. The development of the film industry is heavily dependent on the technological revolution.

Under the influence of 5G technology, technological development and advancement in the film industry is accelerated. From silent film to sound film, black-and-white film to color film, all of these epoch-making films rely on the advancement of science and technology.

The core of 5G technology is "high speed" and "wide connectivity", which will undoubtedly and profoundly impact film production, distribution, and dissemination. Under the influence of 5G technology, the high-definition experience of movie pictures, the sense of wonder of movie images, and the interactive sense of movie appreciation will be enhanced, and watching movies will become more "beautiful" and "fun".

To acknowledge that technical narration is increasingly intricate and pervasive, we must recognize its potential benefits for narration to be valued in technical communication. What are the possible benefits of narration?

The advantages of technical narration intrigue the technical communicator when viewed globally: Compared to expository texts, narrative texts are read faster (Graesser, Hoffman, & Clark, 1980), processed more effectively (Britton), and remembered better (Graesser, Hoffman, & Clark). Narrative texts are more credible and persuasive than expository ones; their greater rhetorical power stems from their being more concrete and easily understood. Experiments conducted by Nisbett et al. demonstrate the compelling ability of the concrete over the abstract and the former's connection to the narrative. Perhaps their illustration illustrates the point more eloquently than their investigation's report, which is therefore worthy of being quoted.

7.2.1 New Style: Virtual Reality

New materials and digital technology techniques create the miracle of the film. When digital technology is used, the real world can be made, and a dream world like virtual reality and the future world can be set up. We have seen it directed and designed (Bian, 2013).

Virtual reality (VR) is a computer-generated simulation of a three-dimensional environment. VR prioritizes the experience over the interface for observation. The immersive technology lets users interact with objects, physically explore the VR world, and do designated tasks. Most virtual reality is viewed through a headset. However, more complex VR utilizes gear like hand-held controllers, special gloves, headphones, or omnidirectional treadmills. VR is also making ways to create ripples in the film industry. The film crew has now begun to use 4K 3D cameras to leverage VR technology.

7.2.1.1 The Development of VR Technology and VR Films

Virtual reality technology creates a three-dimensional virtual environment through computer simulation. Through external interactive gadgets, users receive authentic visual, auditory, and tactile feelings, generating a sense of immersion. The booming VR movie concept mixes films, games, theaters, and other elements. Several games currently utilize cinematic language to further their narratives. Plays and films will be combined in VR films to create immersive dramas. Existing VR video production and hardware playback technologies can provide viewers with a more immersive experience and film. As virtual reality technology progresses, head-mounted displays and smartphones are increasingly adopting panoramic video services. VR and film are still being investigated. Wearing head-mounted devices allows individuals to feel engaged in cinema. Users of virtual reality may view their environment realistically and engage in activities.

The possibilities of VR are much more vast than we initially thought they would be. Because you matter in that story, the way you experience the story matters.

—Saschka Unseld, Pixar Creative Director & Founder of Oculus Story Studio

Cinematic VR technology simulates sight, sound, and touch, immersing viewers in a virtual experience. Filmmakers use this technique to engage the audience with the tale and characters. The technology of virtual reality produces the illusion that the scene is genuine. The closest approach to generating empathy through movies is virtual reality filmmaking. The realistic and immersive experience provided by VR cinema is what draws people in. Creators have long struggled with interaction in VR movies and television. Currently, show characters interact with viewers. VR is an intriguing and innovative medium.

The technological revolution, such as AI, big data, have increased the appeal of virtual reality. The adaptability and subjectivity of VR contradict conventional films and animations. Virtual reality presents an entirely generated image and employs head and motion tracking to track the user's movements and provide an immersive experience. "VR emotionally engages viewers with global social problems" (Gillespie, 148). Existing 2D screens are superior for video games, immersive films, television, etc., to this technology. VR games and movies are trendy. Hollywood is also developing virtual reality films, and some technology companies are constructing virtual reality amusement parks with expansive settings, motion-tracking technologies, and video game-like scenario design.

7.2.1.2 The Role of VR/AR in the Film Industry and the Development Trend

Cinema in VR/AR might not merely be a technological development like the switch from silent to sound, black and white to color, or 2D to 3D. The sensitive nature of these new "realities" will determine a new era in communications and entertainment (Schütze, 2018). It could be more of an artistic progression, similar to the transition from painting to sculpture or photography to the cinema. The two-dimensional screen of the movie suddenly transforms into a three-dimensional environment. The lack of a better-developed model for narrative logic and camera language in VR/AR films and the limited availability of VR/AR filmmaking technology that can reach the standards of film level prevent VR/AR movies from being widely popular soon.

7.2.1.3 VR Filmmaking—Oculus

Oculus Story Studio is an original animated virtual reality film studio division of Oculus VR.

Immersiveness exemplifies the newly discovered power of VR (particularly VR films). Participation is what drives the medium. It is enveloping and thoroughly fuses the observer with the art.

The possibilities afforded by virtual reality filmmaking will expand the scope of stories beyond our wildest imaginings. This access is unique and requires our attention as the storytellers of tomorrow's virtual reality films.

Henry (2015)

One of the first VR movies was Oculus' premiere *Henry*, which introduces a virtual hedgehog telling the narrative of how the medium of virtual reality may be used to connect people.

This virtual reality filmmaking example is essential to comprehending the dynamic capabilities of virtual reality in films. This is the first character who breathes and lives alongside the audience in his narrative experience.

Virtual reality films are distinguished from classic films' capacity to provide first-person access to characters and their firsthand experiences.

It's not pre-recorded—it's alive in this reality. Virtual reality filmmaking might be its closest iteration if the film is a tool for empathy. Even elite Hollywood players like Oscar-winning actress/producer Geena Davis are taking note and becoming involved in VR movies. In Oculus' *Dear Angelica*, she premiered at Sundance in 2017.

7. 3   Interactive Narration

Digital technology impels new film types' appearance and changes viewers' viewing habits. In the context of genre cinema conventions, there have been attempts to categorize films based on their overall narrative structure. In other words, movies that belong to the same genre should have a comparable organization and narrative progression.

The interactive film genre has been conceptualized in terms of branching, multi-linear narratives that rely heavily on computer game mechanics. The nature of the film, computer games, and interactive cinema are compared in the following table.

The Comparison of Classical Film, Computer Games, and Interactive Film (Abba, 2008)

	Classical Film	**Computer Game**	**Interactive Film**
Logical Consistency	The author is in control—characters behave within guidelines.	The plot and circumstances of action constrain player engagement.	The player has free will and will probably act on it.
Framatic Climax	The pace and story threads determine the point of the narrative climax.	Driven by level, score, and the linear direction of play.	The reader will choose when to finish the story.
Character Amnesia	The third-person viewing perspective affords the writer control over information.	The artificial-second-person player perspective only allows information to be released as and when required.	The first person viewer perspective results in the character/reader not understanding the scenario.

As proposed by a remediation strategy, a hybrid interactive film form appears problematic in this light. Considering an interactive film as a discrete object makes reconciling the author's and audience's conflicting desires challenging.

7. 3. 1   Case Study: Netflix and Interactive Films

Netflix is an American production company and subscription streaming service offering a library of films and television series through distribution deals and original works. Netflix attracts viewers with its seemingly endless selection of films, television series, documentaries, etc. However, the streaming platform giant's turning point has been its Netflix Original movies and series.

The entire premise of these interactive titles gallows viewers to choose how they want the movie to play out.

Before 2017, Netflix had released interactive programs for children, beginning with *Puss in Book*. In November 2018, Netflix released the interactive series *Minecraft: Story Mode from Telltale Games*. *Black Minor: Bandersnatch* was their first adult-oriented release. Netflix produced additional shows utilizing the Branch Manager application. Bear Grylls' interactive reality series *You vs. Wild*, consisting of eight episodes modeled after *Man vs. Wild*, premiered in April 2019. In May 2020, an interactive special for the comedy *Unbreakable Kimmy Schmidt* was released.

Black Minor: Bandersnatch is the first adult-oriented interactive film. Charlie Brooker wrote the script, while David Slade directed the film. The film's Netflix debut occurred on December 28, 2018. Its release date was only officially announced the day before. Before *Black Minor: Bandersnatch's* release, Netflix did not confirm the interactive nature of the film, despite widespread media speculation. The movie incorporated the "choose-your-own-adventure" concept, allowing viewers to choose how they want the story to unfold. This occurs throughout the film, interspersed with numerous cutscenes.

Black Mirror: Bandersnatch is no different from other interactive films in interaction design, but the film also uses a more complex cross-layer narrative form.

First, the film has a metaphor for the concept of "game" from content to form. The line between interactive movies and games themselves is not clear. Many works are presented on interactive films, all games released on SONY game consoles but classified as interactive films in many discussions. Thus, an interactive film showing the making of a game has a certain meta-narrative quality: a narrative that tells itself. This crossing of narrative layers usually signifies the maturation of a narrative genre or at least the beginning of its reflection.

Black Mirror: Bandersnatch

Second, the film uses a double conation sexual narrative structure to complete the interaction account. The cross-layer narrative presents attempts at this structure to the audience. The so-called narrative stratification is to tell a story in the language of the characters narrated to become a narrative text, not only the narration in the narrative appears. At this point, the characters in one level of the record become the narrators of another level. That is, one level provides the narrators with another level. The level at which narrators are provided can be considered one level above the level at which narrators are provided.

For one, it offers an alternative concept to the conventional model. Instead, we are given the opportunity to, so to speak, "direct" how the movie unfolds. Netflix also offers a greater variety of interactive films than is currently available.

7.4　Conclusion

Although we all are familiar with movies, their theories behind the screen are not necessarily like what you think. This lecture mainly talked about cinematography and explained a series of technical skills with many kinds of vivid examples. Until now, you should distinguish different camera angles in the movie scenes. Camera distance and the aspect ratio are vital in expressing various emotions and feelings. You should form your unique opinions about mobile framing during the discussion section.

The knowledge of this lecture is the fundamentals of other learning processes. This lecture aims to help you handle the basic framework of cinematography and understand the process and important details of making movies.

7.5　Extended Readings

Scan the QR code to get extended reading materials.

7.6　Post Questions and Discussion

(1) After learning this lecture, how can the director arrange the camera movement to sculpt a tense feeling in your opinion?

(2) How many aspects are being included in cinematography?

7.7　Bibliography

Brian, H. (1976). The Long Take. In B. Nichols (ed.), *Movies and Methods: An Anthology* (p. 315). Berkeley: University of California Press.

Bruce, M. (2013). *Film Production Technique: Creating the Accomplished Image*. New York: Cengage Learning.

Chris, C. (2012). *Chris Crawford on Interactive Storytelling* (2rd ed.). Indianapolis: New Riders Publishing.

Tom, A. (2008). As We Might Watch: What Might Arise from Reconsidering the Concept of Interactive Film? *Journal of Media Practice*, 9: 1, 19-27.

Graesser, A. C., Nicholas, L., & Leslie, F. Clark. (1980). Structural Components of Reading Time. *Journal of Verbal Learning and Verbal Behavior* 19(2): 135-151.

Thorndyke, P. W. (1977). Cognitive Structures in Comprehension and Memory of Narrative Discourse. *Cognitive Psychology* 9(1): 77-110.

Britton, B. K., Arthur C. G., Shawn, M. G., Tom, H., & Margaret, P. (1983). Use of Cognitive Capacity in Reading: Effects of Some Content Features of Text. *Discourse Processes*, 6(1): 39-57.

Ciaran, G. (2020). Virtual Humanity—Access, Empathy and Objectivity in VR Film Making. *Global Society*, 34: 2, 145-162.

Stephan, S., Anna, I.-S. (2018). *New Realities in Audio: A Practical Guide for VR, AR, MR and 360 Video*. Boca Raton: CRC Press.

LECTURE & SEMINAR 8
Consumption of Image Representation Discourses

This lecture focuses on the consumption of images. We will introduce three approaches widely used in recent media products and visual consumption analysis: the semiotic approach, media analysis, and culture analysis. Specifically, as the representatives of modern media products, modern adverts, teleplay and reality shows will be introduced in the following three cases.

After learning this lecture, students are expected to acknowledge the method to consider the media products from critical and theoretical perspectives.

Framework

8.1 How to Analyze Images
8.1.1   Theories of Signs: Linguistics and Semiotics Approaches
8.1.2   Culture Study Approach: Hall's Representation Theory
8.1.3   Foucault's Discourse Theory: Power and Discursive Practices

8.2 Case Study
8.2.1   Case 1: The Semiotics Analysis in the Advertisement Stereotyping
8.2.2   Case 2: Representation of Girlfriend in the TV Drama

8.3 Conclusion   8.4 Extended Readings
8.5 Bibliography

Terms

image power, denotation, connotation, signifier/signified, discourse analysis, representation, stereotype, gender essentialism

Pre-lecture Discussion

(1) How should we understand an image? How should we understand photos and movies? Do you think of photos as windows on the world?

(2) Seeing advertising as a visual culture, how do we analyze an advertisement? Choose an advertising campaign, and provide a critical discussion of how representation may enhance or impair prejudicial depictions of a certain genre.

8.1 How to Analyze Images

8.1.1 Theories of Signs: Linguistics and Semiotics Approaches

First, let's answer the question, "How should we understand an image?"

We know that images can be split into different elements by different categories. In most of the time what they are meant to express is not as clear as the text or the verbal language. As the images are arbitrary and the languages are specific, here is a question that how to analyze the images. It may surprise you that the answer might be "as a text". The linguistics focused on text and verbal languages helps us understand images better, because all signs are cultural creatures and have been constructed by the social and collective use with meanings from what we've learned.

The meanings of images are often unclear, fleeting or plural, which makes them remain more possibilities for further explanation (Gripsrud & Toynbee: 32). Learning to understand images is important. The first tool that may help us is theories of signs into linguistic approaches.

Once in the situation where signs are utilized as cultural objects, they would work just like how the languages do. As the same, they surely can be analyzed in linguistic concepts. Before understanding the concept, we should first understand the process of "making meaning". When people are speaking, the listener cannot understand the meaning of a sentence until the speaker finishes it. And this is the process of making meaning. In short, the language/image consists of symbols and meanings. Meanings are showed according to the situation in which symbols are the images or sounds of words and letters, while archetypes are the half-done words.

Seemingly, when it comes to the analysis of images, we should see the coding/decoding process in signs.

An image is a form of documentation that shows particular people, places and things. Usually, analyzing what an image denotes means to analyze "who and/or what is depicted in the image".

Denotation

It refers to the simple, basic descriptive level, where consensus is wide and most people would agree on the meaning.

Images usually represent particular people, places, things and issues, but **"denotation"** is not their essential purpose. Images depict certain people, places, things and events to get general or abstract ideas across. They use them to connote ideas and concepts. So asking what an image connotes is to

Connotation

It signifies that we have been able to "decode" at a simple level by using our conventional classifications to read their meanings, and enter a wider, second kind of code. Here we are beginning to interpret the completed signs in terms of the wider realms of social ideology —the general beliefs, conceptual frameworks and value systems of society.

ask "what ideas and values are communicated through what is represented, and how it is represented" (Machin, 2010: 35-36).

Here is an example that helps us to understand the code in signs:

"Since the meaning of a sign depends on the code within which it is situated, codes provide a framework within which signs make sense. Indeed, we cannot grant something the status of a sign if it does not function within a code... does transcend single texts, linking them together in an interpretative framework" (Daniel Chandler).

Take the picture below as an example.

To understand a notice like this, both the situation and the common sense need to be included. We need to know that there is a so-called "code of reference" lying behind these words instead of mechanically reading the words one by one.

Firstly, the sign is to be taken as referring to the behavior of actual dogs and passengers on actual escalators.

Then, we understand the notice by interpreting it in terms of certain codes that seem appropriate (Eagleton, 1983:78).

Though philosophers have been studying the relationship between the world and the symbols used to describe it for thousands of years, the term semiotics was first used by early 20th century followers of the American pragmatist philosopher **Charles Sanders Peirce** (1839–1914). During the early 20th century, Swiss linguist Ferdinand de Saussure (1857–1913) came up with a theory system for understanding signs and outlined an approach to understanding how language makes meaning instead of merely conveying an already existing meaning. That was called semiotics.

Overall, semiotics brings the idea that any social phenomena is a communicative process. Semiotics is the study of everything that can be used for communication: words, texts, images, signs, creatures, music, medical symptoms, and so on. "Semiotics studies the way such 'signs' communicate and the rules that govern their use." (Seiter, 1992: 31)

In short, semiotics originated in the study of language, but it can be used to analyze everything that can communicate meaning. It is both a theory and a method. Semiotics is concerned with how meaning is created and communicated through.

Charles Sanders Peirce

8. 1. 1. 1 Peirce: 3 Types of Signs

The role of Charles Sanders Peirce and Ferdinand de Saussure is particularly prominent in the development of semiotics, with both of them being recognized as the "leading modern semioticians" in the academy. So next, we are going to study the semiotic theory of Peirce and Saussure respectively.

According to Peirce, signs can be divided into three kinds according to their relation to the object: **iconic signs**, indexical signs, and **symbolic signs**.

Iconic Signs

The signifier physically or perceptually resembles or imitates the signified indexical signs.

The signifier is directly connected in some way (physically or causally) to the signified—this link can be observed or inferred.

Symbolic Signs

The signifier does not resemble the signified; the relationship is "arbitrary" or purely conventional—it must be learnt.

Examples:

Icon/iconic: The signifier physically or perceptually resembles or imitates the signified. (can be seen; resemblance)

Iconic Signs

Index/indexical: The signifier is directly connected in some way (physically or causally) to the signified—this link can be observed or inferred. (can be figured out; cause and effect)

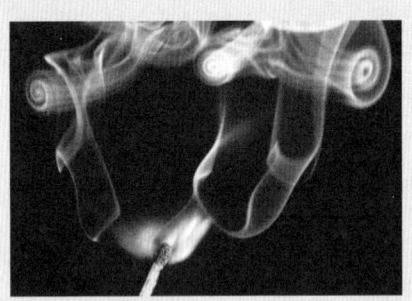

Indexical Signs

Symbol/symbolic: The signifier does not resemble the signified; the relationship is "arbitrary" or purely conventional—it must be learnt. (must be learnt; convention)

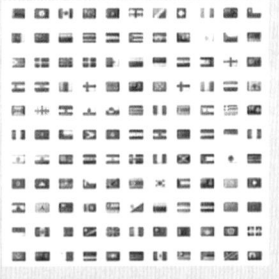

Symbolic Signs

Adapted from Chandler, 1994

8.1.1.2 Saussure: "Signifier" and "Signified"

Ferdinand de Saussure, known as the "father of modern linguistics", argued that language is a "system of signs". He divided "the sign" into two elements: "signifier" and "signified".

Here are some examples that help to understand the concept of "**signifier**" and "**signified**".

The Shape of Snow (examples as external referent)

The sign "snow" is made up by the sound produced by the word snow (the signifier) and the concept of soft white matter which falls from the sky (the signified). Saussure argued that the signified concepts themselves are more arbitrary than the verbal language. As there is nothing about actual snow that confirms that the sound "snow" is confined to it. As it can be called xue (雪) in China and yuki in Japan.

In comparison of images, visual signs are different. If on the television screen or the books we see the shape that looks like snow, we would say that what we see is a signifier that refers to the signified "snow".

So the "signifier" means the physical existence of the sign and it is an expression, while the "signified" refers to the mental concept which means the exact content.

Imaging here is a tree in front of you, and a child asks you, "What is this?" How are you going to tell him about this strange object with many leaves and branches you see? The tree is objective and it is the source of all the signifiers and signified associated with it, known in semiotics as reference.

Originating from the reference, "signifier" refers to all the phonetic and literal symbols that people assign to the tree. In Chinese, the phonetic name for it is shu, or "树"; in

Ferdinand de Saussure

Signifier

The form (actual word, image, photo).

Signified

The idea or concept in your head with which the form is associated.

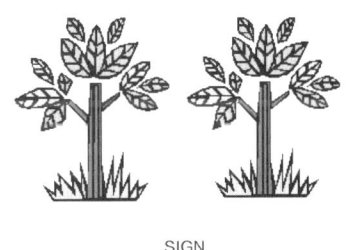

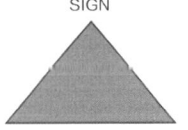

SIGN

SIGNIFIER
the physical
existence of the sign

SIGNIFIED
mental concept

English, it is also pronounced /triː/ , which is spelled "tree"; in French, it is pronounced /aʁbʁ/ and written "arbre"; in Latin it is pronounced /arbor/ and written "Arbor". Different people and different languages may assign different signifiers to it.

In contrast with the "signifier", "signified" means when others read or write the word "tree" to you, you'll retrieve out with a flourishing woody stem in the field of the image of a plant, like the tree in front of you being in your memory. It could be a tree that you have seen elsewhere, or a similar image or concept, but to you the image is "tree", neither "grass" nor "flower", neither "sun" nor "snow", because in your perception those symbols indicate something else.

8. 1. 1. 3　Roland Barthes: "Culture Context"

Roland Barthes (1915–1980) brought a semiotic approach to reading popular culture, treating wrestling matches, soap operas, etc. And he is also a leading figure in applying semiotic theory to the field of visual communication. His *Mythology* (1957) and *Rhétorique de l'image* (1964) both vividly discussed the relationship between semiotic theory and visual images. Roland Barthes' writings show that image symbols are more popular than text symbols in visual communication. At the same time, Barthes also explains the differences between photos, films and paintings, using the framework of cultural contexts.

Roland Barthes

Let's take a look at the cultural texts.

Based on previous theoretical studies, we can know that image makers rely on established connotators. The more abstract an image is, the more its connotative communicative function is foregrounded. Also, context is key.

Context shapes the meaning in the whole process of communication. We can't understand and communicate with each other correctly without a certain context. Considering the context also helps to improve our communicating efficiency. Imagining the scene when your message is delivered in one context but received in another, it doesn't harm to guess the misunderstanding and miscommunication that this is likely to lead to.

What's more, context includes many types. Here are some examples.

Examples:

The presentational context

The production context

The historical context

The textual context

The context of reception

8. 1. 1. 4 Understand the Images: From Photo to Moving Series

Look at the picture below carefully and here are some questions for you.

Reading the materials on the content about how the visual cue works to produce meaning (e.g., color, symbols, lighting, framing, foreground, background, angles, timing). Make a detailed expression of all you see in the picture above and answer these questions about the relationship between signs.
- What is the purpose do you think of the author to create this work?
- Analyze the various contexts of the work production, display and reception.
- Think about how it relates to other elements (textual, graphical, etc.).

After the short introduction of linguistics and semiotics theories, let's try to understand images to this approach. Learning to utilize the analysis framework may offer you ideas to answer the questions better.

According to Gripsrud, "The photographer has to make several choices, of framing, points of view, lenses, lighting, film, speed, etc.—plus all the choices in the darkroom. All of these choices provide the photographer with… space for her or his subjectivity" (Gillespie, & Toynbee, 2006: 30).

When it comes to the comprehension of specific photos, we can analyze it from the perspective of both visual and contextual levels. Here are some examples.

On August 15, 1945, Japan declared its unconditional surrender, and the Second World War ended in victory for the Allies. In Times Square, New York, a young sailor could not contain his joy, took a white uniformed nurse, whom he did not know, in his arms and kissed her boldly.

This is a photo of a German soldier after he was captured by the American army prisoners of war. The German soldier was called Hans, and he was only 16 years old. The American army correspondently took pictures of little Hans and used Hans' pictures as propaganda to tell the German army and the world that Germany had used children as instruments of war. Like his contemporaries who also lived in the same period, he experienced trials and tribulations throughout his life.

And then, moving images emerged. In contrast with the still image, moving image referred to the actual films and videos with actual framings in the repetitions of slow-motion. However, because of the camera will keep us a distance from what's happening, when the vedio sequence was perceived by the TV viewers, they seemed sometimes to lack the moral and emotional significance.

8. 1. 2 Culture Study Approach: Hall's Representation Theory

Apart from the linguistics and semiotics theories above, Stuart Hall's Representation Theory is also widely used in cultural studies and media studies. In this section, we will briefly introduce his theory of encoding/decoding and cultural representation and explain how to use this theory approach to analyze a culture text or project.

Stuart Hall is an essential representative of the British School of cultural studies. Nourishing structural linguistics, semiotics and Foucault's Power Discourse Theory, Hall forms his cultural Representation Theory.

Here let's see what the Representation Theory is.

8. 1. 2. 1 Representation Theory

According to Hall (1997), **representation** makes meanings and exchanges them through the language system consisting of "signs". As we mentioned above, the signs made of the signifier and signified can vary in forms like words, texts, images, etc. In other words, the process of representation can be explained as we use signs to "refer to" or "represent" something in the objective world, while others interpret it following the subjective concepts in their heads. Hence, according to Molina-Guzmán (2016: 440), while presentations are constructed by social norms and values, the interpretations can vary from person to person.

More specifically, as context shapes the meaning in all communication, "representation" also works in the context. Paul du Gay etc. (2013) mentioned that representation is a component in the Circuit of Culture through which any analysis of a cultural text or artefact must pass if it is to be adequately studied. **The Circuit of Culture** contains five major cultural processes in the culture study process: representation, identity, production, consumption and regulation. He argued that when doing culture studies, one should at least explore how it is represented, what social identities are associated with it, how it is produced and consumed, and what mechanisms regulate its distribution and use (Paul du Gay et al., 2013: 5).

Hall (1985: 112-113) considered representation a battleground for "ideological struggle". As Orgad mentioned, "Representation is fundamentally and inextricably inscribed in relations of power. Power relations are encoded in media representations, and media representations, in turn, produce and reproduce power relations by constructing knowledge, values, conceptions and beliefs. It is for these reasons that

Representation

An essential part of the process by which meaning is produced and exchanged between members of a culture... (involving) the use of language, of signs and images which stand for or represent things (Hall, 1997:1).

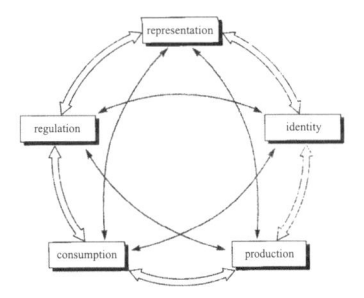

The Circuit of Culture (Paul du Gay et al.,1997)

Misrepresentation

Consciously or unconsciously inaccurate and misleading representation.

Underrepresentation

Insufficient, inadequate and disproportionately low representation.

representations matter" (Orgad, 2012: 2182-2185). Representation is contributed to meaning-making and socio-shaping, but also to power relations, ideology and hegemony, which is even more critical (Ograd, 2012; Molina-Guzmán, 2016).

To summarize, representation matters because it reflects the ideological struggle, power reflections and constructs our social practice. But, in the same time, some scholars argued that representation may also bring problems (Saha, 2012). For example, problematic representations may cause misunderstandings, stereotypes or neglect, and may develop into discrimination or exclusion in the reality.

8. 1. 3 Foucault's Discourse Theory: Power and Discursive Practices

Despite the approach of semiotics, **discourse** analysis is also a prevailing way of image interpretation. Discourse analysis is the study of language and its effects.

Foucault viewed "discourse" as a reference to the rules and practices producing meaningful statements and regulating what could be imagined and communicated in different historical situations.

Discourse

All forms of talk and texts, whether it be naturally occurring conversations, interview material, or written texts of any kind (Gill, 2000: 174).

The broader idea communicated by a text (Hansen & Machin 2013: 117).

Discourse analysis examines "what and how language communicates when it is used purposefully in particular instances and contexts" and with what effect (Cameron, 2001: 13), and the aim is to "identify the functions or activities of talk and texts, and to explore how they are performed"(Gill, 2000: 176).

In summary, discourse involves social conditions at three levels:

• the immediate level of the social situation (social condition of production and interpretation);

• the level of social institution which constitutes a wider matrix for the discourses (combination of discourses);

• the level of the society as a whole (structural characteristics and tendencies of the society).

Discourse analysis is an analysis of texts. We can analyze the text for its words (lexical), or for its structure of the sentences (syntax).

8.2 Case Study

8.2.1 Case 1: The Semiotics in Advertising

After talking about the image, we will look forward to the power of image in aspects of charity advertising.

An ad is never the program people are watching, never the letter people are waiting for, never the website people are seeking, not the part of the newspaper people are reading. However, when asked what do people think about an ad, it may trigger a battle in the emotional and ideological waves in their mind.

"Advertising is the most influential institution of socialisation in modern society" (Jhally, 1990). Because of this, some famous brand companies tend to use specific advertising strategies to improve their sales and deliver their corporate culture and values to the target audiences. In other words, they consist of a specific stream power of social changes.

How to analyze an advertisement?

You can refer to the following points:

- textual form;
- list the signs, think about the interplay between them;
- think about cultural codes;
- technical effects.

The visual and verbal discursive strategies in the advertisements significantly influence the transformation of socio-culture values and stereotypes in public. As Hackley (2005) mentioned, "Advertising has been cited as a force for cultural change of many kinds. Changes in the portrayals of brand consumption in advertisements both reflect and legitimize changes in the social world beyond advertising" (Chris, 2005). Namely, brands use discursive language to induce people to buy their products decorated by beliefs, values, and ideas.

> Look at the two pictures below and think about three questions:
> (1) What do you feel about seeing this kind of image?
> (2) Does this kind of image help you identify the sufferer / victim? (or the donor / volunteer?)
> (3) What is the likelihood of you being motivated to donate money or volunteer your own time and resources upon seeing such images?

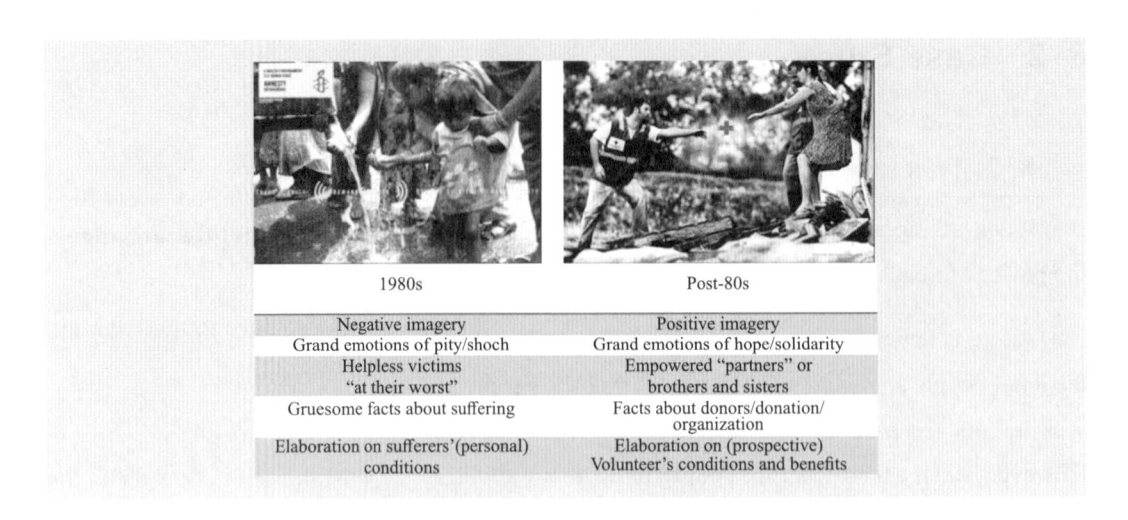

1980s	Post-80s
Negative imagery	Positive imagery
Grand emotions of pity/shoch	Grand emotions of hope/solidarity
Helpless victims "at their worst"	Empowered "partners" or brothers and sisters
Gruesome facts about suffering	Facts about donors/donation/organization
Elaboration on sufferers'(personal) conditions	Elaboration on (prospective) Volunteer's conditions and benefits

8.2.2 Case 2: Representation of Girlfriendship in the TV Drama

This case will take the Chinese TV series *Ode to Joy* (2016–2017) as an example to show how to examine the representation in the TV play.

Among numerous forms of rising cultural productions (such as fictions, animations, movies, reality shows) in China, TV play has took up a central place; for the sake of huge amount of population and time spent watching screens, the Chinese market has cultivated the biggest numbers of consumers for the TV play in the world (Zhang, 2007). According to the statistics, female viewers have taken up 70% among all the Chinese viewers (Jin et al., 2017). Specifically, women's stories occupy a large amount of Chinese TV serials and could own the market more easily (Yau, 2020). That's why the research on the TV serires is so popular. It can reveal the social interactions and tasty trend of the main force of Chinese cultural market.

Ode to Joy tells the story of five women in different social states with different backgrounds. They met each other on the twenty-second floor of an apartment in Shanghai called "Ode to Joy".

As shown by *Ode to Joy*, the representation of girlfriendship in the modern TV series is typical. It is put in the post-feminist context in which the women from upper class with professional success are portraed as female models, capable to provide unidirectional support to their relationship and other females in their economy and work life. Simultaneously, this relationship constructed between different classes is cultivated through the mutual interchange of care and support in both physical and psychological among which romance is a center concern. The benefits that they obtain from this cross-class strategic girlfriendship can enable them to achieve a more fulfilling life.

This show reveals the different consumption habits and lifestyles between different women from different social classes.

There are also predicaments and conflicts among them. Researchers have concluded the discourse of "the girlfriend gaze" according to this show. "The girlfriend gaze" refers to the mutual monitor of each other's heterosexual relationships appropriateness. In this program, women prone to share personal dating experience with their girlfriends to sustain the "strategic sisterhood" and keep active in the female circle. This sharing may induce the unpleasant feelings such as jealousy and inferiority which are also tools for women to internalize surveillance within the optional scope in the need of finding the right one. The women also introduce their male partners into the girl circle or female sphere, where men can make great positive effects on solving women's dilemma and consolidating a patriarchal centrality of men in women's lives.

TV shows could be seen as the main approach to fostering and reshaping the popular imagination of such girlhood community. According to Guo (2017), the eyes-catching appeals in the series resonate with the audience's true-life experiences while presenting a mass-mediated popular imagination of middle-class lifestyle that recipitates "an anxious quest for authorities and models of conduct" in cultural practices (Bourdieu, 1984: 331).

8.3 Conclusion

In the first section, we got to know the key to analyzing what the ideas and values connote in the image with the semiotics method by introducing 4 philosophers' main ideas, including 3 types of signs (iconic signs, indexical signs, and symbolic signs), 2 elements of signs (signifier and signified), as well as cultural texts. Through semiotics, discourse analysis and cultural dimensions theory, the bonds in social values can be reflected in the advertisement.

In the second section, two cases were mentioned to show the image power, charity advertising and global advertising. The image power in photos is that the information hidden in the images can be constructed by photographes. They make detailed inventory of choices of visual cues (e.g., colors, symbols, lighting, framing, foreground, background, angles, timing) to produce meanings that represent her or his subjectivity. There are many interesting issues in the production and dissemination in the global advertising.

8.4 Extended Readings

Scan the QR code to get extended reading materials.

8.5 Bibliography

De Mooij, M., Hofstede, G. (2010). The Hofstede Model: Applications to Global Branding and Advertising Strategy and Research. *International Journal of Advertising*, 29(1): 85-110.

Du Gay, P., Hall, S., Janes, L., Madsen, A.K., Mackay, H., Negus, K., 2013. Doing cultural studies: The story of the Sony Walkman. Sage.

Eagleton, T. (1983). *Literary Theory: An Introduction*. Oxford: Basil Blackwell.

Fairclough, N. (1995). *Media Discourse*. London: Edward Arnold.

Foucault, M. (1971). Orders of Discourse. *Social Science Information*, 10(2): 7-30.

Foucault, M. (2019). *Discourse and Truth and Parresia*. Chicago: University of Chicago Press.

Hall, S. (1985). Signification, Representation, Ideology: Althusser and the Post-Structuralist Debates. *Critical Studies in Media Communication*, 2(2): 91-114.

Hall, S., (1992). Race, Culture, and Communications: Looking Backward and Forward at Cultural Studies. *Rethinking Marxism*, 5(1): 10-18.

Hansen, A., Machin, D., (2013). *Media and Communication Research Methods*. London: Red Globe Press.

Hasinoff, A. (2008). Fashioning Race for the Free Market on America's Next Top Model. *Critical Studies in Media Communication*, 25(3): 324-343.

Hodge, R., Kress, G. (1988). *Social Semiotics*. Cambridge: Polity Press.

Li, L. (2015). If You Are the One: Dating Shows and Feminist Politics in Contemporary China. *International Journal of Cultural Studies*, 18(5): 519-535.

Molina-Guzmán, I., (2016). Oscars So White: How Stuart Hall Explains Why Nothing Changes in Hollywood and Everything Is Changing. *Critical Studies in Media Communication*, 33(5): 438-454.

Mulvey, L. (1988). Visual Pleasure and Narrative Cinema. In Penley, C. (ed.), *Feminism and Film Theory* (pp. 57-68). New York: Routledge.

Pollay, R. W. (1983). Measuring the Cultural Values Manifest in Advertising. *Current Issues and Research in Advertising*, 6(1): 71-92.

Pollay, R. W., Gallagher, K. (1990). Advertising and Cultural Values: Reflections in the

Distorted Mirror. *International Journal of Advertising*, 9(4): 359-372.

Potter, J., Wetherell, M. (1987). *The Routledge Handbook of Discourse Analysis*. London: Routledge.

Saha, A., (2012). "Beards, Scarves, Halal Meat, Terrorists, Forced Marriage": Television Industries and the Production of "Race". *Media, Culture & Society*, 34(4): 424-438.

Sturken, M., Cartwright, L. (2001). *Practices of Looking: An Introduction to Visual Culture*. Oxford: Oxford University Press.

LECTURE & SEMINAR 9
AI in Media

Artificial intelligence (AI) is transforming every walk of life. The integration of AI and media industry has expanded the existing way of content production, distribution and consumption. In this lecture we will take a look at the history and specific usage scenarios of three representative AI techniques: machine-generated content (MGC), intelligent recommendation and extended reality, so as to unravel the logic behind them and explore the impact of AI on human communication activities.

Framework

9.1 Background

9.2 Theory

    9.2.1 Machine Generated Content (MGC)

    9.2.2 Intelligent Recommendation

    9.2.3 Extended Reality

9.3 Case Study

9.3.1 Case 1: Quakebot: Automated Earthquake Reports

9.3.2 Case 2: Douyin: Intelligent Recommendation for Short Video

9.3.3 Case 3: Motion-Driven VUPs and Data-Based Virtual Anchors

9.4 Conclusion

9.5 Extended Readings

9.6 Post Questions and Discussion

9.7 Bibliography

Terms

machine generated content, VR/AR/MR, AI, journalism, intelligent recommendation

Pre-lecture Discussion

(1) What opportunities and risks will the emerging technologies (e.g., VR/AR/MR) bring to the journalism?

(2) With more and more robots "joining" the media, journalists and editors will be completely replaced one day. Do you agree or disagree with this statement?

9.1 Background

The history of **artificial intelligence (AI)** starts from the 1956 Dartmouth Summer Research Project on Artificial Intelligence in New Hampshire, where the term "artificial intelligence" was first used. According to the project proposal, this project aimed to shape the field of AI in which "every aspect of learning or any other feature of intelligence can in principle be so precisely described that a machine can be made to simulate it" (McCarthy et al., 2006).

What is intelligence? In McCarthy's (2007) words, intelligence is the computational part of the ability in humans, animals and some machines for achieving certain goals in the real world. The fact is that what can be characterized as "intelligence" is ambiguous in the history of AI. The goal for early AI attempts is to perform tasks that reproduce intelligent human behavior as human intelligence is deemed the central exemplar (Dick, 2019). Today, however, AI has been proved to equal or outperform humans in several areas, and is predicted to outperform humans in all areas in the future (Kaplan & Haelein, 2019). Therefore, research in AI is not only the study of humans, but the study of the problems the world presented to intelligence (McCarthy, 2007).

Since the Dartmouth Conference, early AI studies focused on the research area of symbolic AI on the basis of logic-based reasoning and heuristic search (Zhao, 2019), and the field of AI has experienced nearly two-decade-long significant success (Haenlein & Kaplan, 2019). In view of the great success achieved in AI research, Marvin Minsky stated that a machine of average human intelligence can be developed in three to eight years in an interview with *Life Magazine* in 1970[1]. But the funding cut in Britain, the disappointing project of the fifth-generation computer in Japan

Artificial Intelligence

A branch of computer science that deals with making machines do things that would require intelligence.

Neural Networks

Also known as artificial neural networks, the bionics branch of AI inspired by the natural neural networks of humans and animals.

Algorithms

A sequence of finite instructions entered into a machine to solve a particular problem or perform a computation.

---
1 Retrieved from https://quoteinvestigator.com/tag/marvin-minsky/.

Machine Learning

An AI technology that enables computers to learn and improve from past experience, and make accurate predictions or perform tasks automatically.

Deep Learning

A complex form of machine learning inspired by neural networks. In deep learning, computer models are trained through multi-layered approach to process increasingly abstract data.

Heuristics

Techniques used in AI to constrain a given problem's search space to a manageable size due to limited resources of time and space (Groner et al., 1983).

and the decline of Cyc[1], caught AI research into trouble (Pan, 2016). In the 1980s, AI made a comeback in the form of **neural networks** and resulted in many successful results.

Thanks to the breakthroughs of neuroscience, **algorithms** and big data, the world has witnessed AI research entering a new stage. There are great successes in **machine learning, deep learning**, robotics, **heuristics**, virtual reality, etc., all of which have made great influence on humans from all aspects. In 2016, AlphaGo, a program developed by Google DeepMind, beat the world champion in an extremely complicated board game Go with the assistance of deep learning, representing a great milestone in the history of AI. One year later, Oxford University carried out a large survey of AI experts on their beliefs about AI progress, and it is anticipated that there is a 50% chance for AI to outperform humans in all activities in the next 45 years (Grace et al., 2018).

Now people constantly engage with platforms such as WeChat, Douyin, Facebook, Netflix, Google and Amazon, through which AI advances are going to transform human's daily life by reshaping the media sector. This lecture looks more deeply into the applications and implications of AI in media industry.

9.2 Theory

MGC

Content (e.g., news stories, movie scripts and original paintings) automatically generated by using software or algorithms with limited human intervention.

The integration of AI and media industry expands the existing methods of content production, distribution and consumption. In the section of theory, three representative AI techniques will be discussed: **machine-generated content (MGC)**, intelligent recommendation and extended reality.

---

1 A long-term AI project that aims to construct an encyclopedia of knowledge by attaining human-like reasoning.

9.2.1 Machine Generated Content

In a broad sense, machine generated content has been defined as a supplement to **professionally generated content (PGC) and user generated content (UGC)**, and is expected to become the mainstream for future content generation (Huang, 2017).

PGC

Content generated by creative professionals from the platform/brand itself.

UGC

Content in the form of texts, images, audios and videos that has been created and shared by users though online platforms such as social media and discussion forums.

There are two main application scenarios of MGC in media industry: journalism and art. With the rapid development of AI large model like GPT-3[1], MGC has permeated to the creative industries of script writing, trailer production, poster production, etc. DALL-E2 which can convert text description into image is a case in point. But in this part, robot journalism (Clerwell, 2014; Deng, 2016), algorithmic journalism (Kotenidis & Veglis, 2021) or automated journalism (Graefe, 2016; Ali & Hassoun, 2019) is the focus.

As a type of journalism that occurs at the intersection between journalism and data technology, automated journalism transforms data into news stories by programmed algorithms. In this view, the Associated Press uses the term "augmented journalism" to describe the journalism under the influences of MGC (Marconi et al., 2017).

9.2.1.1 An Overview of Automated Journalism

The beginning of news automation may date back to half a century ago, when the weather forecasts were successfully generated by computer, indicating future possibilities for using automated structured reports (Glahn, 1970). Similar to the template-based software commonly used in automated journalism today, those automated weather news were composed by pre-written statements according to a set of weather forecasting models.

High quality and structured data is the primary requirement for automated journalism (Graefe, 2016). Available with accurate data such as company's revenue and stock prices, finance becomes another domain that utilizes MGC for news production. Since the July of 2014, the Associated Press became the first world-class news agency to automate its quarterly financial reporting by using WordSmith, a **natural language generation (NLG)**

NLG

The software or computer system that automatically transforms digital structured data into natural spoken or written language.

---

[1] Generative Pre-trained Transformer 3, an autoregressive language model that uses deep learning to produce human-like text created by OpenAI (a San Francisco-based AI research laboratory) in 2020.

platform that transforms data into insightful narrative. Now, its smart writing system can automatically produce up to 4,400 earnings reports each quarter, 15 times more efficient than human journalists.[1]

In current applications, MGC has also found its way into newsrooms to address other problems including sports news and reporting on sudden events. An important example is the work at the *Los Angeles Times* on automating earthquake reporting. At 6: 25 am on March 17, 2014, Los Angeles was hit by an earthquake, and three minutes later, the *Los Angeles Times* became the first outlet to report the quake online by Quakebot, a software application developed by programmer Ken Schwencke. According to Schwencke, the underlying logic of Quakebot is extremely simple—sort, classify, associate and filter massive data through algorithms, then adapt and combine the sorted data into corresponding article template (see Case 1 for more details). Schwencke's design is a prominent step for the application of MGC in journalism, showing that simple customized algorithms can effectively promote the speed and breadth of news coverage (Graefe, 2016). Since then, MGC has taken major steps foreword (Kotenidis & Veglis, 2021).

To sum up, automated journalism has been widely used in the domains of weather, finance, sports, and sudden events. With relatively stable writing style and structure, these routine tasks can usually provide reliable, clean and structured data resources (Graefe, 2016), and in practice, they have shown obvious advantages, including faster writing speed with significantly increasing number of news reports and lower probability in making an error, especially the same error occurred before (Huang, 2017). In China, on September 10, 2015, a report entitled "The CPI rose by 2.0% in August for the first time in 12 months" was generated and published online by Tencent Dreamwriter. Following Tencent's step, other domestic media outlets have launched their own MGC applications, including Xiaomingbot from TouTiao, "Kuai Bi Xiao Xin" from the Xinhua News Agency, "DT Gao Wang" from China Business Network, etc. In addition, AI-based platforms such as Wibbitz are already able to convert texts directly into short videos, enhancing the variety and content diversity of news report, freeing journalists from the tedious tasks and leaving time for creative work.

9. 2. 1. 2 The Procedure in News Automation

To help the public understand how auto-writing algorithms work, in 2014, Tow Center for Digital Journalism of Columbia Journalism School carried out an "anatomy" of the robot-writer from Narrative Science, and proposed a "pipeline"[2] for robot journalists. Based on the five-step

---

1 Retrieved from https://automatedinsights.com/customer-stories/associated-press/.
2 The pipeline for robot journalists includes: (1) ingest data, (2) compute newsworthy aspects of the data, (3) identify relevant angles and prioritize them, (4) link angles to story points, and (5) generate the output text.

pipeline from Tow Center and the MGC models illustrated in the studies of Dörr (2015) and Graefe (2016), the whole procedure of automated journalism is summarized as follows.

(1) Data Collection

Data collection is the pre-step of content production. In the era of intelligent media, AI has overturned the traditional way in gathering information, and all intelligent terminals may become information gatherers and disseminators (Xie & Zhang, 2020). Therefore, data can be accessed via both public sources (e.g., the environmental data collected by GPS) and private sources (e.g., personal health status collected by smart wearable devices), ranging from pre-defined data to historical data, new data and context data (Graefe , 2016). And as mentioned earlier, the key drivers for automated journalism is clean and comprehensive data, and therefore, the domains with limited structured data and sparse access are challenging.

(2) Data Processing

Then, algorithms read the data and employ statistical approaches to compute news worthiness. In most cases, the software monitors compare historical data to identify the most important and interesting features of the data. For example, if a stock price is much higher or lower than expected, then this data would be considered to have high news worthiness, regardless of how this expectation is derived (Deng, 2016). Next, the algorithms classify and prioritize the identified data by importance and arrange those "story points" by following pre-defined rules for a certain topic.

(3) Narrative Generation

In the last step, the storyline and news structure are further specified (Graefe, 2016), followed by NLG, the most straightforward but technical aspect of the entire procedure (Deng, 2016). Specifically, content generation routines such as lexical choice, **referring expression generation** and syntactic choice (Dörr, 2015), are used to compose and produce the actual narrative for optimizing MGC from a natural language perspective, to make the algorithmically generated text more readable. After the process of NLG, stories are finally published online or offline through the **content management system** either automatically or under editorial review (Graefe, 2016).

Referring Expression Generation

A sub-field of NLG, focusing on generating referring expressions that identify specific target entities (e.g., a particular person, place or thing).

Content Management System

A computer software used to help news organizations and individuals to create, edit and publish digital content.

9.2.2　Intelligent Recommendation

In 2022 China Internet Network Information Center (CNNIC) released the 49th "Statistical Report on Internet Development in China"[1]. According to the report, by December 2021, China's Internet users has reached one billion, occupying 73.0 % of the total population. Increasing number of netizens not only leads to the reshaping of the media pattern, but also brings profound changes to the social information environment, among which the most prominent one is the so-called information overload problem, which refers to the difficulty to locate the right information effectively in understanding an issue or making a decision from excessive quantity of print, online or digital resources.

Recommender systems emerged as an independent discipline in the mid-1990s, when researchers started to develop new approaches to predict the needs of users and deal with information overload (Liu, 2017). The underlying formulation of recommender systems can be reduced to the process of predicting **ratings** for the items that are unknown to a user (Adomavicius et al., 2005). Recommendations of items can be made to a particular group of users by selecting the item with highest rating among all estimated ratings for those users, alternatively, a set of users recommended to a particular item. Recommendation algorithms from various research fields such as machine learning, information retrieval and various heuristics are employed to estimate ratings in different application scenarios. On the basis of recommendation techniques, recommendation systems can be roughly divided into three groups: content-based recommendation, collaborative recommendation and hybrid recommendation (Adomavicius et al., 2005; Liu, 2017; Sharma et al., 2021).

Rating

The utility of an item in recommender system, indicating how a particular user likes a particular item (Adomavicius et al., 2005).

(1) Content-Based Recommendation

Content-based recommendation is a classifier system with its roots in information retrieval and information filtering. In content-based recommendation systems, profiling information is created to characterize the attributes of each user and item (Shu et al., 2018). Users' profile including tastes, preferences and needs is often obtained by analyzing their previous behavior, while an item profile (e.g., genre,

Content-Based Recommendation

The approach of making recommendations by estimating users' preferences based on their earlier preferred items.

1　Retrieved from http://www.cnnic.net.cn/hlwfzyj/hlwxzbg/hlwtjbg/202202/P020220721404263787858.pdf.

topic, popularity or release date) is usually computed by extracting a set of features from it. If the profile of candidate items best-match the tastes of a user, then these items would be recommended. To put it simply, items similar to those that a user liked in the past are recommended. For example, if a user reads many books on the topic of AI, then content-based recommendation will be able to recommend science fictions for the user.

Pure content-based system relies solely on profile information to make recommendations and therefore has its own limitations (Adomavicius et al., 2005). First, in order to obtain sufficient profile information, the items are always in the form of text-based content (e.g., documents, websites and news messages) as the computer system works well in extracting profiles from textual information automatically. But for the multimedia resources in the formats of image, audio and video, their attributes should be assigned manually due to the limited content analysis of information retrieval techniques. The second problem of content-based recommendation is that the user would never receive a recommendation for an item that dissimilar to those seen in the past or the user would be recommended something that is almost the same as seen before. New user problem is the third problem for content-based systems. Because the users' tastes are predicted on the basis of previously rated-items, recommendations for new users who have few ratings are unreliable and inappropriate.

(2) Collaborative Recommendation

There are three methods in collaborative recommendation: user-based, item-based and model-based. User-based algorithm assumes that it is a good way to predict the target user's preferences based on the similar users. Therefore, in order to find recommended items, user-based algorithm should find the neighbor users who are similar to the target users first (Gong, 2010). Item-based approach looks into the items that have already been rated by a target user and assumes that the user is going to like the items similar to the highly-rated items. Amazon's recommendation system is a typical application of item-based collaborative recommendation. Different from the above two memory-based algorithms, model-based algorithm aggregates the data about users' previously rated items to learn a model by using machine learning techniques, and then the model is used to make recommendation predictions.

Collaborative Recommendation

A memory-based or a model-based approach of making recommendations to users on the basis of the items previously rated by other users.

Collaborative recommenders tackle some of the challenges arising in content-based recommenders since other users' ratings have been taken into consideration in these systems. However, it suffers from three major problems: cold start problem, sparsity and scalability (Gong,

2010; Sharma et al., 2022). Cold start problem, including new user problem and new item problem, occurs when there are few ratings from a new user or of a new item. Sparsity occurs when the user-item rating matrix is sparse, and insufficient number of ratings may lead to less accuracy. Scalability is a critical challenge for collaborative recommendation. Growing number of users and items in the database increases the time and cost of computation, thus an ever-improving computation power is required.

(3) Hybrid Recommendation

Due to limited content analysis, overspecialization and new user problem in content-based approach, as well as cold start problem, sparsity and scalability in collaborative approach, hybrid recommendation is a combination of content-based and collaborative recommendation, in hoping to relieve the problems of the two systems. Scholars have summarized four different ways in combining these two systems: (1) combing separate recommenders and their predictions; (2) adding content-based characteristics to collaborative approach; (3) adding collaborative characteristics to content-based approach; (4) developing a single unifying recommendation model that incorporates both systems (Adomavicius et al., 2005). Although there are few content distribution platforms relying solely on one single system, most platforms are dominated by one system (Brennan, 2020). Douyin is an excellent example that incorporates content-based approach into the collaborative filtering algorithms (see Case 2 for more details).

Hybrid Recommendation

A combination of content-based recommendation and collaborative recommendation that tries to better meet users' needs.

9.2.3 Extended Reality

Remarkable advances in digital technologies and AI completely change how people experience the world. Any technology that augments or alters the way we encounter people or objects in the real environment could be considered as a supplement or extension to the physical world (Greengard, 2019). More formally, it could be defined as "extended reality", including **augmented reality (AR), virtual reality (VR), and mixed reality (MR)**. If VR is de-

AR

An enhanced version of reality where the objects that reside in the real world are enhanced by overlaying digital content on top of a physical environment.

VR

The experience where users feel they are immersed in a simulated world through multiple sensorial channels.

MR

A hybrid of AR and VR settings, in which physical reality and virtual content are blended to enable interaction between the real world and the virtual world.

scribed as an immersive experience, then AR could be an augmented experience, and MR is a blend of the elements in AR and VR.

Unlike the Web 1.0 age featured by one-way communication through traditional mass media, and the Web 2.0 age characterized by two-way interaction through the Internet, immersive communication emerges as the new communication paradigm (Li & Xiong, 2013). With the support of technical breakthroughs such as 5G networks, AR, VR and MR are able to unleash their full potential (Yu et al., 2020), driving people into the new media age.

9.2.3.1 Augmented Reality (AR)

The concept of AR was first proposed by Boeing researcher Thomas Caudell in 1990. AR technology tries to restore reality by introducing multiple layers of digital information to refine the real objects and achieve a seamless connection between the virtual and the real (Shi & Zhang, 2016). "Situated documentary", an immersive narrative system developed by Columbia University in 1999, is an early attempt of using AR as a storytelling medium for journalism. Based on the methods of overlaying 3D computer graphics and sounds onto the real world, "Situated Documentary" works like a tour guide, through which the imagery of the building presented on a head-worn display as the user walks up to it, and an overview of important events that happened in the surrounding environment are displayed in a hand-held computer when the user gazes at or approaches a particular building (Höllerer et al., 1999).

In 2010, newspaper such as *USA Today* and *The Boston Globe* started to adopt an AR browser called Junaio, then *The New York Times* and *The Wall Street Journal* also followed with Aurasma, an AR platform created by the software company Autonomy (Zhang, 2015). In 2012, *Chengdu Business Daily* released an AR mobile app—PaiPai Dong, becoming the first media outlet in China to adopt AR technology. These apps created an enhanced version of reality, and enriched user's experience through multi-sensory input, thus restoring news events more realistically and building a bridge between the limited reality world and the infinite virtual world.

Similarly, on the TV side, American Broadcasting Company (ABC) has used 360-degree video to broadcast the 2018 US presidential midterm elections, enabling the audience to simultaneously learn about the real-time progress of the results while watching ABC experts on the set, and CCTV has made several attempts to use AR techniques in the live coverage of 2016 G20 Hangzhou Summit and other important events. As creative technologist Rex Sorgatz points out, "We have moved passed the era of big data into a period of deep exploration."[1] Under the influence of AR technology, news media is gradually transforming from "narrator" to "aggrega-

---

1 Retrieved from https://medium.com/message/surfing-drowning-diving-122612314fa8.

tor" and from "notepad" to "database" (Shi & Zhang, 2016).

9.2.3.2 Virtual Reality (VR)

Although the term "virtual reality" was first introduced by American computer scientist Jaron Lanier in 1987, the history of VR can be traced back to the 1830s, when stereoscopes were used to create a 3D view of objects (Gu, 2018). Since its introduction, VR has been an ambiguous term, but now, it most often denotes the use of 360-degree videos, 3D models, head-mounted displays, haptics devices, trackers, etc. Apart from allowing people to step outside the physical environment as in the AR scenario, VR technology tries to bring humans into an immersive digital world (Greengard, 2019), and it is valued for its ability to elicit greater empathy, emotion, and understanding from humans.

VR is highly regarded for its unique advantages of creating a realistic-looking world, and has been widely used in journalism, literature, arts, games, movies, stage plays, exhibitions, and other media practices. In the field of journalism, *The Des Moines Register* (a local newspaper owned by Gannett Corporation) first used VR technology in a special interactive project "Harvest of Change", in which viewers were presented with the changes of a local Iowa farm family in the United States. Since then, media outlets such as *Frontline*[1] and *The New York Times*[2] have also begun using 360-degree live action to report news. Scholars have summarized the core features of VR technology as "3I", namely immersion, imagination and interaction (Burdea & Coiffet, 2003). We can also detect these three core features in VR news.

(1) Immersion. The narrative logic of VR news comes from the viewers' perspective, where they are no longer "outsiders", but are at the center of the news event (Yu & Zhang, 2016). With the help of VR technology, people are allowed to maximize their sensory experience and accomplish an immersive "presence".

(2) Imagination. On the one hand, VR journalism requires the VR developers' imagination to provide solutions to the real problems in news production (Burdea & Coiffet, 2003). On the other hand, the immersive quality of VR news allows the audience to freely imagine their own news stories (Jones, 2017).

(3) Interaction. Compared to traditional journalism, VR journalism achieves a more interactive approach in which audience actively request and seek information. VR news not only gives the audience greater autonomy, triggering the "empathy", but also shortens the distance

---

1 *Frontline* magazine released its first newsreel in September 2015, using VR technology to tell the story of how the Ebola virus is spreading and wreaking havoc in Africa.
2 On November 7, 2015, *The New York Times* produced VR newsreel "The Displaced", in which the difficult lives of child refugees were explored through the stories of three children.

between journalists and the audience.

9. 2. 3. 3 Mixed Reality (MR)

While VR/AR technologies are evolving rapidly, MR technologies are gaining importance in the field of extended reality. Unlike AR, which mainly refers to the digital images superimposed on the real world, and VR, which creates a completely virtual environment, MR is able to digitize the physical environment, while retaining its authenticity, so that the real and the virtual are intertwined. MR users may not be able to distinguish between what is real and what is virtual, as if they have entered a new hybrid world.

MR aims to connect humans with the virtual world and the real world simultaneously, so that people can return to the original sensory channels and intuitively understand the real world and the virtual world by forming a human-computer interaction interface where "what you see is what you get" (Chen & Qin, 2016). At present, the application of MR in the media field focuses on virtual performances. For example, in 2020, the live performance of new product launch of the OPPO Reno 4 series used MR technology to present fantastic interaction effects between the virtual and the real.

In general, extended reality is not a simplistic concept and there is no single or paradigmatic type of AR/VR/MR system (Biocca, 1992). Instead, it comprises a wide variety of technologies and devices that reaches every corner between the real and the virtual world. Designing and developing these technologies to realize seamless experience is the core mission for AR/VR/MR research (Greengard, 2019). However, as the technology continues to evolve, the ethical risks it poses are increasingly concerned. Avoiding turning the "public" into the "crowd" or even into "brains in a tubs" has become the research focus of deep immersion (Deng, 2016).

9. 3 Case Study

9. 3. 1 Case 1: Quakebot: Automated Earthquake Reports

Since automated journalism is objective, efficient, and it never forgets facts or gets tired, Latar (2014) foresees that "the new leader of the newsroom will not be the experienced journalist, but the computer engineer". For sudden events like earthquake, the reporting speed is the first priority. If the underlying data are available, real-time reports can be generated automatically and presented to the public as soon as possible. Here, we start from the case of Quakebot from the *Los Angeles Times* to explain the inner logic of how to give an efficient and accurate earthquake report.

As early as 2011, the *Los Angeles Times* began the project of Quakebot, a news robot that can write earthquake-related news as fast as possible. As mentioned above, Quakebot first got the public attention on March 17, 2014, when it automatically generated a news brief three minutes after an earthquake, beating other news outlets such as *Los Angeles Daily News* and *Los Angeles Weekly*. The initial Quakebot report wrote[1]:

A shallow magnitude 4.7 earthquake was reported Monday morning five miles from Westwood, California, according to the U.S. Geological Survey. The temblor occurred at 6:25 a.m. Pacific time at a depth of 5.0 miles.

According to the USGS, the epicenter was six miles from Beverly Hills, California, seven miles from Universal City, California, seven miles from Santa Monica, California and 348 miles from Sacramento, California. In the past ten days, there have been no earthquakes magnitude 3.0 and greater centered nearby.

This information comes from the USGS Earthquake Notification Service and this post was created by an algorithm written by the author.

The data of this report came from the US Geological Survey's (USGS) Earthquake Notification Service. Once USGS released an earthquake alert, Quakebot received information through an pre-set algorithm, in which relevant data (e.g., location, time and magnitude of the earthquake) were automatically entered into a template to create a draft in the content management system of the *Los Angeles Times*. Then, the draft was reviewed by an editor to avoid potential mistakes before the final publication. To sum up, Quakebot does not have its own earthquake detection system; it relies on the USGS statewide network of geological sensors to detect earthquake-related information. When the USGS detects an earthquake above 1.0 magnitude, Quakebot is notified and generates a story immediately. If an earthquake is predicted to cause significant damage, the editor would add more background and other relevant information on the top of the information provided by Quakebot.

However, the news robot may also provide incorrect earthquake information. Researchers attribute the problem of false alarms to the USGS, since its seismologic sensors may incorrectly identify earthquakes. In 2015, for example, the USGS sensors misidentified earthquakes that struck off the coasts of Japan and Alaska and mistakenly reported them as three separate earthquakes in California. The editor of the *Los Angeles Times* failed to find the error and directly

---

1 Retrieved from https://slate.com/technology/2014/03/quakebot-los-angeles-times-robot-journalist-writes-article-on-la-earthquake.html.

published these three machine-generated reports.

Earle et al. (2011) from the USGS propose a simple way to check the accuracy of earthquake reports by referring to the number of related tweets (postings uploaded to the social networking service Twitter). It is found that the Twitter users will upload the information of earthquake immediately after they experience the shaking, the first tweet sometimes appearing even faster than official seismographic detection, especially for poorly instrumented areas (Earle et al., 2011). Therefore, the number of postings made on social networking platforms is creating a separate data source to verify the correctness of the location, magnitude and other information in automated earthquake reports. Now the USGS updates the number of Twitter postings per minute that contain the word "earthquake" to its Twitter account, and news outlets like the *Los Angeles Times* could add this Twitter earthquake detection into their bots' algorithms (Graefe, 2016).

9. 3. 2 Case 2: Douyin: Intelligent Recommendation for Short Video

Intelligent recommendation is a promising method to help enterprises provide personalized advertisements, news articles, books, movies and other items for customers. Algorithmic recommendation is one of ByteDance's core technologies and the key to its success. Douyin (known as TikTok outside Chinese mainland), is a mobile short video platform launched by ByteDance in September, 2016. It hosts miscellaneous short-form videos that cover all areas of interests, ranging from vlog, news briefing to advertisements and self-made sitcoms with the duration from 15 seconds to 15 minutes. Douyin has gained a massive popularity over the past few years and is recently emerging as one of the world's leading video-sharing platforms. According to "2020 Douyin Data Report"[1], as of August 2020 Douyin's daily active users (DAU) have exceeded 600 million, making it the largest short video platform in China. On the Chinese New Year's Eve of 2021, Douyin's DAU reached a peak of nearly 700 million, accounting for 50% of China's total population.[2] To understand how Douyin attracts users and maintains user stickness, this part carries out an in-depth examination of its recommendation system. Based on the widely used intelligent recommendation algorithms, there are mainly three recommendation patterns in Douyin.

(1) Persona-Based Collaborative Recommendation

Persona refers to the fictional description of users' behavior, experience and goals (Cooper, 1999). In order to understand users' needs and expectations, collaborative filtering algorithms

---
1 Retrieved from https://www.sohu.com/a/442893269_441449.
2 Retrieved from https://new.qq.com/rain/a/20210329A06EP300.

of Douyin create personas on the basis of users' demographic features (e.g., sex, age, income, education, employment, etc.) and their previous engagement with other posts, such as the the number of likes, shares, reposts and comments for videos on different topics. When a new user completes the sign up for Douyin account and logs in through mobile phone numbers or other third-party accounts, the recommendation system quickly process the existing data and estimates the user's basic information. Then, collaborative algorithms screen out the videos that are liked by other similar users, and the videos that receive most clicks and comments are promoted to the homepage. To minimize the risk of cold-start problem, the algorithms will update the users' profile in real time on the basis of their latest viewing behavior. As users spend longer time in Douyin, the algorithms will understand them better (Zhao, 2021).

(2) Decentralized Recommendation

In the era of digital media, users are changing from passive receivers or consumers of information to active content producers and distributors (Han, 2017). Douyin shares videos in a decentralized manner (Brennan, 2020), that is, every user is an independent creator and every post has an equal chance to be viewed. The decentralized algorithms of Douyin work on the basis of strong social networks and weak social networks (Zhao et al., 2019; Ding, 2021; Xu et al., 2022). Strong social networks are often detected when users constantly interact with their close friends, families, colleagues or classmates. The more interactions a user has with a friend, the more likely Douyin is to recommend what the friend likes to the user. By contrast, although there is limited or even no interaction in weak social networks, the algorithms make full of the search history and user habits to predict the preferences and tastes of the users, and recommend the videos created by other users who have similar occupation, hobbies or interests.

(3) Multi-layer Recommendation

Once a video is uploaded, Douyin carries out a series of multi-layer recommendation processes. First, the video is automatically reviewed by a preset model. If the video is suspected of violating the platform's content guidelines, detailed manual reviews will be conducted. After the first screening process, key elements of the video are extracted and tagged with keywords. Then, the categorized video is released to a small pool of a few hundred active users. Parameters such as the number of clicks, likes, shares, comments, average play length and completion rates are analyzed to gauge the video's popularity within its vertical category (the style/topic to which the video belongs). Douyin will stop the recommendation if a video got poor feedback, by contrast, the video with active feedback overflows into a medium pool with thousands of active users. Again, more strict filtering processes are carried out, passing the video with the top-performance to the large pool, where it gains exposure to potentially millions of users. In general, this multi-layer recommendation mechanism is an effective method to guarantee the popularity of the content.

While recommendation algorithms have brought us great convenience, problems including privacy invasion, **information cocoons** and algorithm bias also cause trouble. Thus, in January 2022, four departments[1] in China issued "Regulations on the Management of Algorithm Recommendation of Internet Information Services"[2], which emphasizes users' right to know and choose recommendation algorithms. All Internet companies that provide algorithmic recommendation services, as prescribed by regulations, should provide users with options that are not based on their personal characteristics and allow users to turn off personalized recommendations with one click. This will undoubtedly bring uncertainty to the development of the social platforms that highly rely on intelligent recommendation.

Information Cocoon

A communication environment where people tend to hear only what they want to hear, and choose only what comforts and pleases them (Sunstein, 2006), just like silkworms making cocoons for themselves.

9.3.3 Case 3: Motion-Driven VUPs and Data-Based Virtual Anchors

Now, extended reality technologies create the digital representation of humans, who are reshaping the way we communicate and how we get information. Since the Press Association, a UK news agency, launched the first virtual newscaster "Ananova" in 2000, virtual humans have emerged around the world by employing various kinds of AR/VR/MR techniques in different scenarios. At present, the most common AI characters are motion-driven virtual uploaders and data-based virtual anchors.

9.3.3.1 Motion-Driven Virtual Uploaders

Virtual uploader (VUP), the newest form of Internet celebrity, has engaged in creative activities such as live-steaming, online interaction and video sharing on platforms like Bilibili, YouTube and Twitch. In most cases, VUPs are 2D or 3D virtual animated characters generated by capturing the facial expressions and body movements of a real human, who is known as "Nakanohito" (『中の人』) in Japanese. In

Avatar

A concept derives from Sanskrit word "avatāra", specifically referring to the incarnation of a deity on earth. In extended reality, an avatar is a digital representation of a person, or the person's character/persona in the virtual world.

---
1 They are: Cyberspace Administration of China, Ministry of Industry and Information Technology of the People's Republic of China, Ministry of Public Security of the People's Republic of China, and State Administration for Market Regulation.
2 Retrieved from http://www.cac.gov.cn/2022-01/04/c_1642894606364259.htm.

this view, it can be said that VUPs are the **avatars** of actual live streamers. Just like real people; they read and respond to viewers' comments in real time, however, the real identity of VUPs is not disclosed to the audience, and the audience always identify VUPs as virtual characters rather than the real persons.

On November 29, 2016, Kizuna AI[1], the first virtual uploader with a mature operation model released her first video on YouTube, officially establishing the concept of VUP. After that, Mirai Akari, Siro and other VUPs emerged one after another, spreading the culture of VUPs to Chinese video platforms. At this time, the virtual anchor mainly adopts video activities, similar to the virtual characters in Japanese animation. With the growing popularity of motion capture software on smartphones such as Animoji, the threshold for live streaming of VUPs has been lowered. At the same time, the number and popularity of VUPs have seen explosive growth and the emergence of well-known projects such as Hololive and Nijisanji has transformed the way of interaction between virtual anchors and audiences from "posting videos" to more efficient "virtual live stream".

In 2019, Nijisanji and Bilibili, a very popular video platform among Generation Z and Millennials in China (Bredikhina, 2020), released a virtual uploader project named VirtuaReal, which leads to the further development of the local VUP industry in China. A year later, Yuehua Entertainment and Nuverse of ByteDance jointly launched a five-member virtual girl idol group, A-SOUL[2]. As the first VUP program established and operated by a real company, A-SOUL made virtual live-streams on Bilibili or Douyin, and quickly attracted a large group of audience and set new highs in viewership and number of subscribers. The development of VUPs is shown in the following table.

The Development of VUPs

Time	Issue
December 1, 2016	Kizuna AI released a self-introduction video, marking the establishment of the VUP/VTuber concept and the beginning of the culture.
August 12, 2017	Bilibili's first VUP Xiaoxi released her first video.
February to October, 2018	The number of VUPs has expanded from less than 50 to more than 5,000 with the burgeoning of VUP agencies such as Nijisanji and Hololive.

1　キズナアイ, A female Japanese VUP (also known as a VTuber because she is primarily active on YouTube). Kizuna AI officially debuted on December 1, 2016 (her first video was released on November 29, 2016). On December 4, during her fifth anniversary stream, she announced an indefinite hiatus following her "hello, world 2022" concert on February 26, 2022.

2　A five-member female VUP group consisting of Ava, Bella, Carol, Diana and Eileen. They debuted in November, 2020. Nuverse is responsible for their underlying technical support, and Yuehua Entertainment is responsible for their content planning and operation.

Continued

Time	Issue
January 7, 2019	Hololive cooperated with Bilibili to station all of its VUPs, setting off a boom of overseas VUP/VTuber in Bilibili.
April 19, 2019	Bilibili and Nijisanji partnered to launch the VirtuaReal program to develop recruitment plans for local VUPs.
November 23, 2020	Yuehua Entertainment announced the establishment of VUP group A-SOUL.
January, 2022	A-SOUL members Diana and Carol became the top 100 uploaders of Bilibili.

Currently, Bilibili becomes a center for VUPs in China and has attracted many VUPs who already have a large group of followers on foreign video platforms. By November 2, 2021, there had been 3,606 VUPs on Bilibili, including over 170 new VUPs added in one year, and 39 VUPs with more than 500,000 followers, and from January 2020 to September 2021, the overall revenue of VUPs increased at an average monthly growth rate of 10%.[1] The number of paid viewers and the total number of bullet screens of the VUPs on Bilibili also showed a steady increase over time. According to the "Report on the Development of China's Virtual Human Industry in 2022" released by iMedia (a consulting company), the overall market size and core market size driven by China's virtual humans were said to be CNY 107.49 billion yuan ($16 billion) and CNY 6.22 billion yuan ($ 0.93 billion), respectively.[2]

9.3.3.2 Data-Based Virtual Anchors

The production of VUPs based on motion capture technology still relies heavily on the real human, so that it is impossible for VUP projects to be released automatically on a large scale, or to be used in daily news broadcast. However, the comprehensive and in-depth application of AI technologies have given virtual humans the ability to "interpret external data correctly, to learn from such data, and to use those learnings to achieve specific goals and tasks through flexible adaptation" (Kaplan & Haenlein, 2019). Thus, we get another type of virtual humans, data-based virtual anchors.

Virtual anchor is developed based on the technical breakthroughs in natural human-computer interaction and knowledge computing (Li & Mao, 2019), and there are mainly three technical dimensions: text, voice and image. The "text" refers to the machine-generated content—through big data and algorithms, virtual anchors can achieve the automation of text writing; the "voice" refers to the audible language expression—through recognizing and learning the language expression habits of real anchors, virtual anchors can form a voice with no difference from the real one; the "image" refers to the appearance of the anchor—by "cloning" the expres-

---

[1] Retrieved from https://www.thepaper.cn/newsDetail_forward_18022449.
[2] Retrived from https://report.iimedia.cn/repo13-0/43198.html?acPlatCode=bj&acFrom=bg43198.

sions and lip shapes of the real anchor, people can see a virtual anchor as real as possible (Zhou & Hao, 2022).

Compared with motion-driven virtual uploaders, data-based virtual anchors emerged later. Initially, such anchors were still portrayed as 3D animated characters that could not replicate the facial features of real people. In November 2018, Xinhua News Agency and Sogou jointly released the world's first synthetic news anchor "Xinxiaohao" (modelled on the host Qiu Hao) at the Fifth World Internet Conference. Xinxiaohao and another virtual anchor Xinxiaomeng (modelled on the hostess Qu Meng) express, move and speak similarly to their prototypes. Different from real anchors, they can provide news broadcasting services 24 hours, all year round, or appear on different websites to broadcast information simultaneously. Their appearances in the coverage of important events such as the Spring Festival travel rush have received widespread attention from domestic media.

Data-based virtual anchors have also gained high attention from foreign media. For example, the ROK's MBN TV launched an AI anchor modelled on its news anchor Kim Joo-ha in 2020, and it is said that the virtual anchor can generate a 1,000-word news broadcast in one minute; the British Reuters News Agency developed the world's first automated presenter-led video sports report based on its editor Ossian Shine... In addition to traditional newscasts, data-based virtual anchors are also used in other audiovisual media such as chat apps and TV shows, breaking the inherent model of interpersonal communication to a certain extent.

To add with, virtual humans cannot be easily distinguished as motion-driven or data-based, and there are some avatars that fall in between, such as the virtual singers represented by Hatsune Miku[1]. The creator should first sample voices of real singers/voice actors from a voicebank, and use the singing voice synthesizer software, such as Vocaloid to synthesize "singing" by entering lyrics and melodies, so as to form the voices of virtual singers, and then make them "appear" on stage through stage projection technology. Thus, the synthetic process of virtual singers is the combination of a fully physically driven VUP and a fully technologically synthesized virtual anchor.

---

[1] 初音ミク, a female Japanese VUP with a voicebank developed by Crypton Future Media and anthropomorphic images. Its original audio data was sampled from Japanese voice actress Saki Fujita and synthesized by Vocaloid. She is also the first virtual singer in the world to hold a concert using holographic projection technology.

9.4 Conclusion

"AI + media" is an important means for the transformation of traditional media and the rise of new media. New media formats and models such as machine generated content, intelligent recommendation and artificial anchors are constantly emerging. In content production, intelligent techniques have already infiltrated in the whole procedure of automated journalism from data collection, data processing to content generation. At present, automated journalism is mainly used for generating weather forecasts, sports coverage, financial reports and news on sudden events, all of which are objective reports with plenty of accurate and structured data. In terms of content distribution, algorithmic recommendation solves the problem of information overloading and recommends personalized content for users through content-based recommendation, collaborative recommendation and hybrid recommendation. Apart from freeing humans from repetitive and tedious work, AI also helps to bridge the physical and digital realms through extended reality technologies. Trough AR/VR/MR techniques, AI extends and changes the way people experience the world, creating a fascinating, immersive, imaginative and interactive VR world for human beings.

At the same time, intelligent media industry also faces many ethical challenges. Algorithms and other AI technologies are difficult to describe or understand for the ordinary users, but they are widely influencing the way people access information and services through platforms such as Douyin, Toutiao and Xiaohongshu. By the end of 2021, the Internet Development Research Center of Peking University and 360 Group jointly released the "Report on China's Great Security Perception" (2021), showing that 70% of the respondents felt that algorithms can manipulate their opinions by gaining access to their preferences and interests, 60% were concerned about revealing personal information, and nearly half said they would like to escape the Internet and stay away from their phones when feeling constrained by algorithms. Therefore, in the era of AI, ethical challenges faced in the traditional media industry, such as the objectivity and impartiality of news reporting, personal privacy and copyright issue, still have important research value.

9.5 Extended Readings

Scan the QR code to get extended reading materials.

9.6 Post Questions and Discussion

(1) Have you ever read any automated news before? If the credibility of MGC is equal to human-written news, would you prefer to read an automated news report? Why?

(2) Do you always receive too similar or uninteresting recommendations on short video platforms like Douyin and Xiaohongshu? What will make you opt out the customized recommendation function on these apps?

(3) Will you be the follower of a virtual VUP who can fit all your imagined ideals? What would you like to get from following the virtual idol?

9.7 Bibliography

Adomavicius, G., Tuzhilin, A. (2005). Toward the Next Generation of Recommender Systems: A Survey of the State-of-the-Art and Possible Extensions. *IEEE Transactions on Knowledge and Data Engineering*, 17(6): 734-749.

Ali, W., Hassoun, M. (2019). Artificial Intelligence and Automated Journalism: Contemporary Challenges and New Opportunities. *International Journal of Media, Journalism and Mass Communications*, 5(1): 40-49. http://dx.doi.org/10.20431/2454-9479.0501004.

Biocca, F. (1992). Virtual Reality Technology: A Tutorial. *Journal of Communication*, 42(4): 23-72. https://doi.org/10.1111/j.1460-2466.1992.tb00811.x.

Burdea, G. C., Coiffet, P. (2003). *Virtual Reality Technology.* Hoboken: John Wiley & Sons.

Chen, B. Q., Qin, X. Y. (2016). Composition of Virtual-Real Worlds and Intelligence Integration of Human-Computer in Mixed Reality. *Scientia Sinica (Informationis)*, 46(12): 1737-1747.

Clerwall, C. (2014). Enter the Robot Journalist: Users' Perceptions of Automated Content. *Journalism Practice*, 8(5): 519-531. https://doi.org/10.1080/17512786.2014.883116.

Cooper, A. (1999). *The Inmates Are Running the Ssylum.* Indianapolis: SAMS/Macmillan.

Earle, P. S., Bowden, D., & Guy, M. (2011). Twitter Earthquake Detection: Earthquake Monitoring in a Social World. *Annals of Geophysics*, 54(6): 708-715. https://doi.org/10.3929/ethz-b-000364555.

Deng, J. G. (2016). Robot Journalism: Principles, Risks and Implications. *Shanghai Jour-*

nalism Review, (09): 10-17.

Dick, S. (2019). Artificial Intelligence. *Harvard Data Science Review*, 1(1). https://doi.org/10.1162/99608f92.92fe150c.

Ding, H. R. (2021). Research on the Intelligent Algorithmic Mechanism and the Problems of Douyin. *New Media Research*, 7(10): 10-12.

Dörr, K. N. (2015). Mapping the Field of Algorithmic Journalism. *Digital Journalism*, 4 (6): 700-722. https://doi.org/10.1080/21670811.2015.1096748.

Glahn, H. R. (1970). Computer-Produced Worded Forecasts. *Bulletin of the American Meteorological Society*, 51(12): 1126-1132. https://doi.org/10.1175/1520-0477(1970)051%3C1126:CPWF%3E2.0.CO;2.

Grace, K., Salvatier, J., Dafoe, A., Zhang, B., & Evans, O. (2018). When Will AI Exceed Human Performance? Evidence from AI Experts. *Journal of Artificial Intelligence Research*, 62: 729-754. https://doi.org/10.1613/jair.1.11222.

Greengard, S. (2019). *Virtual Reality*. Cambridge: MIT Press.

Groner, R., Groner, M., & Bischof, W. F. (1983). The Role of Heuristics in Models of Decision. *Advances in Psychology*, (16): 87-108.

Gu, J. Z. (2018). VR, AR and MR-Challenges and Opportunities. *Computer Applications and Software*, 35(03): 1-7, 14.

Haenlein, M., Kaplan, A. (2019). A Brief History of Artificial Intelligence: On the Past, Present, and Future of Artificial Intelligence. *California Management Review*, 61(4): 5-14. https://doi.org/10.1177/0008125619864925.

Han, B. (2017). *In the Swarm: Digital Prospects*. Cambridge: MIT Press.

Hollerer, T., Feiner, S., & Pavlik, J. (1999). Situated Documentaries: Embedding Multimedia Presentations in the Real World. In IEEE, Digest of Papers, Third International Symposium on Wearable Computers (pp.79-86).

Huang, Y. L. (2017). From Mass Media to Personalized Media: The Impact of AI Technology on News Production. *China Publishing Journal*, 24. 9-12.

Jones, S. (2017). Disrupting the Narrative: Immersive Journalism in Virtual Reality. *Journal of Media Practice*, 18(2-3): 171-185.

Kaplan, A., Haenlein, M. (2019). Siri, Siri, in my Hand: Who's the Fairest in the Land? On the Interpretations, Illustrations, and Implications of Artificial Intelligence. *Business Horizons*, 62(1): 15-25. https://doi.org/10.1016/j.bushor.2018.08.004.

Kotenidis, E., Veglis, A. (2021). Algorithmic Journalism—Current Applications and Future Perspectives. *Journalism and Media*, 2(2): 244-257. https://doi.org/10.3390/journalmedia2020014.

Li, Q., Xiong, C. Y. (2013). Immersive Communication: The Third Media Age. *Journalism & Communication*, 20(02): 34-43.

Li, R. H., Mao, W. (2019). The Integration, Innovation and Development of Xinhua News Agency from the Perspective of "AI Synthetic Anchor" and "Media Brain". *Chinese Journalist*, 8: 36-39.

Liu, K. (2019). How AI Can Help Media Production and Operation. *Shanghai Journalism Review*, 3: 8-9.

McCarthy, J., Minsky, M. L., Rochester, N., & Shannon, C. E. (2006). A Proposal for the Dartmouth Summer Research Project on Artificial Intelligence, August 31, 1955. *AI Magazine*, 27(4): 12. https://doi.org/10.1609/aimag.v27i4.1904.

McCarthy, J. (2007). What Is Artificial Intelligence? http://www-formal.stanford.edu/jmc/whatisai.pdf.

Pan, Y. (2016). Heading toward Artificial Intelligence 2.0. *Engineering*, 2(4): 409-413. https://doi.org/10.1016/J.ENG.2016.04.018.

Sharma, S., Rana, V., & Malhotra, M. (2022). Automatic Recommendation System Based on Hybrid Filtering Algorithm. *Education and Information Technologies*, 27(2): 1523-1538. https://doi.org/10.1007/s10639-021-10643-8.

Shi, A. B., Zhang, Y. Z. (2016). The Rise of VR/AR and the Shift of Traditional Journalism. *Shanghai Journalism Review*, 1: 34-41.

Shu, J., Shen, X., Liu, H., Yi, B., & Zhang, Z. (2018). A Content-Based Recommendation Algorithm for Learning Resources. *Multimedia Systems*, 24(2): 163-173. https://doi.org/10.1007/s00530-017-0539-8.

Xie, X. F., Zhang, J. Q. (2020). AI Empowerment: Artificial Intelligence and Media Industry Chain Reconstruction. *View on Publishing*, 11: 26-29.

Xu, L. P., He, D., & Lu, Y. W. (2022). Research on Intelligent Recommendation Based on User Persona—A Case Study of Douyin. *Media*, 12: 53-56.

Yu, G. M., Yang, Y., Qu, H., Geng, X. M., & Yang, J. Y. (2020). The Video Industry in the 5G Era: Trends and Overall Impact. *Youth Journalist*, 22: 38-41.

Yu, G. M., Zhang, W. H. (2016). VR Journalism: Reconstructing the News Media Format. *News and Writing*, 12: 47-50.

Zhao, C. W., Liu, T., & Du, H. H. (2019). Research on Video Recommendation Model of Douyin Short Video Platform from the Perspective of Algorithm. *View on Publishing*, 18: 76-78.

Zhang, Y. (2015). An Exploration of News Narrative Innovational Model Based on Augmented Reality. *Chinese Journal of Journalism & Communication*, 37(04): 106-114.

Zhao, Y. (2019). Research Trends of Journalism Ethics in the Age of Artificial Intelligence. *Journal of Zhejiang University (Humanities and Social Sciences)*, 49(02): 100-114.

Zhao, Z. (2021). Analysis on the "Douyin (Tiktok) Mania" Phenomenon Based on Recommendation Algorithms. In E3S Web of Conferences (Vol. 235, p. 03029). https://doi.org/10.1051/e3sconf/202123503029.

Zhou, Y., Hao, J. Y. (2022). Constructing and Domesticating: The Technical Path and Evolutionary Logic of Artificial Intelligence Anchors. *Chinese Journal of Journalism & Communication*, 2: 115-132.